GUIDANCE MONOGRAPH SERIES

Series I: Organization and Administration

The Function of Theory in Guidance Programs

Merville C. Shaw

GUIDANCE MONOGRAPH SERIES

Shelley C. Stone

Bruce Shertzer

Editors

GUIDANCE MONOGRAPH SERIES

The general purpose of Houghton Mifflin's Guidance Monograph Series is to provide high quality coverage of topics which are of abiding importance in contemporary counseling and guidance practice. In a rapidly expanding field of endeavor, change and innovation are inevitably present. A trend accompanying such growth is greater and greater specialization. Specialization results in an increased demand for materials which reflect current modifications in guidance practice while simultaneously treating the field in greater depth and detail than commonly found in textbooks and brief journal articles.

The list of eminent contributors to this series assures the reader expert treatment of the areas covered. The monographs are designed for consumers with varying familiarity to the counseling and guidance field. The editors believe that the series will be useful to experienced practitioners as well as beginning students. While these groups may use the monographs with somewhat different goals in mind, both will benefit from the treatment given to content areas.

The content areas treated have been selected because of specific criteria. Among them are timeliness, practicality, and persistency of the issues involved. Above all, the editors have attempted to select topics which are of major substantive concern to counseling and guidance personnel.

Shelley C. Stone

Bruce Shertzer

THE FUNCTION OF THEORY IN GUIDANCE PROGRAMS

MERVILLE C. SHAW
CHICO STATE COLLEGE, CHICO, CALIFORNIA

HOUGHTON MIFFLIN COMPANY · BOSTON
NEW YORK · ATLANTA · GENEVA, ILL. · DALLAS · PALO ALTO

COPYRIGHT © 1968 BY HOUGHTON MIFFLIN COMPANY. *All rights reserved. No part of this work may be reproduced or transmitted in any form or by any means, electronic or mechanical, including photocopying and recording, or by any information storage or retrieval system, without permission in writing from the publisher. Printed in the U.S.A.*

CONTENTS

EDITORS' INTRODUCTION	vii
AUTHOR'S INTRODUCTION	ix
1. The Current State of Affairs: Theory, Practice, and Research	1
2. A Theoretical Model for Guidance Services	13
3. Objectives, Values, and Assumptions	21
4. Utilizing Theory in Guidance Program Development	31
5. An Illustration of Program Building Based on Theory	43
APPENDIX	63
BIBLIOGRAPHY	77
INDEX	81

EDITORS' INTRODUCTION

This monograph tells the story, at least in part, of how theory can function in guidance programs. Few would doubt that theory influences guidance program operation. However, explicit statements sketching out the theoretical basis for program operation are rarely available.

It is to be noted that the author has not given merely an historic interpretation of the function of theory; rather, he has worked out and sought to demonstrate how a guidance program functions *because* of the theory upon which it is built. Professor Shaw points out the consequences of implicit rather than explicit theory in guidance. After conceptualizing the present state of guidance theory, practice, and research, Shaw presents six basic approaches, anyone of which could serve as the primary focus of a guidance program, and interprets the theory upon which each approach is based. He also examines the values and assumptions inherent in each approach. His suggestions for utilizing theory in guidance program development are most cogent, systematic, and timely.

In our judgment, after reading this book, few directors of guidance or counseling practitioners will believe that employing a theory is equivalent to impracticality. If personnel are to deal effectively with problems, they must comprehend them fully. Problem comprehension and solution depend upon theory because theory permits systematization of a body of pertinent knowledge which in turn can generate insight and understanding.

SHELLEY C. STONE
BRUCE SHERTZER

AUTHOR'S INTRODUCTION

The people involved in public school guidance programs are usually action-oriented people. They are faced constantly with problems which often appear to demand immediate resolution. As a result of the pressures which they experience in their work, most public school guidance specialists have become thoroughly disenchanted with theory and with theorists. It is difficult to understand how they could feel otherwise. They do not have time for theory as theorists know it. They regularly deal with situations which require immediate attention, and there is little room for vague, untried, and apparently irrelevant theories when action is required.

In the minds of many guidance practitioners, theory is associated with the idealistic pronouncements of college professors or with guidance texts which have not proved helpful to them. There is a definite lack of communication between those who are practitioners and those who are considered to be theorists. This latter group seem almost unaware of the disenchantment of the practitioner with the theorist and his theorizing. This lack of communication is rather dramatically illustrated in a study done by Herr (1965) in which a number of counselor-educators and a number of practitioners of public school guidance were asked to rank the major influences on the conduct of guidance in the public schools. The counselor-educators ranked themselves as being the primary influence on public school guidance practices. The practitioners ranked the counselor-educators tenth out of twelve possible influences. This rather devastating difference of perception between those who are guidance practitioners and those who are ordinarily considered to be the guidance theorists would seem to be a fair measure of the worth of theory in the minds of practitioners.

This situation is most unfortunate. Whether the guidance worker is aware of it or not, there is *some* theory underlying every guidance program. It may be an unspecified theory or even a bad theory, but it exists nevertheless. It is somewhat like mental health. We may choose to say that we are not concerned with mental health. This does not mean that mental health does not exist, nor that, in ignoring it we rid ourselves of the problems related to it. Simply saying that theory is impractical and that we do not need it is not proof that it doesn't exist, nor that in fact it might not be helpful.

It would be unrealistic to deny that theory in the area of public school guidance is both amorphous and confused. Theorists still confuse the act of counseling with the total guidance program (e.g., Beck, 1965). Philosophy is often confused with theory. We have not even resolved yet the problem of whether or not guidance is a field which can have a theory of its own, or whether it must continue to borrow from other fields, such as personality, motivation, and measurement.

In a review of the literature on guidance theory encompassing the years 1962 through 1965, Kehas (1965) states, "Only one article formulated a theoretical model of guidance . . . ." He further states, "There is a consensus that lack of theory impedes research and development in the field; and a conviction that guidance needs theory of its own is growing."

It is greatly to be doubted that guidance specialists in public schools share these sentiments. A review of the literature prior to 1962 reveals much the same state of affairs. We have talked much about what the functions of the guidance worker should be, and we have freely philosophized about guidance programs, but hardheaded attempts to develop theoretical models are primarily notable for their absence.

The basic purpose of this monograph is to make theory useful to the practitioner of guidance. To accomplish this aim, theory must provide a structure or model which describes a wide range of possible objectives, which delineates the point in time at which guidance intervention takes place, which describes the population to be worked with, and which at least implies the kinds of functions which a guidance specialist is expected to carry out in any situation.

In order to achieve the purpose of this monograph, the current status of theory, practice, and research will be briefly reviewed. This will be followed by presentation of a general model which permits the derivation of six basic positions with regard to guidance services. The relationship of value judgments and assumptions necessary for making decisions relevant to guidance programs, as well as the need for establishing program objectives, will be examined. The six approaches based on the model will each be studied from these points of view, and the problem of promoting change in guidance programs will be considered. Finally, for illustrative purposes, a specific point of view will be presented and its implications for a number of current problems will be discussed.

M. C. S.

1

The Current State of Affairs: Theory, Practice, and Research

It will prove helpful to our understanding of guidance theory and its place in the development of guidance programs if the present state of affairs with respect to theory, practice, and research in the guidance field is considered first. For present purposes, a *guidance specialist* is considered to be a person employed in the public schools whose primary training has been in the area of the applied behavioral sciences and whose primary task within the framework of public education is the application of that training to the significant educational role groups, including children, teachers, parents, and administrators. The job titles which are most frequently encompassed by the general term guidance specialist include school counselors, school psychologists, and school social workers. While it is certainly to be hoped that other professions involved in the educational enterprise will apply principles derived from the behavioral sciences, their task is considered to be fundamentally different from that of the guidance specialist. A more precise definition of what guidance is depends upon a more precise definition of the objectives of guidance services, since different objectives will result in different definitions of the term.

The Current Status of Theory

It has already been intimated that theory, particularly theory developed by guidance experts for utilization in the public schools, is almost nonexistent. This situation should not be construed negatively. Guidance has grown largely in response to social and cultural pressures which have arisen outside the field of guidance itself. Thus, in the early 1900's, Parsons (1909) developed ideas relative to vocational guidance primarily in response to the increasing industrialization and urbanization which were taking place in this country. More recently, the pressures of the atomic age and of competition with other nuclear powers have resulted in passage of the National Defense Education Act, which made specific provisions for certain guidance services. A variety of other examples could be cited. The point is that guidance has not experienced an orderly growth process directed from within the ranks of the profession, and for this reason, at least in part, there is little theory available to explain the guidance process.

A second factor which explains the current lack of theory is the relative newness of the guidance profession. Although it is typical to date the actual beginning of the guidance movement from the early 1900's, this is probably a misleading date, because, from that time until the end of World War II, public school guidance was actually limited almost exclusively to *vocational* guidance. A variety of theories has already appeared in connection with this limited aspect of the guidance movement, and such theories continue to appear on the scene, but it was not until after World War II that the horizons of guidance specialists were broadened to include activities other than vocational guidance. It would therefore seem reasonable to take the position that guidance, broadly conceived, did not actually have its birth until after World War II.

The Need for Theory

There appears to be at the moment a rather smug satisfaction among some guidance professionals, both in the public school and at the college level, with the current state of affairs in guidance. There certainly are some reasons to be satisfied. Since the passage of the National Defense Education Act in 1958, the number of school counselors has increased considerably. Somewhat similar kinds of gains can be seen in the other guidance professions, particularly the field of school psychology, which, for all practical purposes, did not even exist prior to World War II. The criteria for certification have been considerably toughened, and guidance professionals leaving colleges and universities at this time are generally much better prepared to carry out their tasks than their counterparts of just ten years ago. There is clearly a move away from part-time guidance specialists to full-time guidance specialists in those professions where it has previously been held that part-time guidance and part-time teaching were a desirable combination.

These are all positive indications, and yet, all is not well. It seems generally true that present guidance programs reflect lack of purpose. Many things are being done; tests are given and interpreted, group guidance classes are held, educational objectives are discussed with students, parents are increasingly included in guidance activities, and still such programs are often seen as unrelated to the basic educational endeavor by teachers and laymen alike. Guidance specialists are increasingly involved in non-guidance activities (Gibson, 1962), and students do not see the role of the guidance specialist as it is seen by the specialist himself (Heilfron, 1960; Barahal and Brammer, 1950). In addition, potentially serious role conflicts exist among various practitioners of guidance. The school social worker, the school psychologist, and the school counselor are in profound disagreement both within and among the several professions with respect to their appropriate responsibilities within the school situation (Shaw, 1967). Attempts to divide professional guidance responsibilities have thus far been generally unsatisfactory to all parties.

What accounts for this state of affairs? Could it be that the rapid and externally induced growth which has resulted in lack of theory formulation is at least one of the factors which accounts for this kind of situation? It is at least a possibility and one which needs to be explored. It seems logical to assume that, without some congruence between theory and practice, we will continue to have the same confused and essentially purposeless jumble of "services" currently being provided by guidance specialists. It also seems logical to believe that the availability of an adequate theoretical model for guidance services might help in the resolution of the role delineation problem among guidance professionals.

Ways of Constructing Guidance Theory

Several options are available with respect to the problem of how to go about constructing guidance theory. To date, most of those who have theorized about the guidance field appear to have assumed that guidance is not a discipline in itself, but rather one which is comprised of bits and pieces of a variety of other disciplines. Thus, the main attempts to theorize about guidance have involved borrowing from other areas. Such fields as the psychology of motivation, personality, and measurement have all been heavily used to propound guidance theory. Most of such theory has, however, been an attempt to explain individual behavior, either that of the student or of the guidance worker. The possibility of viewing guidance theory as a separate entity has seldom been explored.

Perceptions of what a guidance theory might attempt to accomplish have been extremely narrow to date and have resulted in a relatively narrow definition of roles. Thus, the public school counselor, for example, now tends to perceive individual counseling with students as the *sine qua non* of his profession, while the school psychologist tends to see individual diagnostic testing as his major function to the general exclusion of a number of other significant functions. School social workers have, in general, been able to maintain a somewhat broader point of view, although they have at times insisted that anything which happens to the child outside of school is their area of focus (Cook, 1945). These narrow points of view, however, are very probably the outgrowth of narrow kinds of theories.

Only a few serious attempts have been made to theorize about guidance as a separate discipline within the educational framework. Two examples of this kind of theorizing are represented by Mathewson (1962) and Tiedeman and Field (1962). The end result of the theorizing in both of these cases was an original formulation delineating a particular approach to guidance. An even greater need at the moment is for a general model of guidance which would conceivably encompass those of both Mathewson and Tiedeman and Field and almost any other specific theory which might be derived.

The Need for a General Theoretical Model

Any attempt to propound a model such as that suggested must be undertaken with the greatest humility and, considering the current state of guidance theory, should probably be as simple as possible. Such a model should not be specific to any particular academic level, but must in some way span all age levels encompassed by the public schools. It should, in other words, be a general model for the provision of guidance services at all public school levels. This stipulation is necessary, since the model should say something about *when* guidance intervention should occur.

Theoretical discussions bearing on the question of when guidance services should intervene in a child's educational career have been largely overridden by the weight of actuality. Historically, guidance services were introduced at the secondary school level and have largely continued to receive emphasis at that level. It has often been suggested that preventive intervention at an earlier date might reduce problems

The Current State of Affairs: Theory, Practice, and Research

at the later academic levels, but, in actual practice, guidance at the elementary school level appears to deal mainly with already existing problems.

The significance of guidance at the elementary school level was undercut by the original National Defense Education Act, which limited federal support of guidance to the secondary level. A later change in this law broadening such support to include the elementary years is providing the stimulus for more adequate investigation of the effectiveness of guidance services during the earliest school years. There is currently a great deal of ferment relative to guidance in elementary education, and changes do appear to be imminent. In the meantime, decisions relating to *where* guidance emphasis should be placed appear to be dictated more by history than by the potential effectiveness of such services.

Another variable which a general model must take into account is the problem of *whom* guidance services are intended to reach. The issue of whether guidance services are intended only for a small (and presumably deviant) segment of the population, or whether they are for the benefit of all, or nearly all, of the student population is, at least in part, a value judgment. Certainly a case can be made for dealing with almost any segment of the population, and therefore any general model for guidance services must take this possibility into account. There does appear to be consensus among those who have expressed written opinions on this problem that guidance services should be available to the larger rather than to the smaller segment of the student population. There is every reason to doubt, however, that this is the case in actual practice.

A useful theoretical model should include, by implication at least, some indication of *how* guidance services may be rendered. This problem is not wholly separate from the problem of what proportion of the student population guidance services are intended to reach. In addition, the criterion of effectiveness must be injected at this point. Conceivably, it is possible for a school counselor with a ratio of 500 students to one counselor to see each of his students once each semester, as some insist he must (California Association of Secondary School Administrators, 1965), but obviously such contact would be short, and there is no reason to believe it could be other than meaningless to the student. It might keep the counselor busy, but it would be ineffective. It seems apparent that the problem of how guidance services might be effectively rendered will differ from situation to situation, depending upon such factors as the ratio of guidance specialists to students, school size, and the nature of the student population.

The range of choices available for providing guidance services is rather broad. We may choose to reach children *directly* through personal contact. If a decision is made to reach the child directly, further decisions must be made with respect to whether or not such contact should be made individually or in groups. Still further decisions must be made with respect to the purpose of such contacts.

Rather than reaching children directly, it is also possible to decide that effectiveness could best be achieved through working with those who have more time and influence upon the child than the counselor can possibly have. Teachers and parents would certainly be foremost in such a consideration. In this case, it is elected to reach children *indirectly*, but it should be borne in mind that should such a choice be made, the focus is still the child. Decisions with respect to the method and purpose of reaching intermediaries must also be made.

The final variable which a general model should take into account has to do with *why* guidance services are being rendered. What are the goals of the service? How can guidance personnel tell when they have achieved their objectives? While such purposes could not be spelled out in detail in any general model, it is necessary that some indication of purpose be reflected.

The Current Status of Practice

If lack of theory has had any negative impact on practice, then examination of the roles and functions of various guidance specialists should reveal a certain amount of disagreement and confusion. This, in fact, turns out to be the case. Literature dealing with these topics, in marked contrast to the situation with respect to theory, is voluminous, and only the highlights can be suggested here.

School Counseling

In the field of school counseling, it appears to be increasingly assumed that counseling, narrowly defined as a direct relationship with students, is the main job of the counselor (Loughary, 1965). Assumption of this position commits the fundamental error of defining a total profession in terms of a single function. The fallacy of doing so is illustrated by another statement from the source just quoted, which says, "The majority of ASCA members were more articulate regarding what they should do than why they should do it." It is just a bit difficult to understand how decisions can be made relative to *what* should be done without first considering *why* it should be done.

In spite of the presumably large amount of agreement obtained from school counselors with respect to functions, there is clearly profound disagreement among those who write on the subject. Among those who have pointed up this disagreement are Warren (1963), Hill and Nitzschke (1962), Fossett (1960), Pierson and Grant (1954), and Hoyt (1961).

Among the basic issues on which there is disagreement is the question of who constitutes the counselor's appropriate clientele. Johnson, Stefflre, and Edelfelt (1961) state that the counselor works mainly with those whose ". . . school functioning or personal stability is questionable." This point of view with respect to clientele has also been espoused more recently by Berlin (1963). The opposite point of view has been taken by Miller (1961), Mathewson (1962), and Eckerson and Smith (1963), all of whom maintain that guidance services are intended for all children in the school. Still a third point of view has been forcefully articulated by McCully (1963), who maintained that the guidance counselor should observe process in the student's transaction with content, should interpret his observations to teachers, and should demonstrate process in group situations.

Still another difference among counselors centers around the *generalist versus specialist* issue. In broad terms, the specialist is generally seen as spending his time primarily in counseling with students, while the generalist point of view maintains that the counselor should function more as a consultant within the school system, working less with students and more with staff and parents. In the last analysis, one is left with the impression that those who advocate that the counselor operate as a specialist are, in effect, advocating that he work directly with individual pupils who have specific personal problems. Those who argue that the counselor should operate as a generalist appear to be insisting that he deal indirectly with the developmental problems that all children have.

It is apparent also that counselors are sometimes misunderstood by other professionals. A study by Russell and Willis (1964) indicated that a high proportion of teachers believed that there was not good communication between teachers and guidance workers. The feeling was also expressed by teachers that counselors tend to overprotect students, and that many guidance practices could be carried out by teachers if they had more time to do so. Teachers also felt that they were left out by the guidance specialists when decisions about children were being made. Other studies have tended to reflect somewhat similar findings.

Pupils, as well as teachers, are often confused and uncertain about the guidance program. Gibson (1962) reported on a study conducted in twelve high schools with well organized and well established guidance programs. Students in these schools were queried with respect to various aspects of the guidance program. One-half of these students reported that they were not cognizant of the activities of the program in their schools, and one-third of them stated that the functions of the program had not been outlined or explained to them in any way while they were in school. Gibson also found that students preferred counseling from fellow students and parents rather than from school personnel.

School Social Work

There is also substantial evidence of confusion with respect to roles and functions in the area of school social work. Here, too, we find disagreement among professionals with respect to the appropriate clientele of the school social worker. Cook (1945) takes the point of view that events occurring outside of school are the appropriate province of the school social worker, while that which occurs in school is the appropriate concern of the counselor and school psychologist. This position is refuted by Lundberg (1962), but the schism still exists.

Social workers likewise have difficulty in differentiating their role from that of the school counselor and school psychologist. Kelly (1964), in referring to school social work, says:

> In the forefront now are programs for preventing delinquency, identifying and helping the potential dropout, and strengthening the educational accomplishment of the gifted and the under-achiever. The earlier focus on children with particular symptoms or problems has been broadened over the years to provide for a potential contribution to all children.

Would the school counselor or the school psychologist identify any of these areas as his special concern? The answer seems firmly Yes. On the other hand, is there any reason why they should not be the concern of the school social worker?

In addition to the question of how to cut the pie, there is another area of sharp disagreement among school social workers. This question relates to the problem of whether the school social worker should be identified primarily as a social worker or as a *school* social worker. This problem is not unique to school social work. A similar situation exists within the ranks of school psychologists. Nebo (1960) firmly takes the point of view that the school social worker is a special kind of social worker who is clearly part of the school staff. In sharp contrast, Guzzetta (1964), in an intemperately worded statement where all who agree with him are referred to as "superb" and their work as "useful," while those who disagree with him are branded "witless," "preposterous," and their work as "trash," argues that social work must *not* be integrated into education. He states, "The whole trend toward total integration of social work into education must be reversed and propelled in the opposite direction."

The Current State of Affairs: Theory, Practice, and Research / 9

A final illustration of the current confusion of role and functions within school social work is seen in a report by Leton (1958) to Division 16 of the American Psychological Association. After sending a questionnaire to a sample of school social workers representing city, regional, and national areas, Leton reported that social workers perceived the main function of the school psychologist to be that of diagnosing learning and behavior problems. Conversely, social workers indicated that the school psychologist should *not* play a role as consultant to parents and teachers, as a specialist in psychological treatment, or as an individual who performs diversified personnel services. This position would clearly meet with opposition from school psychologists. On the other hand, social workers relegated to themselves and *not* to school psychologists the functions of adjustment counseling, case studies of the handicapped, case studies of the disturbed, parent interviews regarding problem behavior, and personal counseling. They assigned only two tasks to the counselor. These were group guidance and vocational counseling.

The School Psychologist

School psychologists have been less prolific than the other two professions in discussing their role and function. This situation has been commented on relatively recently by Elkin (Gottsegen and Gottsegen, 1963). When psychologists have written about their functions, they have tended to be vague about some of the most crucial issues. For example, Cutts (1955), in summarizing the deliberations of the Thayer Conference, takes a highly equivocal position with respect to the extent to which psychotherapy can be regarded as an appropriate function for the school psychologist. This pattern has been followed by those who have written more recently on the subject. The treatment issue is essentially avoided by White and Harris (1961) and is quite hazily dealt with by Vallet (1963).

An extremely broad definition of what constitutes the primary purpose of school psychology has been presented by Gottsegen (1960), who states: "School psychology as a practicing discipline is concerned with the manner in which educational, social, and emotional growth is affected and modified by the school experience." Here again is a definition which might fit school counseling and school social work equally well.

Theory and the Confusion of Roles

The main thing that is clear after examining statements regarding the roles and functions of various guidance specialists is that there is a tremendous lack of clarity both within and among each of these professions with respect to what their appropriate responsibilities are. It may well be that this lack of clarity exists, and will continue to exist, primarily because an adequate theoretical framework for guidance has not been developed. Until such framework is developed, the guidance professions may continue to be confused with respect to their responsibilities, internecine warfare will continue among the professions, and the effectiveness of guidance programs will be vitiated. The real losers in this struggle, of course, are the children in public schools. The existence of this situation alone demands greater attention to the construction of theory within the guidance field and the development of models for guidance services.

The Current Status of the Evaluation of Guidance Services

It is a fundamental tenet of measurement that whatever is to be measured must be carefully defined prior to the time that measuring instruments are developed. In other words, the purpose for measuring must be clearly specified before any measuring is done. It follows from this that attempts to evaluate current guidance services must, for the most part, be invalid. Without any clearly specified goals prior to the institution of guidance procedures, it is impossible to determine the effectiveness of these procedures. At the same time, nearly everyone connected with guidance in any way gives the deepest obeisance to the concept that evaluation (and even research) are fundamental responsibilities of guidance professionals (Loughary, 1965).

Aside from the problem of not having clearly defined objectives to evaluate, there is another major deterrent to the appropriate evaluation of guidance programs. Interest in evaluation and its first cousin, research, probably reflects rather deeply ingrained personality characteristics. The same can be said for some of the kinds of motivations which propel people into such occupations as counseling, school psychology, and school social work. The problem is that the characteristics which go with the evaluative attitude are not correlated with the characteristics which often interest people in the guidance professions. Thus, most guidance people are not anti-evaluation, they are simply a-evaluative. Basic concepts of measurement, experimental design, and research are far from exciting to most practitioners of guidance. This is not in any way to be considered a condemnation. It seems rather to be a fact of human existence.

The guidance field currently reflects this situation. Few attempts are made to seriously evaluate ongoing guidance programs. When such attempts are made, those who have the responsibility for doing the evaluating are usually thrust back upon the expedient of asking not

"Did we accomplish what we set out to accomplish?" but rather "What do you think we might have accomplished?" Most evaluations which have been carried out in public schools appear to have asked the question "What do guidance workers do?" but the question "What does guidance accomplish?" is becoming more common (Hill, 1963).

There is one more important characteristic of current evaluations of guidance services. The motivation for such evaluation, rather than springing from the desire of the staff to improve its program, most frequently comes from some outside kind of pressure. It may be that the school board has raised questions about the appropriateness of providing certain guidance services. It may be that teachers are questioning the value of the guidance program, or that the building principal has criticized the guidance staff. In any case, the best kind of motivation for conducting an evaluation is not to prove how indispensable guidance services are, but rather to determine which aspects of guidance services are effective and which are not. Following evaluation, it is necessary to take the next step of modifying practices found to be ineffective. Due to the motivations which usually prompt evaluation in the first place, this step is seldom taken.

Summary

To date, theory in guidance has not proven particularly useful in ongoing programs. This may be due to the fact that attempts to formulate theory have primarily depended upon borrowing from other areas. What appears to be needed is a theory which relates fundamentally to the guidance field alone. Some attempts in this direction have been made, but they have had little impact to date. A general model which permits a variety of specific models to be developed would be extremely helpful at the present stage of theory development in guidance. Such a model should answer, in part at least, such questions as who guidance is for, when guidance services should intervene, how services are to be provided, and what the goals of such services will be.

Investigation of the current status of practice in school counseling, school psychology, and school social work reveals a relatively confused state of affairs. There is profound disagreement both within and among each of these three fields with respect to appropriate roles and functions. There is a great deal of overlap in what each of these three professions claims as its own territory, and the potential for serious interprofessional rivalry exists.

The evaluation of guidance programs has seldom been effectively carried out, primarily because sound evaluation requires that objectives be established prior to the initiation of functions. In the absence of this condition, sound evaluation is not possible. In addition, a relative lack of interest on the part of most guidance workers in evaluation enters to complicate the problem.

It is the sense of this chapter that the development and utilization of guidance theory is vitally necessary if meaningful, effective, internally consistent guidance programs are to be offered, and if damaging interprofessional rivalries are to be avoided. The development of theory is not merely an academic exercise but an absolute necessity for the development of effective guidance programs. Until such theory has been derived, roles, functions, and evaluation of guidance programs will continue to be confused. If theory is to be useful, however, it must be developed in such a way that guidance workers will perceive it to have utility and relevance to their functioning.

2

A Theoretical Model for Guidance Services*

The current status of functioning in guidance programs attests to the need for a theoretical model for guidance. It has already been suggested that public school guidance should begin to consider itself as an entity distinct from other professional educational role groups and also from the other behavioral sciences. This is not to say that guidance is unrelated to other behavioral sciences, or that it will not draw upon the research and techniques which other fields have developed. Neither does it mean that the guidance professions are unrelated to the total school enterprise. It does mean, however, that in order to develop an appropriate conceptual model for guidance, it will no longer suffice to borrow bits and pieces from other disciplines. It has been pointed out that there is undeniably a wide variety of different theoretical positions which can be taken with respect to the guidance field. A major need at the moment appears to be for a simple, broadly conceived theoretical model into which more specific theoretical proposals relative to the guidance operation can be fitted.

---

* Parts of the material in this chapter, including a modification of Figure 1, have previously been published in the *Personnel and Guidance Journal,* April, 1966, under the title "A Focus for Public School Guidance Programs," by M. C. Shaw and J. K. Tuel.

Such a model should provide for various options with respect to *when*, in the school career of each child, guidance services should intervene. It should also delineate *who* would be the recipient of guidance services, as well as having implications for *how* such services will be rendered, at least in a general sense. An additional variable for which a general model might have implications relates to the *why* of guidance services. That is, what are the eventual goals of the guidance program? It is impossible to ignore this variable in any conceptual scheme because of the implications that projected outcomes have for the questions of who receives guidance services, when they are provided, and how they are rendered.

The selection of any specific option encompassed by such a model would be dependent upon the specific objectives established for the program, which would in turn be dependent upon the values and assumptions made by those who devise and operate the program.

A General Model

Figure 1 represents a way of conceptualizing some of the different kinds of choices which are open to guidance specialists with respect to program focus. The two rectangles indicate that guidance services can be rendered either *directly* to those who are the focus of concern, or may be furnished *indirectly* through dealing with the other significant persons in the child's environment who may be in an even better position than the guidance worker to influence the child's behavior in the learning situation. Such significant persons would certainly include parents and teachers, among others.

The vertical dimension within each of the rectangles represents the proportion of the *student* population to be effected, while the horizontal dimension indicates the relative point at which guidance services may intervene in the child's educational career. The extreme left-hand side of the diagram represents the provision of guidance services for *all* children at the earliest possible time in their school careers. Movement to the right-hand side indicates intervention at a later date.

It is assumed that services appearing toward the right-hand side will require more intensive long-term work, while services appearing toward the left-hand side can be accomplished through less intensive treatment and through utilization of group techniques. For this reason, the later that guidance intervention occurs, the fewer will be the number of individuals in the school situation who can be served by the program. It is further assumed that a program of early and continuous intervention by guidance professionals is aimed at the

A Theoretical Model for Guidance Services / 15

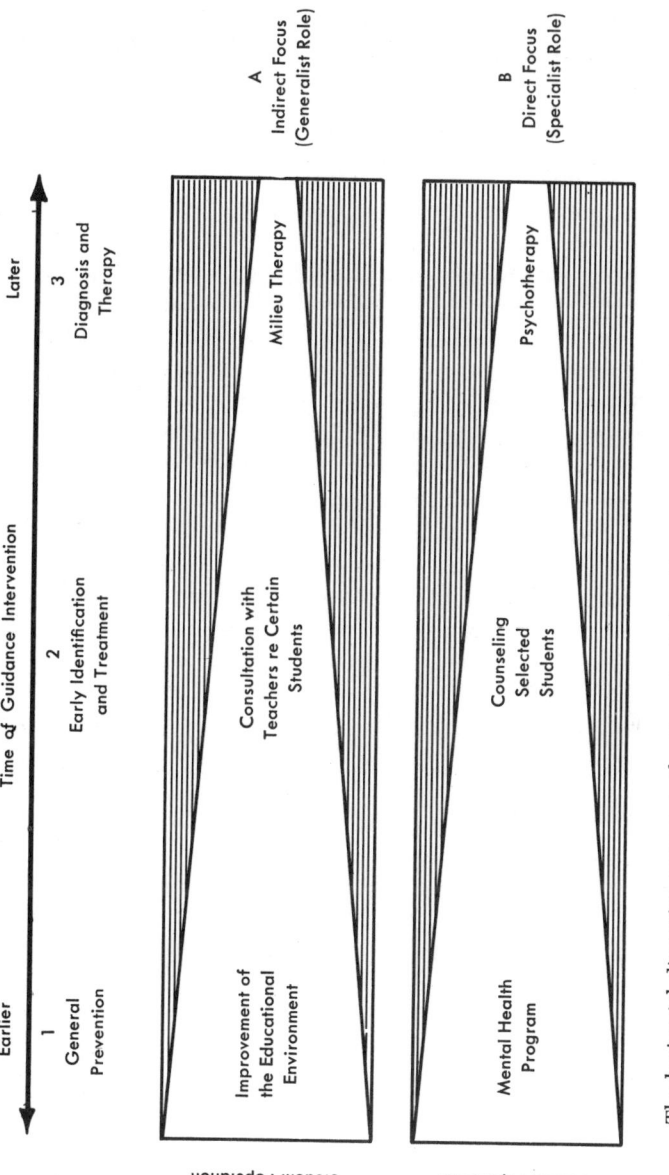

FIGURE 1. A General Model for Guidance Services

The horizontal dimension represents the time at which guidance intervention takes place. The two different rectangles represent two basic techniques for achieving objectives — directly through working with students or indirectly through working with significant adults in the learning environment. The proportion of the population which can be reached through a given technique initiated at a given time is indicated by the white areas. Shaded areas represent the proportion of the population *not* reached by a given program.

prevention of certain kinds of problems, while the opposite extreme represents attention to *the diagnosis and the remediation* of already existing problems.

Thus, the goal of general prevention is aimed at the total school population. Early identification, the second alternative indicated, implies early identification and special treatment of those individuals who either are predicted to have a high probability of developing pathology, or who already show minor symptoms of developing pathology. It should be pointed out that a program of early identification is often called a "preventive" program. This is true only in a relative sense, however, since the fact that specific symptomatology can be identified indicates that a problem already exists. It may be a preventive approach in the sense that it will prevent a small problem from getting worse. It is not a preventive approach from the point of view that it prevents the problem from ever occurring. The third alternative, diagnosis and remediation, represents the normal post facto approach of treating pathology only after it has developed to a point where it is easily recognizable and/or can no longer be tolerated.

The headings across the top represent broad and simplified statements of objectives. It should be emphasized that these three choices represent only three points on a continuum. They are not separate and discrete purposes for guidance programs, but rather the three most widely different choices it is possible to make, given the limits of this particular continuum. It should further be emphasized that these objectives exist only in their most rudimentary form, and further refinement would be necessary before they could become operational in a guidance program.

"Specialist" Versus "Generalist"

Another issue brought into sharper focus by this model is the controversy which exists over the question of whether a guidance specialist should operate as a "generalist" or "specialist." It is quite clear that in dealing directly with children, the guidance worker is operating in what is usually considered to be the specialist role. In dealing primarily with significant others in the child's learning environment, the guidance worker is functioning in what is ordinarily defined as the role of a generalist. Thus, choice of direct or indirect focus identifies the guidance worker as specialist or generalist. It might be said that the argument between those who assume opposite points of view in this controversy is somewhat specious since a guidance worker functioning in either role will need similar skills and knowledge.

If all assumptions made with respect to this diagram are correct, then the interrelationship between the vertical and the horizontal

A Theoretical Model for Guidance Services / 17

dimensions results in the fact that fewer students are affected by the guidance program when the intervention of the program comes later rather than earlier. This is reflected in the cone-shaped portion of the diagram, with the small end of the cone at the right.

Six Basic Approaches

Indicated within the diagram are six basic approaches, three of which are related to direct focus on the child himself and three of which are related to influencing the child's learning environment. It should be pointed out that these approaches are not mutually exclusive, and that, in most guidance programs, some smattering of each is likely to be found. Nevertheless, each of the six approaches indicated sometimes forms the major focus for guidance programs. Further, if the criterion of *effectiveness* is introduced with respect to outcomes of the guidance program, then from a purely practical point of view it may be necessary to utilize staff for the accomplishment of a *single* approach, to the relative exclusion of others. For this reason, the implications of each position will be considered separately.

The Direct Approach

Mental Health Programs

This kind of an approach is begun early in the child's school career, and is intended to reach the total student population. Its basic purpose is to prevent certain difficulties. Another way of making the same statement is that the program is intended to assist the student in developing along optimum lines (the so-called developmental approach). A variety of kinds of approaches has been made to this problem (APGA, undated), but perhaps the most sophisticated, consistent, and far-reaching attempts have been made by Ojemann (1959) and his associates at the University of Iowa.

In such a program, children themselves are the primary target of an approach which is intended to prevent interpersonal and other problems from occurring. Diagnosis and treatment in the usual sense of the word do not enter into the picture. Although the teacher may be the primary instrument of carrying out the mental health program, the guidance specialist might well function as the initiator and supervisor of such an endeavor. The program is intended to influence all children, not just those who manifest interpersonal difficulties. The specific goals of such a program may be quite varied. In the approach utilized by Ojemann, the aim of the program is the development of skills in interpersonal relationships. Other goals might be selected.

Identifying and Counseling Selected Students

This approach may involve the use of personality screening devices in order to determine which children show signs of developing pathology. It may also be carried out on a less formal basis by utilizing teacher referrals to the guidance practitioner who then makes the decision as to whether or not the child is an appropriate candidate for counseling. When counseling is carried out, it is typically of a limited and problem-centered variety. Such concerns as study problems, shyness, classroom misbehavior, failure to complete academic work in appropriate ways, and misunderstandings with parents are typical of the kinds of situations which might be dealt with in this kind of program. Either group or individual procedures may be utilized, although, in practice, emphasis is clearly on the latter technique.

Diagnosis and Psychotherapy

Implementation of this focus clearly indicates the carrying out of intensive diagnostic procedures followed (sometimes) by intensive psychotherapy. In some instances, the intensive diagnosis is followed only by reports to teachers with suggestions as to what steps a teacher might take in order to help the child. When therapy is carried out, it is typically done on an individual basis.

The Indirect Approach

Improvement of the Educational Environment

The major thrust of this focus is to bring about conditions within the child's educational environment that will lead to maximum utilization of abilities within the school situation. Environment as utilized in this instance is conceived of as including not just the school situation, but also those elements of the environment outside of the school situation which have a bearing upon the child's school performance. Such an approach is intended to reach all children through influencing the behavior of significant persons in the child's environment. The possibilities of reaching all children are greater with this approach, since any single teacher works with a large number of children and most parents have more than one child. Further, the contacts that teachers and parents have are of longer duration and are potentially more meaningful. Thus, what is done for parents and teachers to change their attitudes and behaviors will result in reaching a relatively large number of children. Tests of the effectiveness of this approach are being carried out at the Western Regional Center of the Interprofessional Research Commission on Pupil Personnel Services under direction of the author.

Consultation with Teachers about Selected Students

Utilization of guidance specialists as child behavior consultants is receiving increased attention. Efforts are under way, both at the Eastern and Southwestern Regional Centers of the Interprofessional Research Commission on Pupil Personnel Services, to test the effectiveness of this approach.* Briefly, it involves making the guidance specialist available to teachers to consult with them about children in their classes who are having learning difficulties. Such learning difficulties may be directly related to the curriculum and the child's mastery of it, or may be indirectly related to it in the form of behavior difficulties which in turn are impeding the child's progress. The problems which teachers bring to the child behavior consultant vary considerably and may be either minor or serious. Part of such a specialist's role may involve teaching the teachers what kinds of symptoms to look for and what kinds of problems are appropriate to bring for consultation. Child behavior consultants do not deal directly with children.

Milieu Therapy

This approach involves changes in the normal placement of students within the school situation. It normally occurs at a later time with respect to developing pathology, and therefore more intensive treatment is indicated. Children may be moved from one class to another on the basis of the fact that a particular teacher may be better able to deal with a particular child. Another variation of the theme involves placing children in special classes. The placement of a child in a special class for the emotionally disturbed would be an example of this kind of environmental intervention. Placement in a special school represents an even more drastic therapeutic technique which is sometimes employed. It is a concept which has gained importance in public education in recent years, and has also received attention in the institutional setting (Cumming and Cumming, 1962; Bockoven, 1963).

Summary

An attempt has been made to present a general model for guidance services which makes the various significant options open to guidance specialists easier to conceptualize. Four main variables are taken into

---

* The centers are sponsored by the Interprofessional Research Commission on Pupil Personnel Services, a group of sixteen professional organizations with interests in research and demonstration in the general area of pupil personnel services. The Eastern Regional Center is located at the University of Maryland and is under the direction of Dr. Richard H. Byrne. The Southwestern Regional Center is located at the University of Texas and is under the direction of Dr. John Pierce-Jones.

account by the model. They include consideration of why guidance services are rendered, who should receive guidance services, at what time such services should intervene in the child's life, and how such services might be rendered.

It is assumed that these four questions must be answered in order to develop any meaningful guidance program, and further assumed that in order to be effective the program must pick a primary point of emphasis. Three general objectives of guidance programs were postulated, and six different basic approaches to the rendering of guidance services were suggested. The three objectives represent three points on a total continuum and do not represent all possible alternatives. The same must be said for the six programs derived from these three objectives. Each of the six programs has much to recommend it, and each will find advocates within the school system.

3

Objectives, Values, and Assumptions

It appears much simpler to build a guidance program or to settle problems of role delineation and function simply by asking the question, "What should we do?" than it is to determine first what outcomes should be sought. Selection of the first alternative, however, results in the fact that what a staff elects to do determines what its goals are. This will be immediately recognized as a reversal of what is desirable. It is necessary to decide *first* what the goals are, and only then to determine what functions follow from the goals which have been decided upon. It is also necessary to examine the assumptions and the values upon which different choices of objectives and functions are based. Again, this is an easy task to overlook, but one that must be undertaken if the program is to have meaning.

The Current Status of Objectives

It is a fundamental premise of most purposeful activities carried out in our society that such activities must have a clearly defined goal or objective; something must be specified about what the outcomes are to be *prior to* the time the activity is undertaken and prior to any decisions relative to the functions that people will perform in order to meet the objectives.

This is not an area where public school guidance programs have performed adequately, nor is it an area where those who have written about guidance have been thorough. Examination of the material contained in guidance texts or district guidance handbooks generally reveals that one of four conditions prevails. In the first place, some publications of this sort completely overlook the issue of establishing program objectives. It appears to be assumed in these situations that purposes grow out of the kinds of services which the guidance worker is supposed to render. In such cases, the program tends to be built around the personal interests of the people who staff the program and as personnel change, program emphases shift.

A second common condition is that many guidance specialists confuse guidance functions (services) with guidance objectives (outcomes). Thus, the administration of group tests is, in some instances, viewed as a goal rather than as a step towards the accomplishment of a goal. Individual counseling is frequently viewed as an end rather than a means, as is the discussion of educational programs with high school students. While it is certainly true that objectives and functions form a continuum rather than a dichotomy, it is both possible and necessary to make distinctions between the two. When means become ends, we have placed the cart before the horse and the ends can hardly be expected to be clear-cut, measurable, or worthwhile.

A third general observation is that in most guidance texts and district guidance handbooks, consideration of goals receives but little attention. Treatment of this topic may cover anywhere from one paragraph to a few pages, but seldom more than this. This means that guidance services are discussed without much relevance to the purposes which these services are supposed to accomplish. Without a thorough statement of what the goals are, it is impossible to develop logical, unified functions clearly related to desired outcomes, and it is likewise impossible to evaluate performance with any degree of clarity, specificity, or meaningfulness.

A final observation relative to existing statements of objectives is that they tend to be vague, general, and at times appear to include almost everything that goes on in the school setting with the exception of instruction. To individuals outside the guidance profession, it must sometimes appear to be a case of the guidance tail trying to wag the educational dog.

The Adequacy of Guidance Objectives

In order to be at all purposeful, in order to provide meaningful, unified, and effective services, and in order to make it possible to determine the outcomes of the efforts of the guidance staff, it is imperative that the objectives of the program be stated prior to the development of the functions. If goals are not stated, how can it be known what the program is attempting to accomplish? How can the program be evaluated? How can others know what the accomplishments of the guidance staff are? Indeed, can there be such a thing as a "guidance program"?

It is possible to establish some general criteria by which *any* objective or any set of objectives postulated for the guidance program can be evaluated. What should these criteria be? In the *first* place, objectives should be stated in clear and unequivocal terms. If it is really necessary to utilize certain vague and loaded words, such as "adjustment," "happiness," or "self-understanding," then it is necessary that these terms be defined so that the meaning of the objective is clear. A corollary of this criterion is that objectives should be stated in such a way that outcomes are open to assessment and evaluation. This procedure will enable guidance specialists to avoid the situation in which the evaluation of programs must be carried out in the absence of any stated objectives, resulting in essentially meaningless evaluations.

A *second* criterion that should be applied to the objectives of guidance programs is that they should be related to the basic purposes of public education. One of the factors which has tended to push guidance out of the educational picture from the teachers' point of view, one of the things which has caused laymen to regard it as a frill, and has caused teachers and laymen alike to wonder if the guidance function is really related to education, has been the propensity of the guidance worker for dealing with situations that do not, in the eyes of others, relate to learning. The objectives of guidance programs should be such that both educators and parents can see that guidance does have an impact on the kinds of things about which they are most concerned, particularly the learning of all children in the school system.

A *third* criterion which should be utilized in evaluating the appropriateness of guidance objectives is that such objectives should be capable of accomplishment. While this may appear to be only common sense, examine any half dozen guidance texts or a similar number of guidance handbooks from different school districts. After reading them, ask yourself if what such material suggests is capable of accomplishment even if the 250 to 1 counselor ratio suggested by American School Counselor Association and the 1,000 to 1 pupil-school psychologist ratio suggested by American Psychological Association exists. If, for example, an objective implies intensive individual work with all students in the school (as some do), then it can hardly be held to be capable of accomplishment.

On the other hand, let it be made clear that this criterion does not imply the desirability of establishing mundane objectives which are absolutely certain of accomplishment. An experimental attitude is among the most valuable assets a guidance staff can have. The central issue here is that guidance staffs should not establish objectives that, by their very nature, rule out the possibility of their accomplishment.

A *fourth* criterion against which any objective can be measured is that objectives for guidance services should be stated in such terms that they are applicable to all academic levels and in different places. To state, for example, that the provision of educational and vocational guidance is a purpose of guidance services is to confuse the issue. This is not a purpose; it is a function. It is something that is *done,* presumably along with other things, in order to achieve a more distant goal. Further, it is limited to fairly specific grade levels and is not generally considered to be applicable, for example, in the primary grades.

Likewise, statements of purpose should be made in such a way that they are applicable in different places and with different kinds of populations. This does not mean that functions will not differ from one age level to another, or that functions will not differ from one particular community to another, but guidance workers tend to use the excuse, "Our situation is different," as a means of explaining essentially directionless guidance programs, or as a means of justifying the carrying out of functions which they happen to like to perform.

A *fifth* criterion which should be applied to guidance objectives is that such objectives should imply both unique and professional services. At the present time, a high proportion of the smorgasbord of services rendered by guidance staffs cannot be classed as professional. Included here might be such tasks as the registration of new students, the administration of group tests, much of what is called programming, and, in addition, the whole welter of clerical and quasi-administrative kinds of work that guidance specialists are often called upon to do.

In addition to being professional, services should be unique. It is necessary to identify guidance as a profession separate and distinct from both teaching and administration, but one that is *equally involved* in the educational process. Teachers frequently tend to identify guidance staff with administration and, if one examines the proportion of administrators who were first guidance specialists (Fisher, 1966) or looks at the tasks that guidance staffs often carry out, this is an entirely understandable position for teachers to take. Likewise, the former professional identity of most counselors as teachers is not helpful in attempting to establish for guidance workers a unique identity. Unless the functions performed by a guidance specialist are clearly unique, he may be regarded by his former teaching colleagues as just a teacher with a new title.

These, in brief, are criteria which should be applied to any statements of objectives for guidance services. It is not a matter of applying three out of five or four out of five. Unless all are taken into account in the establishment of objectives, guidance programs will suffer.

Values, Assumptions, and the Guidance Program

Although the importance of establishing objectives for guidance programs is commonly ignored, failure to take into account the values and assumptions which underlie specific objectives is even more common. The terms *values* and *assumptions* will be used interchangeably in what follows, since it is frequently impossible to differentiate between the two. For example, Beck (1963) in listing "assumptions" includes, among others, the following one borrowed from Cribbin (1960): "Guidance is student-centered, being concerned for the optimum development of the whole student and the fullest realization of his potentialities for individual and social ends." This might quite clearly be considered a statement of values as well as a statement of assumptions. Rather than create a semantic jungle, the words will be used synonymously in what follows.

Attempts have been made to assemble common assumptions which underlie all guidance (Cribbin, 1960), but while it is perfectly possible to indulge in such sweeping statements as, "Guidance is based on the recognition of the dignity and worth of the individual and on his right to personal assistance in time of need," this is the kind of generality that could be applied to a variety of other social institutions in addition to guidance. The assumption quoted, for example, might just as well be applied to a mental hygiene clinic, mental hospital, and even to the instructional aspects of education. The kinds of values and assumptions which it is most necessary to specify, from the present point of view, are those which relate specifically to guidance and to specific objectives of guidance programs, for it needs to be recognized that different objectives do involve different assumptions and values.

It should be emphasized that it is impossible to implement a guidance program (just as it is impossible to implement any other aspect of the educational program) without making value judgments and assumptions. Partly as a response to the scientism which prevails in our culture today and partly as a result of guidance workers' desires to be "objective" in all matters, there is a tendency to avoid making value judgments and a tendency to equate not talking about value judgments with never having made them in the first place. Whether we like it or not, the necessity for making such judgments exists, and it is far wiser to make them explicit than to pretend they do not exist by ignoring them.

The selection of specific guidance objectives is essentially a process of making value decisions. Decisions about whom guidance services are for, to what end and for how long, all involve value decisions (or assumptions). This is not a matter for apology or regret. All of the basic sciences ultimately rest upon certain unprovable assumptions. It is only when assumptions are clearly and deliberately studied that appropriate decisions about their tenability can be made. Such scrutiny may well reveal that assumptions are being made which are patently untenable, or even that assumptions are being made of which there is no awareness.

Values and Assumptions Involved in the Postulated Model

The point of this discussion may be made clearer if specifics are considered. In order to do this, it will prove helpful to consider the six basic approaches to guidance suggested by the model (see Figure 1, pg. 15). Note that one assumption has already been made; namely, that, in order to have an effective guidance program, it is necessary to select a focus, and that, if no focus is selected, the guidance program will prove less effective.

Certain values and assumptions are inherent in connection with each of the three general objectives. Further, there are values and assumptions implied by the selection of a direct or indirect focus for guidance services, and there are assumptions and values related specifically to each of the six options specified by the model.

The Three General Objectives

Certain values and assumptions are specific to each of the three general goals of guidance specified by the model. For example, specific to the objective of general prevention (prevention of *what* has not yet been specified) are at least three values and/or assumptions. First is the implicit idea that all children *need* guidance, since a major emphasis of this approach is the attempt to provide guidance services for all children. A second value of this sort is the notion that all children are *entitled* to guidance within the framework of public education. The third notion inherent in this general goal of guidance is that prevention is better than cure, in the sense that it can be more effectively accomplished, and may rule out the eventual need which some children might otherwise have for more intensive treatment.

Selection of the second general class of objectives, namely, those related to the early identification and treatment of pupil problems, also involves a different set of values and assumptions. It assumes that not all children need guidance, and further, that not all children are entitled to guidance. Beyond this, it assumes that those who need guidance most are entitled to it, and it defines "those who need guidance most" as children who are just *beginning* to develop particular problems. Thus, an additional assumption is that early identification and treatment of problems is better than dealing with fully developed problems.

The third general alternative involves still a different set of assumptions and requires a different kind of value judgment. In the first place, it is assumed that relatively few children need guidance and that relatively few children are entitled to guidance. It is further assumed that the children who need guidance are the ones who have the most serious problems, regardless of the nature of the problems. It is assumed also that it is the purpose of guidance services to provide very intensive and extensive services to meet the therapeutic needs of relatively few children. Perhaps it goes without saying that adoption of any one of these three objectives also involves the assumption that the objective is capable of accomplishment.

Direct and Indirect Focus

A decision to work directly with children, as opposed to the option of attempting to reach children through changing the behavior of significant adults in their environment, also involves differing assumptions. The former choice obviously implies the assumption that, in order to have an impact on child behavior, it is more effective to deal directly with the child himself. The second alternative just as obviously assumes that children can be reached more effectively through attempting to influence the behavior of significant adults in their environments who may be in a better position than the guidance specialist to influence children.

The Six Positions

Additional assumptions are involved in the selection of any one of the six specific procedural options delineated by the model. In some cases, these are only extensions of assumptions already mentioned in connection with either the three objectives or the two different focuses which have been delineated.

To elect to approach general prevention through improvement of the educational environment (1A) is to reaffirm the assumptions already made in connection with the general option of prevention, and to assume beyond this that the educative process requires that the guidance specialist assist parents, teachers, administrators, and possibly others in carrying out their respective responsibilities more effectively. It should also be pointed out that there is an implication that the student himself may be almost unaware of the existence of a guidance program, since, if this approach is rigidly interpreted, he may seldom come in contact with a guidance specialist in the lower grades and may therefore be almost unaware that those concerned with his education are being assisted by a guidance specialist. This position may also tend to focus more narrowly on the relation of the guidance specialist to the learning of children than any of the other positions.

If the second alternative of utilizing guidance personnel primarily to consult with teachers and/or parents about certain students who are developing problems (2 A) is selected as a focus for a guidance program, further assumptions are necessary. It is assumed that the teacher and the guidance specialist will cooperate in the identification of children who are beginning to manifest problems. It is also ordinarily assumed, within the framework of this kind of procedural option, that the teacher will initiate the contact with the guidance specialist. It is probably also true that there are fewer limits on the kind of problem which the guidance specialist will consult about than was true of the previous option.

If the alternative of special placement or milieu therapy is selected as a focus (3 A), it is assumed that the teacher's responsibility will end when a referral has been made. From this point on, it is the function of the guidance specialist to complete a diagnosis and to make an appropriate placement. It is further assumed that the "teacher" in the special placement program will himself be either a guidance specialist or highly trained in the behavioral sciences as well as in the area of specialty (emotional disturbance, mental retardation, etc.) which he is teaching; in effect, a behavioral specialist takes over the teaching function. It is assumed that accuracy of diagnosis is of paramount importance in the placement of children, and further assumed that the child cannot function adequately in the normal classroom situation.

If a general mental health program aimed at prevention is selected as a major focus for the guidance program (1 B), it is assumed that children need to be specifically and directly taught techniques of "mental health." These techniques will vary depending on the more specific objectives of the program. If a program such as that of Ojemann is selected for emphasis, then the techniques taught will relate to improving the child's interpersonal relationships. In such a case, an additional assumption is being made, namely, that the school's role includes the responsibility for developing and facilitating the child's socialization. Assumptions of this character are frequently associated with the mental hygiene approach.

If the option of counseling with selected students (2 B) becomes the focus of the guidance program, then it is assumed that problems which have developed minimally can be handled through a relatively brief series of counseling sessions with students involved. Note that it is also assumed that it is possible to make an early diagnosis of most problems with which the school may be concerned. At the present time, it also appears to be assumed that such counseling should be primarily individual in nature. It is further assumed that other significant adults in the child's life will be only minimally involved in the guidance process.

If the final option, that of diagnosis and psychotherapy (3 B), is selected, then the guidance process becomes almost exclusively a matter for the guidance specialist. It is assumed that children being thus treated *can* function in the regular classroom situation while they are in therapy. Within the framework of this option, diagnosis is assumed to be a great deal more significant than was true of any of the other five options. An additional assumption is that it is the role of the school to provide psychotherapy to children with personal problems without much regard to whether that problem is related directly to or stems from the child's school experience.

The reader may be able to determine still other values and objectives associated with the model which has been presented. The important point is that when various aspects of a guidance program are under consideration, the assumptions and values which are attendant upon certain choices which must be made need to be examined. Some of these assumptions may be found to be untenable, or at least distasteful, and objectives and procedural options may be legitimately rejected on these grounds.

The Interrelationship of Objectives, Assumptions, and Values

It is quite normal for most guidance staffs to *attempt* to carry out *all* of the kinds of options that have been suggested by the model, and to attempt to meet all of the objectives as well. This may well be the crux of one of the most serious problems in guidance today, and is just the point at which theory may be of some utility. From the point of view of feasibility and effectiveness and of all the other criteria which have been suggested as being standards by which to judge the appropriateness of objectives, it can only be concluded that the dispersion of effort involved in attempting to carry out all of the procedural options outlined can only result in failure to achieve any of the objectives satisfactorily. The poorer the ratio of guidance specialists to students, the more narrowly will any given program have to focus, but, even under conditions which are presumed to be ideal (ideal, in this instance, defined as the guidance worker-student ratio recommended by appropriate professional organizations), it is probably true that only one of the general kinds of objectives could be effectively achieved.

The objective to be selected should be tested against the criteria suggested. Beyond this, however, it is necessary for those involved in the development of guidance programs to look carefully at the assumptions that any particular program makes and see if they are willing to accept them. Does the staff believe that guidance is for all children or not? Does the staff believe that they can most effectively achieve their goals through dealing directly with children or through dealing with significant adults in the child's environment? These and other issues must ultimately be resolved, and there may be some who will be dissatisfied even after extensive consideration and discussion.

Values, assumptions, and objectives are unavoidably interrelated. It is simple, in the development of a guidance program, to avoid serious consideration of objectives. It is simpler still to avoid the issue of values and assumptions. To the extent that these two areas are not taken into account, however, the ultimate value of the guidance program is lowered.

Summary

It has been emphasized that, in order to build a sound guidance program, the objectives of the program must be specified before any functions can be decided upon. It has further been emphasized that those responsible for determining what the guidance program should be like must also give conscious scrutiny to the values and assumptions which underlie any given objective. Five criteria for determining the adequacy of guidance objectives were suggested, and it was indicated that *all* criteria would need to be met in order for guidance objectives to be considered sound.

The values and assumptions related to various aspects of the guidance model which was outlined in Chapter 2 were delineated. Some of these assumptions were specific to particular objectives, others were specific to the question of whether services would be rendered directly or indirectly, and still others, specific to one of the six basic approaches suggested. Examination of assumptions and values and application of the suggested criteria to potential guidance objectives will result in laying the groundwork for a sound guidance program.

4

Utilizing Theory in Guidance Program Development

To this point there has been an attempt to show that, while theory has not been of great utility to most guidance specialists and of little use in program development, it nevertheless has the potential to be of real value and, further, cannot be ignored if programs are to be soundly constructed. Emphasis has been on the importance of selecting appropriate kinds of options for guidance programs and on the prior task of clearly examining and stipulating the values, asssumptions, and objectives which inevitably accompany such a program.

One assumption being made that is important to reiterate is that, in order to be effective, any guidance program must select a primary focus. Neither current nor anticipated ratios of guidance specialists to children provide any reason to believe that more than a single primary focus can be effectively implemented. It is further assumed that one difficulty most operating guidance programs have experienced has been that they attempt to do almost everything represented by the general model rather than zeroing in on a specific goal. This is a position which will surely go against some of the basic feelings of many guidance specialists, but in the light of the situation as it exists and as it is likely to exist in the foreseeable future, it cannot be ignored.

To this point it has been suggested that there is a schema for viewing guidance services and that two kinds of significant variables which are necessarily involved in any such general scheme are values and assumptions on one hand and program objectives on the other. Nothing has yet been said about functions, and detailed discussion of this aspect of the guidance program will be covered in monographs which follow. It is appropriate at this time, however, to discuss the interrelationship among values, objectives and functions. Figure 2 indicates the nature of this relationship. It is to be noted that a one-way relationship exists among the three main types of variables which have been suggested.

Non-Behavioral   *Behavioral*

Values ⟶ Objectives ⟶ Functions

FIGURE 2. The relationship among the three basic elements of the guidance program

The figure makes clear that there is a hierarchy among these three variables. In moving from values to objectives to functions, we are moving from the abstract to the concrete, or from the non-behavioral to the behavioral, or from the passive to the active. The position is taken that this is (or should be) a one-way relationship, because what we *do* (functions) should not determine our goals nor should our goals determine the kinds of values and/or assumptions which we are willing to make. It is, rather, the opposite which holds true. Value systems should dictate the goals or objectives of the program. Objectives in turn should dictate the functions which guidance specialists perform or the roles which they assume. Therefore, the process of building a guidance program utilizing theory *must* logically begin with a consideration of the more abstract variables in Figure 2, namely, values and objectives.

A Suggested Procedure

The following approach is offered as a reasonable way to effectively utilize theory in the development of guidance programs. It is assumed that what is being considered is the formulation of guidance policy which will result in providing a framework for the activities of guidance workers either within a specific school or in an entire district. It is clearly most appropriate to try to form *district* guidance policy rather than school-by-school within the district. Although the argument is often made that "our situation is different," such differences can best be taken into account at the level of *functions* rather than at the level of *objectives*. One of the main problems in guidance appears to be the lack of continuity which children experience with respect to the guidance program. The elementary program frequently has little or no relationship to the junior high program, and the junior high program may have little relationship to the senior high program. If objectives differ from one level to another, then whatever guidance specialists do or are attempting to do at one level may well be lost when children leave particular schools.

In addition to having the advantage of providing a certain uniformity of objective from school to school within the same district, a district guidance policy has the further advantage of ensuring that guidance staff will not be used for administrative or other unrelated purposes in specific schools; the district guidance director need only consult district guidance policy in order to determine whether guidance staff assigned to a specific school are being used for non-professional or inappropriate purposes.

Who Should Be Involved in Program Development

The question of who should be involved in the development of guidance policy or in the alteration of present guidance policy is a significant one. Since such a proposal will ultimately have to be accepted at the administrative level, it is certainly appropriate to include administrative representation in such deliberations. If the program to be developed is at the district level, then, in addition to representation from building principals, there should also be representation from central office administrative staff who have responsibilities in relation to guidance.

Teachers also have a stake in the development of the guidance program. Regardless of what options may be selected, teachers will be involved to one extent or another. They may constitute the main referral sources to guidance services, or they may be much more actively involved in the program. In any event, their understanding and active cooperation is necessary. Because this is so, then teachers should likewise be appropriately represented in such an undertaking. Again, if a guidance program for the entire district is being considered, teachers from all academic levels should be involved in such considerations.

Naturally, there should also be representation from the guidance fields, and perhaps this should be the heaviest representation of all. No precise percentages of representation for any group can be given. The main purpose of including teachers and administrators is to obtain their points of view and ultimately to gain a general acceptance of whatever program may result from such deliberations. Such acceptance will be easier if teachers and administrators have been involved in the development of the guidance program.

The task of these two groups goes beyond mere attendance at meetings. It is also their responsibility to actively solicit the ideas and opinions of their co-workers in the teaching and administrative fields as the program is being developed. They should, in other words, represent not only themselves but make some attempt to represent their professional subgroup generally.

The size of the group is an important factor. Since it is a working group which will meet in an extended series of meetings, it must be small enough to provide every group member ample opportunity to interact with the others. Group leaders differ in their ability to manage groups of various sizes, but a maximum of twenty participants should be kept in mind. With this size group, or one somewhat smaller, there should be ample opportunity for all group members to participate.

A Line of Procedure

The major task of a group of the sort suggested will initially be limited to consideration of values, assumptions, and objectives of the guidance program. In order to deal adequately with the problem of functions, it will be necessary to discuss specific levels (elementary, junior high, secondary), and this would indicate the necessity for forming groups with specific responsibilities at different educational levels.

While values occupy the primary place in the hierarchy, this is a highly abstract topic and will be extremely difficult for many groups to deal with. It is probably better to begin with a consideration of the objectives or goals of the guidance program. Under such circumstances, a typical group will be repeatedly tempted to discuss "What should we do?" rather than sticking to the topic of goals. Various group members will find it frustrating to attempt to deal with a definition of outcomes. They may term it a discussion of the "philosophy of guidance" in the most negative sense, or may be tempted to take the point of view what is being done is available in textbooks and that one should rely on the "experts" for answers to such questions. It must be made clear that these questions have not been adequately dealt with previously and that answers of the kind being sought do not exist in the literature. It also must be made clear that when discussing objectives, the task is to establish the outcomes that the program is intended to have, not to define a "philosophy of guidance." Philosophical considerations have little bearing on the issue after values have been delineated.

The group leader in such a situation may find himself hard pressed to keep the topic on the subject of goals. In such a task-oriented group, however, the role of the leader is not just to act as a catalyst, but also to keep the group oriented to the task at hand. It will be necessary to establish criteria by which to judge objectives, such as those suggested in Chapter 3, and to *continually bring these criteria into focus* as objectives are considered.

The group may also be tempted to consider such questions as "What do we like to do?" or "What do we do best?" Such considerations are not appropriate, since the program should not be built around the needs of staff, but rather around the needs of children. It is the staff who should fit the program, not the program which should fit the staff. This is a fundamental tenet of program development. Apart from the ethical considerations involved, the fact of turnover in staff makes building a program around staff analogous to building a bridge on the sand.

The Role of the Group Leader in Program Development

It has already been intimated that the role of the discussion leader in a situation of this sort will be most difficult. He cannot be a person who has the intent of enforcing his own hidden agenda on the group. For this reason, it is sometimes wise to consider the utilization of an outside consultant to fulfill this role. The consultant will not be seriously influenced by existing professional or interpersonal problems in the group. While he may bring his own biases, he should be carefully apprised of the fact that his role is seen as that of facilitating discussion. The group leader should utilize his position to make sure that the group takes into account all criteria established for the evaluation of objectives at all times and to point out alternative courses of action to the group. He should further point out ultimate consequences of specific positions the group is taking. His field of primary interest and experience should naturally be that of guidance. He should be a person of integrity and one who can take a firm position with respect to keeping the group oriented to their task.

In entering into this kind of a situation, all parties involved should understand that a fairly long period of intensive work will be required. The problem to be dealt with is not one which can be resolved in a few meetings with no work going on between. Participants will need to use time between meetings to obtain ideas and opinions from their co-workers.

The group leader will need to keep in mind the task-oriented nature of this group. The assumption is that everyone present has a contribution to make to the resolution of a common problem. The group leader will have to take a firm position if some members of the group persist in dealing with questions which are not relevant. It is impossible to emphasize strongly enough the extent to which it will be tempting to many group members to do so. It appears to be much easier to answer the question "What should we do?" than it is to answer the prior significant question "What should our outcomes be?" and the group leader must be alert to forestall the switch in the easier direction.

It is difficult to estimate the amount of time that may be necessary for the development of a series of acceptable objectives. Various staffs are in different stages of readiness with respect to a task of this kind. Where the attitude is such that change is easily possible and where some thought and dialogue have already begun on the general topic of desirable change in the guidance system, the problem may be considerably less complex. Even at this, it does not seem reasonable to assume that such a group will be able to produce a set of appropriate objectives in much less time than an academic year. While this may surprise many, it is based on the observations of the author who has attempted to do this in a number of different school districts. The task is surprisingly difficult. Guidance workers are not used to thinking in hardheaded terms when it comes to goals or objectives, and will be tempted to provide glittering generalities or to discuss what the counselor ought to do as opposed to what the school psychologist ought to do. These kinds of directions need to be avoided, and objectives must be produced in line with the criteria established.

The Problem of Change

It should be recognized that typically the task under discussion involves changing an ongoing guidance program rather than beginning to build a new one. This is one of the most difficult kinds of efforts which can be imagined. Zander (1950) has clearly pointed out the natural tendency of most human beings to resist a change in what they are doing. He indicates that this is not a problem unique to the school system, but one that may be found in industry as well. He says, further, "Obvious improvements have sometimes caused intense resistance. Research shows that *any* change may be resented unless intelligent planning is done in advance to help the 'changees' understand their own feelings." People tend to become comfortable with what they are doing. The suggestion that they might need to change not only raises the possibility that they might have to learn new skills and do things in different ways, but also carries with it the implication that what they are doing is not satisfactory. Both of these situations are likely to create resistance to change.

The change agent will need continually to remind himself that the task being undertaken is threatening to a large number of individuals who will be involved in it. If it has been determined that changes are to be made, then this should be made clear to the individuals who are involved in deciding on such a change, but it also should be made clear that the alternatives open to them have not been decided upon in any way and that the group is free to pursue its course. This should have the effect, at least in part, of reducing the threat under which they are operating.

The ease of bringing about change will differ from one situation to another. A variety of factors is related to the relative ease with which change may be brought about. It has already been indicated that prior discussion of the desirability of change among those involved is likely to make acceptance of change simpler and more complete than a situation where the notion of change is dropped like a bombshell on those who will be involved.

Another significant variable in determining the rate of change is administrative attitude. Carlson (1965) demonstrates quite clearly that certain characteristics on the part of the superintendent are directly related to the adoption of new curricula. It has also been demonstrated that the attitudes of principals are significant factors in the eventual success of innovation within the guidance program.[*] It would thus appear that not only is a state of general readiness desirable, but also that change will be brought about more smoothly and more quickly in situations where administrative support is given to the idea of change.

It has been indicated by Gallaher (1965) that a large body of research supports the idea that a climate conducive to the acceptance of change is best created when the individuals whose behavior is to be changed perceive such change as relevant and when they have had a hand in planning the change. Both of these points are significant for the kind of change being considered here. Gallaher makes a further point that those to be involved in the change need to have the capacity for criticism. This is a situation which may not be present in some guidance programs. There appears to be a strong tendency among guidance personnel to accept, in somewhat docile fashion, the situation as it is. Beyond this, there is a tendency to accept the advice of authority with respect to what a sound guidance program should be like, even though the voice of authority may have no sound basis for positions advocated. Imbuing such a staff with a constructively critical attitude may well be the prime task of the change advocate.

---

[*] This fact has been demonstrated by the work of the Western Regional Center of the Interprofessional Research Commission in introducing new modes of operation into ongoing guidance programs. This material has not yet been published. The Western Regional Center is located at Chico State College, Chico, California, and is under the direction of the author.

Changing an Established Program

The problem with which most guidance workers will be faced is that of changing an already existing program rather than developing a new one. From the point of view of simplicity, the latter situation is much to be desired. If the program is already in operation, then those who are associated with it, either in the sense of working actively in the program or as the recipient of services from the program, are likely to have a certain set relative to most aspects of the program. This set, with its concomitant perceptions, attitudes, and beliefs about guidance, will make change more difficult than would be the case in a fluid situation where the program has not yet been put into action. Where the program already exists, those who advocate change should expect such change to be gradual rather than sudden. There should not be an expectation that the enthusiasm of change agents for bringing about change will be shared by others.

It is necessary first to lay the groundwork for change by creating a climate in which change can come about. This can be done in part by inviting comments relevant to guidance services from all segments of the staff and by asking for suggestions for improvement or change in the functions provided by the guidance staff. It should be made clear to those asked for such suggestions that they will not necessarily be accepted, but, on the other hand, it should be clearly indicated that guidance staff are not completely satisfied with the situation as it is.

It may actually be more of a problem to create the same interest in and readiness for a change among guidance staff than among teaching faculty. If the staff has become comfortable with a specific mode of operation, they may be reluctant to change even though guidance services are not effective. It is not to be anticipated that all guidance staff will ever be enthusiastic about change, and no such goal as complete acceptance by the staff of the need for change should be set as a condition for attempting change. As a part of the program to induce acceptance of the need for change among guidance staff, it may be well to attempt to collect information on the opinions of teachers, students, and administrators relative to the guidance program. Such information can be highly convincing evidence of the need for change in systems where guidance services are not effective. In all cases, those who will be affected by the change *must* be involved in the change process and the decisions made relevant to a change in operation.

Finances and Change

It is a real temptation for guidance staff to believe that marked improvement in fiscal backing for the guidance program is necessary prior to making any positive changes. This is probably because, in most instances, changes are thought of in terms of adding personnel to the existing staff. There has been a tendency to equate a good guidance program solely with the existing student-guidance worker ratio. This assumption is, of course, not tenable. It is perfectly possible to have a poor guidance program in the presence of a highly desirable ratio of guidance workers to students, and, within certain limits, it is possible to have a good program with a less than desirable ratio. The point here is that it is not possible to equate a sound program *only* with numbers of staff.

Viewed positively, it should be emphasized that, while appropriate action to obtain an adequate ratio of guidance workers to students should continuously be pressed, this effort should not be confused with the issue of making plans for a more effective program. As a matter of fact, it is highly possible that additional staff members will prove easier to obtain *after* the guidance program has demonstrated its effectiveness to numbers of current staff members.

Building Support for Change

Assuming that the guidance staff itself has agreed to become involved in program change, the question becomes how to get support for whatever changes may be proposed. It has somehow become standard procedure to expect to get support simply because it is asked for. This can be seen in several areas of guidance. For example, counselors are concerned about their status in the educational hierarchy. They frequently raise the question of how to get adequate "recognition" from teachers and administrators with respect to the significance of their job. Another variation of this is seen when guidance workers complain about poor teacher attitudes toward guidance. The other educational professions should not be expected to be supportive of guidance until guidance has demonstrated its contribution to the education of children.

It has already been suggested that non-guidance personnel should be involved in the preparation and planning of the guidance program. Beyond this, care should be taken to prepare a *total* plan to present appropriate individuals and groups. If suggestions are made only with respect to certain specifics, for example, "reduce the amount of clerical work" or "increase the amount of group counseling," not only is the entire message of this monograph negated, but chances of ultimate approval of such a program are considerably diminished. It is much simpler to refuse to approve small changes, which may stem from relatively little thought, than it is to turn down a *total program*, which has obviously taken a great deal of thought and which attempts to take

40 / The Function of Theory in Guidance Programs

into account all of the problems which should be considered in such an endeavor. Further, when a total program is presented, it is not necessary for members of the guidance staff to insist on "less clerical work" because the suggested program may well rule out the possibility of clerical duties.

In addition to presenting a total plan which represents the thinking of a total guidance staff as well as that of representatives from other educational role groups, it is also important to present facts and figures to buttress the report. Too often, such projected changes are accompanied primarily by the opinions of the individuals involved in the preparation of the report. It is an easy matter to oppose one opinion with another, and when the opposer is in a position to enforce his opposition, then a great deal of time has been wasted. Some of the kinds of specific information which might prove helpful would include a thorough documentation of how counselors are currently spending their time, accompanied by documentation with respect to how they would expect to spend their time under a new plan. If counselors can demonstrate with hard facts that they are spending much of their professional time on non-professional functions, this is a powerful argument for change. It would be an unusual situation where the annual salary of one guidance specialist could not cover the annual salaries of two clerical workers. Sometimes, rather than thinking in terms of adding professional staff, we need to think in terms of adding clerical staff so the professional staff can carry out appropriate responsibilities.

Another useful kind of information to accompany proposed guidance program changes is that which reflects the opinions of teachers, students, and administrators about guidance services. If, for example, teachers and students tend to be almost unaware of the kinds of services rendered by guidance staffs (not an unusual condition), then there is powerful argument for changing the mode of procedure. Further, if it is demonstrated that guidance staff are carrying out largely administrative responsibilities, there is again a powerful argument for change.

It should not be expected that other staff members, even those on the guidance staff, will share the initial enthusiasm for change which a few individuals may have. A certain cynicism (usually related in the minds of those who manifest it to "reality" as opposed to the "ivory tower approach") sometimes prevails, and the fact that conditions are not good is sometimes assumed to be indicative of the fact that they can't be any better. Sometimes the reformed reformer is the most cynical of the lot. At one time he may have made the assumption that being "right" ensured success. Having found out through practical experience that it does not, there is sometimes the assumption that being "right" is now equated with a lack of success.

It will be necessary to move slowly. There is no reason to expect immediate acceptance of program changes if such program changes require other professionals to make new adjustments, and particularly if the program changes have removed some tasks from counselors and placed them on others. A corollary to this is that guidance workers should not at any time expect acceptance of the guidance program by all members of the staff.

The Implementation of Change

One of the current attitudes which seems to prevail in our culture is that people can be "sold" anything, and that it is therefore necessary to "sell" the guidance program to the rest of the staff. Actually, the thing which should sell the program is its effectiveness, and at no point should "selling" the program be equated with convincing others that the program has something to offer in the absence of any evidence to that effect. Guidance staff will gain status and recognition to the extent that they make themselves indispensable, in professional kinds of ways, to the educational enterprise. In addition to moving slowly and to realizing that being right doesn't ensure success, an early step in the implementation of a changed program should be the provision of direct and tangible professional services to staff. The focus would still be children, but an attempt should be made to assist teachers and others with their professional problems.

From the point of view of teachers, it is also important that the guidance staff divorce themselves from both administrative titles and administrative duties. It is probably not the best plan to utilize a vice-principal as head of the guidance program within a particular school. The title "head counselor" would be preferable from the point of view of establishing a unique identity for guidance staff.

It is also a good idea to avoid telling faculty that they are the *main* guidance workers. When we say this, we may mean only that the teacher is important in the guidance program, but it is sometimes interpreted to mean that the main guidance functions must be *carried out* by the teacher. Teachers are not the main guidance functionaries within the school. Professional guidance personnel are. If this situation does not obtain, then we need to re-examine the question of whether or not guidance workers are necessary.

In conclusion, it should be said that guidance specialists should be calm, polite, and persistent in presenting a new program. There is no reason to be defensive about a proposal for program change if it has been carefully thought through. Through being persistent, the guidance worker simply demonstrates that the proposals made are not fads or whims, but the result of a carefully thought-out policy which needs to be enacted in order to improve the educational opportunities of the children in the school.

Summary

The interrelationship between values, objectives, and functions has been discussed. It has been suggested that values and objectives must be considered before any consideration of appropriate functions can take place. A procedure for engaging in program development has been suggested. Because of the fact that most counselors will be faced with the problem of making changes in existing programs, the problem of inducing and implementing change has also been discussed. Some of the steps which might be taken to decrease natural resistance to change have been suggested. The need for the use of data and for a calm, though persistent, approach in promoting change has been emphasized, as has been the need to be positive rather than negative in the approach taken. The involvement of those who will be affected by the change in the change process is of prime importance.

5

An Illustration of Program Building Based on Theory

In order to demonstrate how a guidance staff might proceed in the development of a guidance program on a logical, theory-oriented basis, a specific point of view will be taken with respect to the directions in which a guidance program might move and the values (assumptions), objectives, and functions of such a program will be delineated. It should be re-emphasized that the assumptions and objectives delineated might hold for *any* school level, although functions will vary with school level. It will be possible, within the framework of the position taken, to make general statements about how functions will vary from the elementary to the secondary level.

A Point of View*

Several educational and social trends of special significance for guidance specialists are currently taking place. The influence of the family appears to be lessening, especially its role in the inculcation of positive

---

* The material included in this section has previously been published in Shaw, M. C., and Tuel, J. K., *A Proposed Model and Research Design for Pupil Personnel Services in the Public Schools,* Western Regional Center of the Interprofessional Research Commission on Pupil Personnel Services, Chico State College, Chico, California, 1964.

43

values towards education, work, and democratic ideals. As this development has progressed, the public in general, including educators, appears to have assumed that the school should take on the role of surrogate parents. Furthermore, there is some evidence to indicate that the school has done just this, so that, in addition to its traditional and perhaps too narrow role of transmitting knowledge, public education has now assumed a much broader responsibility. Thus, manners, morals, values, attitudes, mental health, driver education, vocational and educational direction, and many other functions previously considered matters of family responsibility are now within the purview of public education. Yet, paradoxically, having relegated these matters to the school, the public now appears to be indicating a desire for a return to "basic education," in effect, a retreat to the views of the nineteenth century and before. Thus we find a strong incongruity: On one hand, the school has taken on a wide variety of responsibilities formerly carried out by the family; on the other hand, though the American family shows little predisposition to reassume these former responsibilities, it appears to be in the process of demanding a "return to fundamentals" in education. In brief, having shifted its own responsibilities primarily to another agency, the family, in the form of the "public," is making it increasingly difficult for the school to carry out these tasks successfully.

Concurrent with the development of the paradoxical situation just described has been the evolution of the professional guidance specialist. This profession has developed primarily in response to demands from *outside* the profession. As a result, no cohesive philosophy has developed which binds the profession together or gives it a set of common objectives. Thus, while most professions are able to speak briefly and to the point with respect to the goals of their profession, counselors find it impossible to do this.

It appears that public school guidance specialists are approaching a choice point and if they do not make a deliberate decision, it will be made for them, either by other groups, particularly school administrators, or by the weight of circumstance, or by a combination of the two. The decision appears to be whether to view guidance services as agencies which will attempt to be parent surrogates or as agencies which attempt through the provision of unique services to make learning possible, more meaningful, and more useful to children. If the former course is chosen, the implication is that guidance personnel will tend to emphasize work with individual children and that they will concern themselves with almost any kind of problem that a child may have developed. From the practical point of view, this means that they will continue to deal with cases primarily of the emergency variety, that they will spend most of their time with a limited segment of the population, and that they will have little impact on the school as a whole. If the latter choice is made, the implications are that guidance staffs will not be primarily concerned with serious mental health problems, but rather will be concerned with problems interfering with learning and the further effective use of learning; that they will be concerned with the majority of children rather than a minority.

Fortunately, other developments in our society in general and in the school in particular do not make this latter choice the hard-boiled abandoning of children in trouble that it may appear to be. Within the educational world itself, there has come about the development of concern for special groups such as the retarded, the gifted, and the emotionally disturbed. In many states, special classes for these groups are now conducted. Outside the field of professional education, there has been a burgeoning of referral sources for a variety of the kinds of human problems for which guidance specialists have often taken responsibility. These two developments, both leading in the same general direction, should make it possible to view the focus on problem prevention without feelings of guilt.

The Purposes of Education

In order to derive a guidance program relevant to the educational process, it is necessary to discuss briefly the purposes of education. To presume to discuss these purposes in any detail in this statement would be pretentious. Volumes have been devoted to the subject and agreement in detail has seldom been reached between those who have varying philosophies of education. There are three basic general responsibilities of education that most persons would agree on, even though there would doubtless still be disagreement about their relative places in a hierarchy of purposes. The first of these purposes is the *transmittal of knowledge and skills*. This purpose encompasses the historic and generally accepted role of education and few, if any, would deny that it occupies a central place in almost any philosophy of education. A second purpose which has gained prominence in more recent times stresses the *preparation of the learner* to actively and effectively appropriate new knowledge and skills. Still a third purpose, closely related to the second, focuses on the preparation of the learner to effectively apply his skills to practical problems, problem solving, or new learning situations. The overall responsibility of education that will find general agreement is thus that education must provide a situation, an atmosphere, if you will, in which the skills and knowledges deemed by society important to learning can be adequately learned in such a way that the student can put his knowledge to effective use. There may be more disagreement about the second and third postulated purposes than there is about the first, but, in the light of a growing and irrefutable body of knowledge bearing on the conditions necessary to learning both in the learning environment and the learner himself, and our growing belief that many who appear to learn are not able to make effective use of their knowledge, we cannot ignore these important objectives.

The Appropriate Focus for Guidance

The question which now becomes appropriate is, "What unique contributions can be made to these goals by the well trained guidance specialist?" The first goal, dealing with the transmittal of skills and knowledge, is primarily the province of the classroom teacher, although the guidance specialist also has some responsibility in this area. In the course of his contacts with teachers, parents, administrators, and children, he will invariably be called upon to behave in relation to this goal, but this is not his primary function nor his *unique* contribution to the educative process.

It seems obvious that it is in connection with the second and third proposed objectives that the guidance professional has the most to offer. Thus, the teacher can be viewed primarily (but not solely) as the conveyor of information, while the guidance specialist fulfills his role by facilitating and enhancing the ability of the students both to appropriate knowledge and to make effective use of it. He will thus be concerned with the overall *learning environment* and with those characteristics of the learner that promote or interfere with learning and the learner's ability to make maximum use of material which he has already learned. Succinctly stated, the basic purpose of the guidance specialist is to assist all students to maximize their learning and to enable them to use their learning effectively through intervention in the learning environment. He will not be interested in treating existing disorders; rather he will be interested in preventing learning disorders from occurring.

Assumptions and Values Underlying the Proposed Focus

Two general kinds of assumptions are involved in any choice of focus for a guidance program. The first of these may be labeled ethical assumptions. These involve the value decisions which are made when a choice of focus for a guidance program is selected. In most circumstances, these kinds of assumptions go completely unregarded. There appears to be some concern that to discuss such value decisions might be regarded as lacking in objectivity and this is somehow perceived as alien to our times. The truth is, of course, that value decisions are implicit in any operational guidance program and the fact that we may choose not to make them explicit in no way expunges them from existence.

The second general kind of assumption may be labeled professional assumptions. These involve the kinds of assumptions we are willing to make about the efficacy of certain professional measures and are an index of the reliance we are willing to place on certain professional skills and techniques. Again, it should be pointed out that these assumptions are seldom clarified with regard to specific guidance programs. We generally assume that *all* of the techniques which we use, including individual counseling, psychotherapy with disturbed children, consultation with teachers, and use of individual tests, are equally efficacious. There is, of course, some reason to doubt that this is so, and it would be wise to attempt to spell out the kinds of assumptions being made relative to certain professional techniques.

Ethical Assumptions

The primary ethical assumption made in the point of view which has been described above is that guidance is for *all* children. This is not a concept which will be new to the seasoned guidance worker. Nearly all texts on the subject make a deep obeisance to this concept, and it is stated with great regularity by directors of guidance services when speaking to the PTA, the Lions, or the Rotary. The fact of the matter is, however, that scrutiny of most guidance systems will reveal that a large share of the guidance time is going to a very small proportion of the student population. The value "guidance is for all children" appears to be widely espoused but rarely practiced.

A second ethical assumption is involved in the narrowing of role which the current focus implies. This implication is to the effect that treatment of existing pathology is not properly within the scope of public education but must be carried out by other social agencies. It is often argued that some children cannot learn in school because of existing emotional difficulties, and this is certainly true. It is further argued that since these children are in school, it is necessary to deal with them in some way and guidance specialists are usually the means elected to accomplish this. There is, however, serious question as to whether this is an appropriate role for either the school in general or the guidance specialist in particular. If schools are to take on the treatment of existing pathology, then one must begin to ask, "Where does the school's responsibility end?" Does it have all the responsibility of the school, plus those of parents, church, mental hygiene clinic, and other significant social organizations? If the school is to maintain its effectiveness, it is obvious that it cannot be all things to all people. The guidance program, as a part of the school, must apply the same logic to its own functioning. It should be pointed out that this ethical assumption intersects with the previous one in that, if time is to be given to treatment, it will be impossible to provide appropriate guidance services to all children.

Professional Assumptions

In addition to those assumptions which involve certain value judgments, certain assumptions are also made in connection with the professional activities to be carried out by the guidance staff. In some cases, there will be only a hairline difference between an ethical and a professional assumption and it is not necessary to argue the difference. It is important, however, to make note of all assumptions basic to a specific guidance program. The primary professional assumption made by the proposed focus is that prevention is more effective than cure. In the previous paragraph, the position was taken that treatment was not an *appropriate* function of the guidance program. The position is now being taken that treatment cannot *effectively* be carried out within the school setting by guidance personnel. A number of conditions combine to make this true. The difficulty of carrying out successful treatment is compounded if, at the same time, there is an insistence that *all* children receive assistance through the guidance staff. Variables of time, professional training, and the nature of the setting conspire to make treatment difficult. This is not to say that attempts should not be made to provide educational settings in which severely disturbed children can function appropriately. The issue is that treatment is not a primary responsibility of the guidance staff. The major advances in physical medicine have been made, not through treatment of disease, but through prevention. The same analogy would appear to be reasonable when applied to learning difficulties.

An additional assumption related to prevention is that an effective program of prevention will result in less need for treatment. If the prevention of learning difficulties is to be the focus of the program, then clearly there should be fewer learning difficulties if the program is effective, and therefore less need for remedial and therapeutic measures in the later school years.

Another assumption of the suggested approach is that it is possible to influence student behavior through influencing the behavior of intermediaries. Since emphasis is on the student's learning environment and since the most important influences in the student's learning environment are the significant people in it, and further, since some of these people, such as parents and teachers, have more sustained contact with students, it is only sensible to focus attention on these individuals as significant environmental factors. At higher age levels, an additional group with significant influence on individual students is the peer group and as the influence of this group becomes more significant, it, too, must be taken into account as an environmental influence.

A final assumption of the proposed guidance program is that children in the elementary school may, in general, be unaware of the existence of guidance professionals, since most of the professionals' time will be spent with parents and teachers. This situation will change as peer group influence becomes stronger and as this fact is taken into account by the guidance program, but clearly at the lower age levels it would be inappropriate to evaluate the guidance program by asking students such a question as, "Has the counselor been helpful to you?" Children will not be able to respond appropriately to this question since they will, in general, have had little direct contact with the counselor.

General Outline of an Appropriate Program

The functions to be delineated are intended specifically to implement the objective which has been established. This is, at least in part, an exercise in logic and, because this is so, continual empirical evaluation of the extent to which objectives have been accomplished is a necessity. The appropriate role of the guidance specialist in this kind of a program is active rather than passive. He will seek out those tasks he should accomplish or persons with whom he should work. He cannot wait passively for situations to arise which call for emergency kinds of activities on his part, but will seek to anticipate and forestall these situations by working with appropriate individuals or groups.

It should also be emphasized in the strongest terms that the guidance specialists cannot be identified in the minds of teachers, parents, or students as an arm of the administration. If a counselor is to successfully carry out the basic and unique responsibilities demanded by the objectives established, it must be as the representative of a profession which is not identified either with administration or with teaching, but which *is* identified with the overall facilitation of the educational process and which has an identity of its own. The categories of responsibility which will be delineated are in line with the objectives cited. They are, however, intended to be suggestive and to allow for flexibility in any given situation.

The concept that guidance programs must differ in different settings is a sound one. This does not mean that basic *purposes* will differ from one situation to another, but rather that variations in *function* may be necessary depending upon circumstances. For example, counselors operating within the present frame of reference will have a definite role to play with parents in every school situation, but the methods used to reach parents, the focus selected for emphasis, and the methods utilized will vary with such factors as grade level, size of the school, student-counselor ratio, and the nature of the community in which the school is located.

The Guidance Specialist's Role with Teachers

Work with teachers, either individually or in groups, is of primary importance to the current objectives. It is the teacher who bears the basic responsibility for establishing the climate of learning within the school. Whether students learn effectively, learn to use their learning effectively, or learn to want to learn will depend in large measure upon the climate created by the teaching staff. McCully (1963) has suggested that "newly inducted teachers may know more about content and less about the educative process" and "newly inducted teachers may be less knowledgeable about students, about individual differences, and about student motivation." If this is true, then the guidance specialist's task, as the individual responsible for the development of an environment which is conducive to learning, becomes of primary importance. Other evidence for the significance of the guidance professional's task in moderating the learning environment is presented by Mallery. In seven out of eight high schools which he studied, Mallery (1962) found that students were quite generally negative in their reaction to the curriculum and to subject matter in general because they seemed to them to be unrelated to their lives and to the community. These students almost appear to regard school as something more for teachers than for students. It is quite clear that the learning environment in these seven schools was not conducive to maximum academic or personal development on the part of the students.

In commenting on the findings of Mallery and others, McCully further stated, "there is grave doubt that a professional could, through the individual counseling of students and performing the other peripheral activities which have traditionally been included in a 'guidance program,' exercise more than a marginal influence at best in those schools. The learning environment and resultant student attitudes would likely frustrate and possibly defeat him."

The guidance specialist's task with teachers falls into three general categories. The *first* way in which the counselor can be of assistance to the teaching staff is to work with them on problems which relate to the effectiveness of their teaching. This is a role which most counselors have deliberately avoided. Administrators are not particularly favorable, either, to the notion that counselors should assist teachers with their professional problems, but the fact remains that the teacher's personality is his primary teaching instrument and where there are problems of teacher personality that interfere with teaching effectiveness, the counselor has a responsibility. This is not to suggest that the counselor should become a psychotherapist for seriously disturbed teachers in the school. It does suggest, however, that such problems as teacher conflicts of attitudes and values with students or minor emotional problems which lessen teaching effectiveness are appropriate areas in which counselors and teachers should interact.

In assisting one teacher to teach more effectively, a counselor is reaching many more students than he could reach in a similarly expended amount of time spent in working directly with students. Further, in helping teachers in this way, teachers may be better able to handle similar problems in the future. This means that the guidance professional's role with a teacher is that of *counselor* and that the guidance worker will resort less to providing information and sympathy and rely more on the utilization of the same professional techniques with teachers that he employs in counseling with students.

Such an endeavor will not be successful simply by advertising the fact that the guidance worker is willing to discuss professional problems with teachers, although it is to be hoped that ultimately teachers may learn to come to the counselor for this purpose. One technique which has proven successful in involving teachers is to provide a group counseling situation in which all members of the faculty are invited to participate. The focus of discussion is the professional problems which teachers face daily. It is wise to establish a limited number of sessions to begin with (about four or five), but there is no reason why discussions cannot be continued beyond this point if they are fruitful. This technique has been tried in four different school districts at all school levels with a surprisingly high proportion of teacher participation and highly positive teacher response.*

Teachers might also learn to call on guidance workers to be present at parent-teacher conferences where the problems under discussion seem relevant for the inclusion of a behavior specialist. Where the teacher suspects the child is being pushed too hard by parents, where the child is not receiving appropriate encouragement for learning from the home, or in cases where differing teacher and parent perceptions of the child are interfering with his work in school, a guidance specialist can serve a useful function.

---

* Data bearing on this study have not yet been published, but have been collected and are in the process of analysis by the Western Regional Center of the Interprofessional Research Commission on Pupil Personnel Services located at Chico State College, Chico, California.

A *second* general area of work with teachers in which the guidance professional has much to contribute relates to the improvement of instruction. A guidance specialist will not set himself up as a subject matter expert, but there are a variety of other contributions to curricular and instructional improvement he is capable of making. The guidance specialist has available a great deal of data which can be useful in considering curricular change and he is the one best qualified to interpret such data. He can assist the teaching staff to better understand the curricular needs of the students; he has test information which suggests the levels at which curriculum should be aimed; he has a variety of information on student characteristics and on the makeup of the community in which the school is located. If he does not have these kinds of data immediately available, he is the one most capable of getting them. In addition, guidance personnel have the skills to assist teachers to recognize the need for establishing objectives for their instruction and, once the need is recognized, to assist them in delineating for themselves appropriate instructional goals.

The guidance specialist is also the individual within the school system best trained to adequately assess the outcomes of instruction. The simplest way in which he can aid teachers with assessment is through helping them to evaluate their own instruction more effectively. It should be emphasized that he is assisting teachers to evaluate instruction and *not* evaluating the instructors. It is also understood that this evaluation is not conducted for administrative purposes, but rather for purposes of helping individual teachers who want such assistance in order to see more clearly the outcomes of their teaching.

The *third* general area of work with teachers relates to students who are already having learning difficulties. In many cases, the guidance worker may well have a threefold goal in dealing with students who have such difficulties. One would be to help the student himself. The second would be to assist teachers and other students through decreasing the interference that such students with learning problems often create in the classroom. The third goal would be to assist the teacher to deal more effectively with similar problems when they arise in the future with less help from the counselor.

Teachers can be helped to deal more effectively with general student problems of attitude and motivation which involve such behaviors as truancy, potential dropout, underachievement, or overaspiration. Teachers can also be helped to deal more effectively in the classroom with behavior and personal problems which interfere with the learning of the individual who manifests disruptive classroom behavior and with the learning of students who are in contact with the student who has the problem.

Teachers should also be encouraged to utilize the guidance specialist as a referral agent for students whose problem may fall outside the concern of the school but where the school has an ethical obligation to make an appropriate referral.

The Guidance Specialist's Role with Parents

While guidance personnel have come to pay more attention to the importance of reaching the parents of the children whom the schools are attempting to teach, such efforts have occurred primarily at the time when the child enters school, at articulation points, or when the school has some information for parents, for example, test data, that is most efficiently dispensed in group situations. Such work with parents is typically of the one-time variety and, like the Sunday sermon, may have little carry-over effect. Still, it is a beginning. While many professional educators claim that parents are not interested enough in their children to make any organized work with parents possible, this does not seem to be true in those cases where well organized attempts to do so have been made and where an appropriate approach has been made to the parents (Shaw and Rector, 1966). The mode of approach appears to be a prime factor in gaining parental cooperation and the key seems to lie in making it clear to parents that their assistance is needed, that no criticism of them is either intended or implied, and that the basic issue is their children's education.

Systematic and sustained parent contact should be a part of the proposed guidance program at all levels. In kindergarten, parents are often interested in the social aspects of their child's behavior. In first grade, they tend to be interested in whether or not he is learning to read as he should, and what they can do about it. In high school, they are concerned with assisting their children to make appropriate vocational choices. All of these interests, and many others, can be utilized to motivate parents to participate more meaningfully in the education of their children, if the opportunities are provided. It is true that parents are deeply involved, in an emotional sense, with their children. Sometimes they appear to the professional educator not to have their child's best interests at heart, but even in such cases it is unwise to assume that the parent is not basically concerned about the child.

At the elementary level, parents can benefit greatly through counselor-led group discussion bearing on normal developmental problems. At this level, emphasis would be on the prevention of problems and such a process would be effective in preventing learning difficulties. In the high school, much counselor time and effort is spent in dealing with the problem of the educational and vocational futures of secondary school students. The school seldom attempts to involve parents deeply in such a process over a prolonged period of time, and yet there is every reason to believe that parental behavior, aspirations, and feelings will be a primary determinant of a child's vocational future. At the high school level, planned parent contacts over a period of time relative to educational and vocational decision-making could be of real assistance to the child.

The role of counselors with parents will be greater at the elementary levels and will tend to decrease somewhat, relative to the amount of time spent with children themselves as the age of children increases. This is the case for two reasons. First, the development of verbal communication is a limiting factor in counseling at lower age levels; therefore, the counselor will necessarily have to work through the significant adults in the child's life. Second, the influence of adults, while it continues to be significant, nevertheless diminishes as the child moves through school and the child himself must increasingly be considered responsible for his own behavior.

Working with parents has the same advantages as working with teachers. In doing so, the counselor is dealing with people who will spend much more time with the child than he will be able to do. In addition, through working with groups of parents, he will be able to reach more children than would be the case through direct work with the children themselves. The counselor thus increases both the breadth and depth of his impact on school children.

In addition to the benefits which children directly derive from the counselor's work with parents, there are some additional positive aspects of this kind of activity. One of the most significant side effects is that when the child of parents who have participated in the parent counseling groups subsequently has difficulty of any kind in school, the attitude with which parents approach the problem is more positive than it might otherwise have been. Where school personnel would sometimes expect the parents to blame the school for whatever difficulty the child finds himself in, it has been found that parents who have participated in counseling groups approach such problems much more in the spirit of "What are we going to do about it?" This is no little matter in some situations where parental tendencies to blame the school not only are hard to take but also interfere with children's learning.

The Guidance Specialist's Role with Children

It has already been mentioned that direct individual work with children will need to be reduced considerably below the level ordinarily considered desirable, if the spirit of the currently proposed rationale is to be carried out. It has also been suggested that work with seriously disturbed children or children whose problems do not seem to interfere with their school learning constitutes an inappropriate focus for guidance specialist activity.

With What Children Should the Guidance Specialist Work Directly?

It has been noted that work with parents will be largely preventive and that the parent groups with whom the counselor should be primarily interested in working are the parents of normal children who have normal problems. The position has also been taken that, in his work with teachers, the counselor will attempt to assist teachers to create more effective conditions for learning within the classroom and to become more effective in dealing with some of the kinds of learning and behavior problems which arise in the classroom. In working with children, the bulk of the counselor's efforts will be expended in an attempt to promote optimal educational development. Thus, the whole area of articulation from school to school, or from school to work, or from school to higher education is one for which the counselor bears much of the responsibility and which will entail direct contact with the students involved.

In addition, and perhaps even more fundamental to the present focus, the counselor will work directly with children when children themselves become a significant determinant of the learning environment. Coleman's (1961) work indicates quite clearly that the peer culture in the high school plays an important part in motivating children to want to learn or not to want to learn. To ignore this segment of the educational environment would be to ignore one of its most significant determiners.

It is difficult to state with any precision the point at which the child culture becomes a significant factor in the learning environment. Existing research does not provide us with this answer. As a rule of thumb, it would appear appropriate to say that beginning at the junior high school level, the adolescent subculture begins to exert increased influence on its members. It is at this point that children should be more actively and directly involved in the guidance process. The establishment of regular group counseling sessions aimed at assisting children to handle their increasing independence more effectively and at assisting them in the development of ego identity would be one direct means of influencing the student aspect of the learning environment. Such groups might well be established on a volunteer basis, as were the parent and teacher groups, on the assumption that if they are successful, social pressure will soon cause additional numbers to be involved. It is important to emphasize that such groups are for the normal child if maximum participation is to be obtained.

Working Directly with Problem Children

The position has been taken that the major emphasis of the proposed guidance program will be on the prevention of learning difficulties, and the assumption has further been made that once such a program has been instituted the number of learning difficulties should diminish. It would not be realistic, however, to assume that such a program could possibly prevent all such difficulties, and there are bound to be cases where learning problems arise. A number of these children can be helped within the framework of the school situation but, if they are going to be helped, they must be reached directly by a professional guidance specialist. Such work must not constitute the bulk of that carried out by the guidance specialist. Rather it should be carried out with a view to preventing more serious problems from occurring in these students at a later date.

The kinds of situations which demand direct counselor contact with the child might include the following, among others: children who are producing academically at a level significantly below that which might be expected; potential dropouts; discipline problems which have not been able to be handled through intervention with the teacher but which, in the judgment of professional personnel, are not in need of referral to other agencies; emergency situations in which the attention of a professional guidance specialist is called for immediately; contact with children who can appropriately be referred to other agencies for assistance, but where there is a problem of deciding what agency is appropriate, or else a problem of helping the child and his parents to accept such a referral.

Further discussion of specific means of dealing effectively with individuals included in these groups is not within the scope of this monograph. It is suggested that a rule-of-thumb limit of 10% of the counselor's time should constitute the maximum spent in carrying out remedial kinds of functions with these groups. To spend more time on such efforts would be to frustrate the preventive-developmental emphasis of this point of view.

Social-Cultural Problems

Recent publicity has forcefully brought to the attention of educators social problems that have been with us for many years and which affect the education of large numbers of children. It has been convenient to ignore these problems, but our growing social conscience, increasing affluence, and changes in technology which necessitate more education for even minimum employability, coupled with demands being made by such groups, have finally forced the schools to face this issue. Further, this kind of concern is clearly within the framework of the guidance program suggested herein because of the relationship of environmental conditions to school learning.

Some full-scale attempts have been made to deal with the environmental problem in its relation to the education of children, as in the Higher Horizons project in New York City. These efforts have typically been made at a fairly advanced educational level and at a time when chances for success were less than they would have been had such efforts been made a number of years earlier. Such efforts have focused heavily on the school and classroom situation and have tended to ignore the emotional and attitudinal factors which predispose children from such environments to lack motivation to secure the maximum education of which they are capable. The Head Start programs improve upon some aspects of previous efforts in the direction of overcoming cultural disability by initiating preventive efforts in the pre-school years, but total efforts to remedy this situation must involve parents and teachers, as well as children, on a very intensive basis beginning in the pre-school years and extending over the period the child is in the public school. To initiate such a program at the high school or junior high school level is to insure defeat. If it is to be maximally successful, it must be started at a time when there is some possibility of changing the attitudes and behavior of both parents and children toward education and its importance for their own future.

The experience of the Western Regional Center of the Interprofessional Research Commission on Pupil Personnel Services has indicated that, contrary to popular opinion, the parents of children in culturally deprived areas are as interested as any other parents in the welfare of their children. The methods used in gaining parental cooperation will differ somewhat for such a group, but it has been demonstrated that they are more than willing to participate in school-sponsored activities aimed at the ultimate welfare of their children. This situation was found to be true even at the junior high school levels.

Teacher attitudes relative to such groups of children are also highly significant. There is often the feeling on the part of teachers that both intellectual and motivational factors conspire to make such children unteachable. With such an attitude, it is not to be expected that outstanding educational results can be achieved. It will be necessary to alter such attitudes and the behavior congruent with such attitudes where it is found to exist. Teacher discussions groups offer a sound means of accomplishing such an objective. It will also be necessary to interest the faculty in bringing about appropriate curricular changes to meet the needs of these children. In this instance, the guidance specialist can serve an important function by providing information descriptive of the intellectual, social, and motivational characteristics of children in the school. It seems evident by now that cultural enrichment in and of itself will not have a significant impact on the attitudes and behavior of culturally deprived children.

The School Testing Program

Counselors have traditionally been called upon to handle all phases of the school testing program, including the preparation of materials, actual administration of the tests, the scoring of the tests, the recording of test results on cumulative records, and feedback of test results to appropriate individuals and groups. The scoring aspect of this task has largely been reduced through utilization of test scoring services (except at the elementary level), but the other tasks for the most part remain. Much of what professional counselors have done and are doing in connection with testing programs cannot be appropriately classified either as unique to the counseling function nor as professional level work. The counselor's general responsibility in connection with the testing program should include the establishment of the testing program, after appropriate consideration of the objectives of the counseling program and of the needs of the teaching faculty. Specific responsibilities include the selection of instruments to be used, supervisory responsibility for seeing that the testing program is carried out, supervisory responsibility for scoring and for whatever statistical manipulations are to be made with the scores, and the feedback of the results to teachers, curriculum committees, administrators, children, parents, and other appropriate groups.

In spite of what test manuals imply and in spite of what guidance specialists might like to believe, there is no real reason why a responsible and intelligent clerk cannot be trained adequately to administer most of the kinds of group tests which are used in the public schools. If there is a state or local requirement to the effect that a certified person must be at all times present in the classroom with children, the classroom teacher can be utilized for this purpose. There seems to be no valid reason to use professional guidance personnel for this kind of responsibility. Utilization of this approach would not only free guidance specialists of an unnecessary burden, but is a method preferable to using the classroom teacher as psychometrist in that a single well trained and supervised clerk can do most of the testing, thus insuring use of correct and standard procedures throughout the entire testing program. The same clerk could also take care of the routine chores, such as inventory and ordering test supplies, sharpening pencils, and preparing materials for testing programs. After testing, the same individual could take the responsibility for seeing that the tests are scored, whether it is to be by hand with the use of clerical assistance or by a test scoring agency.

Under this set of conditions, the counselor would maintain supervisory responsibility for the testing program, but would not be faced with the onerous task of dealing with every facet of it. His time would be freed to deal with truly professional matters, including those related to the appropriate utilization of test results. The major criterion of adequacy of a testing program is not just the kinds of tests that are included in it, but also the effectiveness with which information resulting from it is utilized in the education of children.

Inappropriate Activities for the Guidance Specialist

Certain activities which are considered inappropriate have already been suggested or implied, but it would seem well to specify further those kinds of activities which are inappropriate to the functioning of a counselor within the present framework. Such functions would include substituting for absent teachers or administrators, registration of new students, and clerical work in general. Many school counselors are now fulfilling all three of these functions, particularly the latter. While it is easy to talk in the abstract about hiring a clerk to take over certain non-professional responsibilities, it is often difficult in practice to find the money and willingness to do so.

A part of the problem is that the guidance specialist in many situations is already viewed as a clerical functionary, and it is difficult to change this image enough to persuade administrators that real clerical help is needed and that the guidance staff could function professionally if relieved of such responsibility. It would be wise in many cases, when money becomes available for hiring additional staff, to employ two clerks with the money that might otherwise be utilized to hire one professional. The guidance staff might be further ahead in this way than they would if they had hired only a single new counselor who would soon have to take over his share of clerical responsibilities.

Discipline

There has been much discussion of the role of guidance staff in discipline, and there is no intention of examining this issue further. The point at which there does seem to be agreement, however, is that guidance personnel should not be involved in discipline when discipline is used synonymously with punishment. The concept of the guidance worker as a professional person who is striving to enhance normal development and as a person who behaves punitively is incompatible.

Student Activities

Student activities are often a major responsibility of school counselors. In the past, it was said that teachers could get to know their children better if they would score their own standardized tests. We have largely discarded this myth, but seem to have clung to the myth that the same thing will be true of guidance workers if they supervise student activities. Whether this belief is a sincere one or whether dumping student activities on counselors is simply a convenient way of dealing with unwelcome tasks is impossible to say. In any case, there seems to be no real reason why the guidance professional should be any more responsible for student activities than any other member of the staff.

Programming and Scheduling

In many cases a guidance worker is the professional person most deeply involved in programming students. This is a highly time-consuming activity in which typically counselors are responsible for seeing every student individually and mapping out their academic programs for the coming year or semester. Typically, this "individualized programming" means that a counselor sees each student for 10 or 15 minutes, glances hastily through a cumulative record, asks the student what he wants to take, and then gives him whatever is available that comes closest to meeting his needs. While we may wish to delude ourselves that this constitutes a respect for individuality, it must be admitted that there is very little that is individual about it. Limitations of time, limitations in our personal knowledge of students, limitations in our knowledge of what criteria should be considered in making placements, and limitations in the classes available all militate against doing a truly individualized job of programming students.

Two alternatives are available and neither of these seems particularly palatable to most public school personnel. The first alternative involves the utilization of teaching faculty, under the direction of the guidance staff, in the programming of students. Both administrators and teaching faculty resist this suggestion, but it nevertheless remains a logical thing to do. Guidance specialists could take the responsibility for educating teachers for this function and supervising their activities, but the amount of time spent in this activity by the guidance staff could be grossly reduced through this means. A second choice, and one which guidance workers themselves seem to reject, is to computerize the programming function. A number of schools are already experimenting with this idea, and in terms of what we know at present about computers, it is not unreasonable to say that they will do at least as good a job as the counselor and very possibly a better one. A computer is able to "keep in mind" more variables than the guidance worker is likely to be able to in the rushed time that he has. When a good computer program is adequately written, the computer should even be able to match students with appropriate teachers, something which many counselors claim they now do.

The inappropriateness of excessive individual counseling or therapy with students or of long-term work with serious emotional and behavior problems has already been emphasized. Intensive diagnosis in preparation for individual treatment is likewise inappropriate. It should be stated specifically, however, that there is no limit to the amount of time that *could* be spent in this kind of activity. Any guidance specialist who chooses to do so can easily use up all of his available time in long-term counseling or therapy, if he is a competent practitioner. It is important to remember, however, that the emphasis of the present approach is on prevention, not remediation. Preventive activities in the early school years will diminish the need for remedial work in later school years. In any case, however, prevention appears to promise more positive results for a larger number of children than does a remedial approach.

One School District's Plan

In order to demonstrate what guidance specialists themselves are able to do through utilization of the approach that has been suggested throughout this monograph, an actual framework for guidance services at the secondary level which was developed by school counselors themselves is included in Appendix. This program was developed through consideration first of the assumptions and values which this group was willing to endorse. This was followed by consideration of appropriate objectives, of which there eventually were four. This, in turn, was followed by a description of function. Specific means of implementing each of these functions was also considered, as would be necessary in an operational program. The program was developed for the junior and senior high school levels with a ratio of one full-time counselor to each 375 students.

The basic point of view of the counselors is described under the heading "Philosophy." Then, under each of the four objectives, the functions which are appropriate to the objectives are listed and the implementation of each function is further described. Following its preparation (which took nearly two years), the program was adopted by the junior high school and high school principals and the superintendent as a matter of district policy.

Summary

In this chapter, a rationale for taking a specific position with respect to guidance services in public schools has been delineated. The values and assumptions connected with this specific position have been explored, and the objective of the program which stems from the rationale, values, and assumptions espoused has been stated. The position has been taken that the guidance specialist should be primarily concerned with the enhancement of the learning environment and with the characteristics of the learner that promote or interfere with learning and the learner's ability to make use of material which has been learned. Emphasis is on the prevention of learning difficulties rather than on their remediation.

Guidance functions relative to this objective were discussed in a general way. Emphasis was on enhancing the learning environment through influencing the behavior of significant educational role groups, including parents and teachers. Specific responsibilities of the counselor consistent with this framework were discussed. In addition, a specific program prepared by the counselors in a school district has been presented. This program delineates the values, objectives, functions, and implementation of functions in an actual guidance program, and illustrates how a guidance staff can use the approach herein suggested to develop their own program.

APPENDIX

Philosophy

SECONDARY COUNSELING PROGRAM
ANTIOCH UNIFIED SCHOOL DISTRICT

Counseling is an integral part of the total educational process. Counseling provides services that will lead to the development of knowledge, skills, and the self-reliance needed by the students to make satisfactory adjustments for themselves and to society. The counselor is responsible to ALL students, not to the few. In order to provide effective professional services, it is necessary to work not only with the student but with others who bear responsibility or influence the education of children.

Prepared by the secondary counseling staff of the Antioch Unified School District.

Norris Adams	Helen Hardten
Donal Brislain	Paul Hardten
Eugene Daley	Lucille McBride
Sam DeLoach	Rachel Scott

OBJECTIVE I

To Provide Services which will Enable the Students to Gain the Greatest Benefits from the Curriculum

FUNCTIONS	IMPLEMENTATION
A. RECOGNITION, PREVENTION, AND REMEDIATION OF LEARNING DIFFICULTIES	RECOGNITION, PREVENTION, AND REMEDIATION OF LEARNING DIFFICULTIES
1. Assist teachers in using more effectual approaches in recognition and prevention of learning problems of children.	A. Assist teachers to be more effective in dealing with the learning problems of children in the following ways: 1. Provide regular and routine opportunity, individually or in groups, for teachers to discuss their methods and procedures in relationship to classroom effectiveness. 2. Encourage the establishment of programs for students with learning difficulties. 3. Provide all teachers with cumulative data on the students' learning problems. 4. Assist in follow-up studies related to learning difficulties.
2. Share the responsibility of aiding students who are not receiving adequate benefits from the curriculum.	B. The counselor shares the responsibility of aiding students doing academic work not commensurate with their ability by doing the following: 1. Identifying students with learning difficulties. 2. Ascertaining the probable causes of the learning difficulties. 3. Aiding the student in the recognition of his problems. 4. Aiding the student in discovering methods of overcoming the learning difficulties. 5. Sharing this identifying data with all persons concerned with the development of the child.

OBJECTIVE I (continued)

FUNCTIONS	IMPLEMENTATION
B. CURRICULUM	CURRICULUM

1. Participate in curriculum development.	A. PARTICIPATE IN CURRICULUM DEVELOPMENT
	1. The counseling staff will be alert to opportunities to act as a resource for groups engaged in curriculum studies. Some of the information which might be appropriately provided by the counselor for these curriculum study groups are:
	  a. Ability level of students.
	  b. Achievement level of students.
	  c. Outcome of previous special instructional procedure.
	  d. Social and cultural aspects of the students who will be involved.

2. The counselor may act as a resource person and will provide student data which will assist teachers within a subject area or departments within a subject area to evaluate curriculum outcomes.	B. EVALUATION OF CURRICULUM OUTCOMES 1. In addition to participating in general curriculum development, the skills of the counseling staff will be utilized to assist in the evaluation of curriculum outcomes. This can be accomplished in two general ways: by invitation of the department involved, the counseling staff will assist in assessing outcomes of the total program. At the invitation of individual teachers, assistance will be given in the preparation of classroom tests or other teacher-constructed evaluative instruments. Outcomes are for department or individual usage.

OBJECTIVE I (continued)

FUNCTIONS	IMPLEMENTATION

3. Research to determine if student needs are met by the curriculum.	C. RESEARCH
	1. Because curricular change should be based, insofar as possible, on factual information, the counseling staff will undertake to participate in the collection and analysis of appropriate data. This will be done at the invitation of groups needing such data. In addition to providing information to curriculum groups, the counselors will provide other information to the staff at large. Examples of such meaningful data are:
	  a. Information relevant to potential dropouts.
	  b. Measured achievement scores compared to grades in class.
	  c. Effects of subsequent learning or progress in school.

C. PROGRAM PLANNING To provide the coordination and articulation required to assist the student to make appropriate decisions in his educational planning. 1. Orient the teachers in implementing their functions in student program planning. 2. Inform and interpret the contents of the prescribed school program to the parents.	PROGRAM PLANNING A. After an appropriate schedule of classes has been provided, the counselor's role in programming is a supportive one in the following areas: 1. To orient, with administrative support, in the preparation of teachers for their programming responsibilities. 2. To counsel directly with those students with special programming problems; i.e., learning difficulties, transfer students, health problems, summer sessions, and correspondence courses.

OBJECTIVE I (continued)

FUNCTIONS	IMPLEMENTATION

D. ORIENTATION AND ARTICULATION
1. Orientation of incoming students from feeder schools and from other school districts.
2. Articulation from elementary to junior high school, to high school, and to post-high school experiences.
3. Articulation between levels in school; departments within schools.
	A. ORIENTATION AND ARTICULATION FOR STUDENTS
	1. Junior high school counselors visit sixth grade classes to give programming and other needed information to parents, students, and sixth grade teachers.
	2. Plan a visitation day for the sixth and the ninth grade students. Activities might include assemblies, campus tours, films of school life, etc.
	3. Pre-school enrollment and late student enrollment.
	   a. Reliable student guide should be assigned to help orient new students.
	   b. Plan assembly with a panel of high school students to discuss activities, adjustment problems, etc.
	B. ORIENTATION AND ARTICULATION FOR TEACHERS
	1. Head counselor and counselors in junior high school meet with sixth grade teachers in the spring, prior to registration for seventh grade.
	2. Head counselor and counselors in high school meet with ninth grade teachers in the spring, prior to registration for tenth grade.
	3. Distribute handbooks to seventh grade, tenth grade, and transfer students.
	4. Orientation related to counseling activities prior to the opening of school. This should be followed up later in a faculty meeting.
	5. Alert teachers to any student adjustment problems.

OBJECTIVE I (continued)

FUNCTIONS	IMPLEMENTATION
4. Orientation of parents.	C. ORIENTATION AND ARTICULATION FOR PARENTS 1. Counselors should be involved in the "return to school" night. 2. Contribute information relative to counseling for principal's bulletin to parents. 3. Assist in planning a "career night" with the administration. 4. Interpret test results (individually and in groups) to parents. 5. Orientation for parents of students new to the district.
E. TESTING PROGRAM 1. Assist in a comprehensive testing program.	TESTING PROGRAM A. ASSIST IN A COMPREHENSIVE TESTING PROGRAM 1. The counselor will provide the administration and teachers with advice, data, and recommendations which will aid them in the selection and administration of testing programs. 2. The counselor will collect data that would indicate need for special tests involving personal needs of the students. The counselor would recommend such tests to the head counselor.

OBJECTIVE I (continued)

FUNCTIONS	IMPLEMENTATION
2. Provide for test information and interpretation.	B. TEST INFORMATION AND INTERPRETATION 1. Test data will be interpreted to the students and teachers individually or in groups. 2. Test data will be interpreted to the parent upon request or when considered useful. 3. The counselor will advise the head counselor in the recording of test data on the students' records.

OBJECTIVE II

To Provide Services for Personal Development As It Relates to Educational Development

FUNCTIONS	IMPLEMENTATION
A. IDENTIFICATION OF LEARNING DIFFICULTIES 1. Systematically identify the student with problems which interfere with appropriate school progress including such difficulties as: reading problems, social maladjustment, academic underachievement, etc.	A. IDENTIFICATION OF LEARNING DIFFICULTIES 1. Use appropriate data including test scores and cumulative records. 2. Give proper notification to teachers and parents. 3. Use the case conference as an aid to identification and appraisal of the symptoms of those students with learning difficulties.
B. PREVENTION 1. Work with parents and teachers on growth and development characteristics and problems of students. 2. Assist students, teachers and parents in the prevention of students' learning difficulties.	B. PREVENTION 1. Teachers will be invited to participate in group discussions dealing with problems of students' behavior, discipline, and children's learning problems. 2. All parents will, at some time, be invited to participate in group discussions dealing with matters of child development, educational development, and other issues of common parental concern. 3. Direct work with students in prevention includes provision of: self-information, orientation, program decision-making and vocational and educational guidance (see other sections).

OBJECTIVE II (continued)

FUNCTIONS	IMPLEMENTATION
C. REMEDIATION 1. Initiate remedial action concerned with the problems affecting the student's progress in school.	C. REMEDIATION 1. Work with individuals and groups of students who show symptoms of behavior which affects educational development. 2. Through conferences, work with parents of students who show evidence of educational difficulties. 3. The counselor will initiate individual or group conferences with teachers of students who have problems. 4. Parent-teacher-counselor conferences will be arranged when appropriate.
D. REFERRAL AND FOLLOW-UP 1. Refer students to the appropriate individuals or agencies when considered necessary. 2. Follow up and maintain liaison with proper individuals and agencies.	D. REFERRAL AND FOLLOW-UP 1. Follow established procedures in referring to an available agency those cases which give little promise of responding to services which the school is able to give. 2. Make appropriate follow-up on referrals to outside agencies (district, psychologist, county, health, probation, etc.) through the proper channels.

OBJECTIVE III

To Provide Services which will Enable the Students to Make Appropriate Plans for their Educational and Vocational Futures

FUNCTIONS	IMPLEMENTATION
A. COUNSELING WITH STUDENTS	A. COUNSELING WITH STUDENTS
1. Assist the students to understand their vocational aspirations in relationship to ability and achievement.	1. Through planned group or student initiated conferences, the counselor assists the student in self-identification as related to his environment, objectives, aims, or goals.
2. Assist the students to explore broad areas of work in order that they may make realistic educational and vocational decisions.	2. Bring appropriate students into contact with other agencies which provide advisory services relative to the educational and vocational future of youth, such as California Employment Service.
	3. Encourage students to explore various educational-vocational materials and inform them of the availability of these materials.
3. The counselor will inform the students of the availability and purpose of various tests.	4. Provide specific information to appropriate students on relevant testing program, such as College Entrance Examination Board, American College Test, etc.
4. The counselor will interpret test results to students.	5. Utilize special testing when deemed necessary for individual needs.
	6. With the teacher's assistance, test results are provided and interpreted to the students in planned groups.
	7. At the request of the student, counselor will provide individual test interpretation.

OBJECTIVE III (continued)

FUNCTIONS	IMPLEMENTATION
B. COUNSELING WITH PARENTS AND TEACHERS 1. The counselor assists parents and teachers in understanding adequate methods of aiding students in making educational and vocational decisions. 2. The counselor actively utilizes parents, teachers, and other resources in the process of educational and vocational guidance.	B. COUNSELING WITH PARENTS AND TEACHERS 1. Provide planned parent-group counseling sessions and/or individual conferences. 2. Inform parents regarding information available at the school which may affect their child's educational and vocational future, including vocational, financial, college, apprentice, and technical school training, etc. 3. Through planned groups and/or individual conference, provide test results and interpretation related to the child's educational and vocational future. 4. Provide in-service orientation to teachers on the purposes, availability, and scheduling of various tests, including College Entrance Examination Board, American College Test, Merit, and others. 5. Students will be referred to appropriate teachers for information on specific educational and vocational problems.

OBJECTIVE III (continued)

FUNCTIONS	IMPLEMENTATION
C. EDUCATIONAL AND VOCATIONAL PLANNING 1. The counselor will act as a resource person in assisting the administration, staff, and other agencies in providing appropriate materials, programs, and information which will assist the students in educational and vocational planning.	C. EDUCATIONAL AND VOCATIONAL PLANNING 1. The counselor will assist the administration in planning special career programs, such as college night and career days. 2. At the administration's direction, the counselor may provide information to outside agencies, i.e., mental health agencies, employers, juvenile authorities, armed forces, F.B.I., welfare and community agencies. 3. The counselor will, upon request, act as a resource person for guidance information in certain activities connected with organizations, such as Future Teachers, Medical, Art, Future Business Leaders of America, etc. 4. The counselor will act as a resource person to those appointed to the responsibility of such activities as awards, scholarships, summer programs, etc.

OBJECTIVE IV

To Provide Routinely an Internal and Ongoing Evaluation of the Effectiveness of the Counseling Program under Administrative Supervision and, when requested, Provide Similar Evaluative Services for other Aspects of the Educational Program

FUNCTIONS	IMPLEMENTATION
A. EVALUATION	A. EVALUATION
1. Under supervision of the administration provide evaluation of the counseling program effectiveness.	1. Criteria to be utilized in the determination of counseling program outcomes are established by the stated objectives and their resultant function. Examples of the types of data to be collected: a. Data which reflects reaction of students, parents, and teachers to counseling services. b. Actuarial data which explains what a counseling staff has done. c. Outcome data which describes educationally related attitude and behavioral changes in students, teachers, and parents. Instruments for collecting such data will be developed in conjunction with administrative approval.
2. Provide assistance in the evaluation of teaching outcomes to departments or individual faculty members when requested by the department or the individual.	2. Assistance in classroom testing procedures such as item analysis, selection of appropriate item types, etc. 3. Assistance in evaluation of academic program outcomes.

BIBLIOGRAPHY

American Personnel and Guidance Association, *Basic Approaches to Mental Health in the Schools*. Washington, D.C.: American Personnel and Guidance Association, undated.

Barahal, G. D., and Brammer, L. H., "What Do Freshmen Think of Their High School Counseling?" *California Journal of Secondary Education*, Vol. 25, 1950, pp. 328–331.

Beck, C. E., *Philosophical Foundations of Guidance*. Englewood Cliffs, New Jersey: Prentice-Hall, 1963.

Berlin, I. M., "The School Counselor: His Unique Mental Health Function." *Personnel and Guidance Journal*, Vol. 41, 1963, pp. 202–205.

Bockoven, J. S., *Moral Treatment in American Psychiatry*. New York: Springer Publishing Company, 1963.

California Association of Secondary School Administrators, Counseling and Guidance Committee, *Guidance Programs Guidelines for California Secondary Schools*. Burlingame, California: CASSA, 1965.

Carlson, R. O., *Adoption of Educational Innovations*. Eugene, Oregon: University of Oregon Books, 1965.

Coleman, J. S., *Social Climates in High Schools*. Office of Education, Cooperative Research Monograph No. 4. Washington, D.C.: U.S. Government Printing Office, 1961.

Cook, Katharine M., "The Place of Visiting Teacher Services in the School Program." Office of Education, *Bulletin No. 6*. Washington, D.C.: U.S. Government Printing Office, 1945.

Cribbin, J., *A Critique of the Philosophy of Modern Guidance*, reprinted in Farwell, G. F., and Peters, H. J., eds., *Guidance Readings for Counselors*. Chicago: Rand McNally and Company, 1960.

Cumming, J., and Elaine, *Ego and Milieu: Theory and Practice of Environmental Therapy*. New York: Atherton Press, 1962.

Cutts, Norma D., ed., *School Psychologists at Mid-Century*. Washington, D.C.: American Psychological Association, 1955.

Eckerson, Louise O., and Smith, H. M., "Pupil Personnel Services." *Occupational Outlook Quarterly*, Vol. 7. No. 3, Sept., 1963, pp. 19–23.

Elkin, V. B., "Structuring School Psychological Services: Internal and Interdisciplinary Considerations," in Gottsegen, M. G., and Gloria B., eds., *Professional School Psychology*, Vol. 2. New York: Grune and Stratton, 1963.

Fisher, J. K., "Research Assembly on Pupil Personnel Services." Annual Conference of the Association for Supervision and Curriculum Development, San Francisco, California, March 14, 1966.

Fossett, Katharine, "Guidance Institutes — NDEA." *Personnel and Guidance Journal*, Vol. 39, 1960, pp. 207–209.

Gallaher, A., Jr., "Directed Change in Formal Organizations: The School System," in *Change Processes in the Public Schools*. Eugene, Oregon: University of Oregon Books, 1965.

Gibson, R. L., "Pupil Opinions of High School Guidance Programs." *Personnel and Guidance Journal*, Vol. 40, 1962, pp. 453–457.

Gottsegen, M. G., "The Role of the School Psychologist," in Gottsegen, M. G., and Gloria B., eds., *Professional School Psychology*, Vol. 1. New York: Grune and Stratton, 1960.

Guzzetta, C., "Current Uses of School Social Work in Guidance Programs." Paper presented to the annual workshop meeting of the San Diego and Los Angeles branches of the National Association of Social Workers, School Social Work Section, March, 1964.

Heilfron, Marilyn, "The Function of Counseling as Perceived by High School Students." *Personnel and Guidance Journal*, Vol. 39, 1960, pp. 133–136.

Herr, E. L., and Cramer, S. H., "Counselor Role Determinants as Perceived by Counselor Educators and School Counselors." *Counselor Education and Supervision*, Vol. 5, 1965, pp. 2–8.

Hill, G. E., "Evaluation of Guidance Services." *The Clearing House*, January, 1963, pp. 275–280.

———, and Nitzschke, D. F., "Preparation Programs in Elementary School Guidance." *Personnel and Guidance Journal*, Vol. 40, 1961, pp. 155–159.

Hoyt, K. B., "What the School Has a Right to Expect of Its Counselors." *Personnel and Guidance Journal*, Vol. 40, 1961, pp. 129–133.

Johnson, E. F., Stefflre, B., and Edelfelt, R. S., *Pupil Personnel and Guidance Services*. New York: McGraw-Hill Book Co., 1961.

Kehas, C. D., "Theoretical Formulations and Related Research in Guidance, Counseling and Personnel Services." *Review of Educational Research*, Vol. 36, 1966, pp. 207–218.

Kelly, J. L., "Present Practices in School Social Work," in *School Social Work*. Washington, D.C.: U.S. Government Printing Office, 1964.

Leton, D. A., "Concepts Which School Social Workers Hold of School Psychology." Report of the Committee on Relationship to Social Work, Division 16, American Psychological Association, 1958.

Loughary, J. W., ed., *Counseling, A Growing Profession*. Washington, D.C.: American Personnel and Guidance Association, 1965.

Lundberg, H. W., "Obtaining Improved Coordination and Collaboration in Pupil Personnel Activities." A paper presented at the annual conference of the American Personnel and Guidance Association, Chicago, April, 1962.

Mallery, D., *The High School Student Speaks Out.* New York: Harper and Brothers, 1962.

Mathewson, R. H., *Guidance Policy and Practice*, 3rd ed. New York: Harper and Row, 1962.

McCully, C. H., "Beyond Ritual in Guidance." Invited address at the annual meeting of the California Counseling and Guidance Association, Anaheim, California, 1963.

Miller, F. W., *Guidance Principles and Services.* Columbus, Ohio: C. E. Merrill Books, 1961.

Nebo, J. C., "Some Aspects of School Social Work Practice in Schools," *Social Work in the Schools — Selected Papers.* New York: National Association of Social Workers, 1960.

Ojemann, R. H., *Developing a Program for Education in Human Behavior.* Iowa City, Iowa: State University of Iowa Press, 1959.

Parsons, Frank, *Choosing a Vocation.* Boston: Houghton Mifflin Company, 1909.

Pierson, F. A., and Grant, C. W., "The Road Ahead for the School Counselor." *Personnel and Guidance Journal*, Vol. 32, 1954, pp. 207–210.

Russell, J. C., and Willis, A. R., "Survey of Teachers Opinions of Guidance Services." *Personnel and Guidance Journal*, Vol. 42, 1964, pp. 707–709.

Shaw, M. C., "Role Delineation among the Guidance Professions." *Psychology in the Schools*, January, 1967.

Shaw, M. C., and Rector, W. H., *Parent and Counselor Perceptions of Their Participation in Group Counseling.* Monograph No. 3, Western Regional Center of the Interprofessional Research Commission on Pupil Personnel Services. (Chico State College, Chico, California), October, 1966.

Tiedeman, D. V., and Field, F. L., "Guidance: The Science of Purposeful Action Applied through Education." *Harvard Educational Review*, Vol. 32, 1962, pp. 483–501.

Vallet, R. E., *The Practice of School Psychology: Professional Problems.* New York: John Wiley and Sons, 1963.

Warren, D. M., "High School Guidance in 1970: A New Frame of Reference." *California Journal of Secondary Education*, Vol. 38, 1963.

White, Mary A., and Harris, M. W., *The School Psychologist.* New York: Harper and Brothers, 1961.

Zander, A., "Resistance to Change — Its Analysis and Prevention," *Advanced Management*, Vol. 15, 1950, pp. 9–11.

INDEX

American Personnel and Guidance Association (APGA), 17
American Psychological Association (APA), 23
American School Counselors Association (ASCA), 6, 23
Antioch (California) School District, 63
   Guidance plan, 61
Assumptions, underlying guidance, 25
   underlying postulated model, 26
   ethical, 47
   professional, 48
Barahal, G. D., 3
Beck, C. E., 25
Berlin, I. M., 7
Bockoven, J. S., 19
Brammer, L. H., 3
Byrne, R. H., 19
California Association of Secondary School Administrators (CASSA), 5
Carlson, R. O., 37
Change, 36
   acceptance of, 37
   and finances, 38
   implementation of, 41
   in an established program, 38
   need for data, 40
   support for, 39
Coleman, J. S., 55
Consultation, with teachers, 19, 28
Cook, Katharine M., 8
Cribbin, J., 25
Cumming, Elaine, 19
Cumming, J., 19
Cutts, Norma D., 9
Diagnosis, 16, 18
Direct services, provision of, 17
   compared to indirect services, 26
   to children, 55
   to problem children, 56
Discipline, 59
Eckerson, Louise O., 7
Edelfelt, R. A., 7

Education, purposes, 45
Educational environment, 18, 46
Elkin, V. B., 9
Evaluation of guidance programs, 10
Field, F. L., 4
Fisher, J. K., 24
Fossett, Katharine, 7
Gallagher, A., Jr., 37
Gibson, R. L., 3, 7, 8
Gottsegen, Gloria B., 9
Gottsegen, M. G., 9
Grant, C. W., 7
Guidance functions (practices), 6
   appropriate, 49
   confusion with objectives, 22
   inappropriate, 59
   unique, 46
Guidance program development, 32
   outline of, 49
   personnel involved, 33
   procedures, 34
   role of group leader in, 35
Guidance specialist, defined, 1
   involvement in unrelated tasks, 3
   role, with children, 54
   with parents, 53
   with teachers, 50
Guzetta, C., 8
Harris, M. W., 9
Heilfron, Marilyn, 3
Hill, G. E., 7, 11
Hoyt, K. B., 7
Identification of problems, 18, 29
Indirect services, provision of, 19
Interprofessional Research Commission on Pupil Personnel Services, 19
   Western Regional Center of, 18, 37, 43, 51
Johnson, E. F., 7
Kelly, J. L., 8
Leton, D. A., 9
Loughary, J. W., 6, 10
Lundberg, H. W., 8

Mallery, D., 50
Mathewson, R. H., 4, 7
McCully, C. H., 7, 50
Mental health programs, 18, 28
Milieu therapy, 19, 28
Miller, F. W., 7
National Defense Education Act, 2, 4
Nebo, J. L., 8
Nitzschke, D. F., 7
Objectives of guidance, 21
  adequacy of, 22
  criteria for, 23
  current status of, 21
  interrelationship with values and assumptions, 29, 32
  postulated model, 26
  purpose, lack of, 3
  vagueness, 22
Ojemann, R. H., 17
Parsons, F., 2
Pierce-Jones, J., 19
Pierson, F. A., 7
Prevention of problems, 16, 17, 27, 28
Programming, 60
Psychotherapy, 9, 18, 29
Rector, W. H., 53
Role delineation and theory, 9
Russell, J. C., 7
School counseling, 6
School psychology, 9

School social work, 8
  role in guidance, 8, 9
Shaw, M. C., 3, 43, 53
Smith, H. M., 7
Social-cultural problems, 56
Specialist vs. generalist, 7, 16
Stefflre, B., 7
Student activities, 60
Teachers, communication between counselors and, 7
Testing program, 58
Thayer Conference, 9
Theory, in guidance, 1
  current status, 2
  diagram of model, 14, 15
  model for, 13, need for, 4
  need for, 2
  relation to role delineation, 9
  separate from other theory, 3, 4
  utilization in program development, 31
  ways of constructing, 3
Tiedeman, D. V., 4
Tuel, J. K., 43, 67
Vallet, R. E., 9
Values and the guidance program, 25
Vocational guidance, 2
Warren, D. M., 7
White, Mary A., 9
Willis, A. R., 7
Zander, A., 36

Other Monographs in Series I:

ESTABLISHING GUIDANCE PROGRAMS IN ELEMENTARY SCHOOLS
Verne Faust

ESTABLISHING GUIDANCE PROGRAMS IN SECONDARY SCHOOLS
Anthony C. Riccio
Joseph J. Quaranta

EXPANDING AND MODIFYING GUIDANCE PROGRAMS
Dorothy E. Johnson

STAFFING GUIDANCE PROGRAMS
George E. Hill

GUIDANCE PERSONNEL AND OTHER PROFESSIONALS
Richard C. Diedrich

ETHICAL AND LEGAL CONSIDERATIONS IN GUIDANCE
Wesley Huckins

INTERPRETING GUIDANCE PROGRAMS TO THE PUBLIC
Herman Peters

INTERPRETING GUIDANCE PROGRAMS TO SCHOOL PERSONNEL
Edward Roeber

INTERPRETING GUIDANCE PROGRAMS TO PUPILS
George O. McClary

HOUGHTON MIFFLIN COMPANY · BOSTON
New York · Atlanta · Geneva, Illinois · Dallas · Palo Alto

From Weill Medical College of Cornell University

The Cornell Illustrated Emergency Medicine and First Aid Guide

**Edited By
Antonio M. Gotto, Jr., MD, DPhil**
Dean, Weill Medical College
with
Physicians of the Emergency Medicine Department
NewYork-Presbyterian Hospital,
Weill Cornell Medical Center
Neal Flomenbaum, MD, FACP, FACEP
Emergency Physician-in-Chief
and
Faculty of Weill Medical College

LifeLine Press

A Regnery Publishing Company • Washington, DC

DISCLAIMER

All health and health-related information, including the descriptions and images contained in this book are intended for informational or educational use only and not as a substitute for the diagnosis of a competent health care professional or treatment by a physician. This information is intended to offer only a general basis for individuals to discuss their medical condition and concerns with a health care provider. As medical science is advancing continually, and since every individual's medical condition and needs vary considerably from person to person, this book is not to be considered complete or current in any way. Every effort has been made to make the content of and presentation of information in this work accurate and comprehensive, but that does not preclude the possibility of errors or of the omission of relevant medical information.

No product or treatment method included in this product is to be considered endorsed or recommended by Weill Medical College, Cornell University, medical advisors and consultants, or the publishers, producers, and distributors of this work; nor should the omission of any product or treatment be interpreted as disapproval of that product or treatment method. Readers are advised that they should consult a competent and qualified health care professional and physician in determining their medical condition and needs, and that is the only means of treating health care problems or situations recommended herein.

Produced by: The Reference Works, Inc.
Harold Rabinowitz, Director
Jenna Bagnini, Managing Editor
Stephen Smith, Noam Levy, Editors
Bob Antler, Tina West, Production

Copyright © 2002 The Reference Works, Inc., and Cornell University

All rights reserved. Printed in the United States of America. No part of this book may be used or reproduced in any manner whatsoever in any medium without the written permission of the Publisher, except in the case of brief quotations embodied in critical articles and reviews. Credits and acknowledgments for this book are contained on the last page, which is a continuation of this copyright notice.

Correspondence regarding this book should be addressed to the Publisher: LifeLine Press, a division of Regnery Publishing, Inc., One Massachusetts Ave., N.W., Washington, D.C. 20001

FIRST EDITION

Library of Congress Cataloging-in-Publication Data

The Cornell illustrated emergency medicine and first aid guide: the complete family guide / Antonio M. Gotto, Jr., general editor.
   p. cm.
Includes bibliographical references and index.
  ISBN 0-89526-184-7 (alk. paper)
   1. First aid in illness and injury—Popular works. 2. Emergency medicine—Popular works
I. Gotto, Antonio M. II. Cornell University, Joan and Sanford I. Weill Medical College.
  RO87.C74 2001
  616.02'5—dc21

02 03 04 05 06   10 9 8 7 6 5 4 3 2 1

The Editors

Antonio M. Gotto, Jr., M.D., D.Phil., is the Stephen and Suzanne Weiss Dean of the Weill Medical College of Cornell University. Dr. Gotto attained a D.Phil. in Biochemistry at the University of Oxford and an M.D. at Vanderbilt University School of Medicine. He has received several honorary Ph.D.s and professorships from around the world.

The Emergency Medicine Department at the Weill Medical College of Cornell University

Neal Flomenbaum, M.D., Professor of Clinical Medicine and Emergency Physician-In-Chief at Weill Medical Center at Cornell.
Wallace A. Carter, M.D., Assistant Professor of Emergency Medicine in Medicine and Program Director for the Emergency Medicine Residency.
Richard Lappin, M.D., Assistant Professor of Clinical Medicine.
Sam Senturia, M.D., Assistant Professor of Clinical Medicine.
Renu Mital, M.D., Instructor in Medicine.
Randy Fischer, M.D., Instructor in Medicine.
Charles Kwon, M.D., Instrutor in Medicine.
Eric Maniago, M.D., Instructor in Medicine.

Weill Medical College of Cornell University

Jack Barchas, M.D.
M. Flint Beal, M.D.
David A. Behrman, M.D.
Frank A. Chervenak, M.D.
Ronald G. Crystal, M.D.
John M. Daly, M.D.
Richard D. Granstein, M.D.
Lorraine J. Gudas, M.D.
Barry J. Hartman, M.D.
Joseph G. Hayes, M.D.
Julianne Imperato-McGinley, M.D.
Ira Jacobson, M.D.

Mark S. Lachs, M.D.
Bruce B. Lerman, M.D.
Alvin I. Mushlin, M.D.
Carl F. Nathan, M.D.
Maria I. New, M.D.
Richard S. Rivlin. M.D.
W. Shain Schley, M.D.
Roy L. Silverstein, M.D.
H. Dirk Sostman, M.D.
Manikkam Suthanthiran, M.D.
E. Darracott Vaughan, Jr., M.D.
Russell F. Warren, M.D.

Contents

The Editors	6	Black Eye	46	Crush Syndrome	86
Introduction	9	Bleeding	46	Dacryocystitis	87
		Bleeding, Treatment of	47	Deafness	87
Abdominal Pain	11	Blister	50	Decompression Sickness	89
Accidents	12	Blood Poisoning	50	Defibrillation	89
Acting Out	16	Blood Pressure	51	Dehydration	90
AIDS	16	Boil	52	Dehydration in Infants	92
Airway Obstruction	19	Botulism	53		
Alcohol Dependence	19	Brain Hemorrhage	54	Delirium	93
		Breathing Difficulty	55	Dementia	94
Allergic Reaction	20	Bronchodialator Drugs	57	Dengue	94
Altitude Sickness	21			Dental Emergencies	95
Ambulance	22	Bruise	58	Depression	96
Amputation	23	Burns	59	Detergent Poisoning	99
Anaphylactic Shock	24	Cadmium Poisoning	61	Diarrhea	99
Aneurysm	24			Discharge	102
Angina Pectoris	26	Caffeine	61	Dislocation, Joint	102
Anoxia	27	Carbon Monoxide	62	Dizziness	103
Antepartum Hemorrhage	28	Cardiac Arrest	63	Double Vision	104
		Cardiopulmonary Resuscitation (CPR)	64	Dressing	105
Anthrax	28	Cardiovascular Disorders	67	Drowning	107
Antifreeze Poisoning	29			Drug Overdose	108
Antiseptics	29	Carditis	69	Drug Poisoning	110
Aortic Aneurysm	30	Cauliflower Ear	70	Dysentery	111
Apnea	30	Causalgia	70	Dysmenorrhea	111
Appendicitis	31	Centers for Disease Control	70	Ear, Discharge from	112
Arrhythmia, Cardiac	31			Ear, Foreign Body in	112
Arsenic	33	Chest Pain	71	Earache	113
Asphyxia	33	Childbirth	73	Eardrum, Perforated	114
Asthma Attack	34	Chlorate Poisoning	74	Electrical Injury	114
Atelectasis	36	Choking	74	Embolism	116
Atrial Fibrillation	37	Cold Injury	76	Emergency, First Steps	118
Avulsion	38	Coma	77		
Back Spasms	39	Complication	78	Emergency Hospitalization	119
Bandage	40	Compress	78	Epileptic Seizure	120
Barbiturate Drugs	41	Concussion	79	Extradural Hemorrhage	122
Bends	42	Contraception	79		
Beta-Blocker Drugs	42	Coronary Heart Disease	81	Eye Injuries	122
Betamethasone	43			Eye, Foreign Body in	123
Biliary Colic	44	Coughing Up Blood	82		
Birth Defects	44	Cramp	83		
Bites	45	Crohn's Disease	84		

Facial Pain	125	Kidney Failure	159	Sling	191
Fainting	125	Kidney Stones	160	Snakebites	191
Falls, Preventing	126	Life Support	161	Spider Bites	192
Feces, Abnormal	126	Loss of Consciousness	162	Splint	193
Fever	127			Sports Injuries	194
Food Allergy	129	Menstruation,		Sprain	196
Food Poisoning	130	Disorders of	162	Stings	196
Foreign Body	131	Mercury Poisoning	163	Strangulation	197
Fracture	132	Migraine	164	Stroke	197
Frostbite	135	Morning After Pill	166	Strychnine Poisoning	199
Gallstones	136	Mushroom Poisoning	166	Sucking Wound	199
Gangrene	137	Nausea	167	Suffocation	200
Gastritis	137	Neck Rigidity	168	Suicide	200
Gastrointestinal Bleeding	138	Nerve Injury	168	Swallowing Difficulties	202
Glands, Swollen	139	Nervous Breakdown	169	Swelling	203
Head Injury	140	Nose, Broken	169	Tendonitis	204
Head, Neck, and Back Injuries	141	Nosebleed	170	Trauma	204
Heart Attack	142	Numbness	171	Tropical Diseases	204
Heat Exhaustion	144	Operating Room	171	Urinary Tract Infection	205
Heat Stroke	145	Pain Relief	172	Vaginal Bleeding	206
Heimlich Maneuver	146	Plants, Poisonous	173	Venomous Bites and Stings	207
Hiccup	147	Poison	174	Vomiting Blood	208
Hip Fracture	147	Poison Ivy, Oak, and Sumac	175	West Nile Virus	208
Hives	147	Poisoning	176		
Hospitals, Types of	148	Punchdrunk	177		
Hot Flashes	149	Rabies	177		
Hyperemesis	150	Radiation Sickness	178		
Hyperglycemia	150	Rape	179	Appendix A	209
Hyperventilation	151	Recovery Position	179	Related Organizations	
Hypotension	151	Rib, Fractured	181	Appendix B	213
Hypothermia	153	Running Injuries	181	Further Reading	
Hypovolemia	154	Scorpion Stings	183	Appendix C	215
Ice Packs	156	Seizure	183	Poison Control Centers	
Indigestion	155	Seizure, Febrile	184		
Injury	155	Septic Shock	185	Index	221
Insect Stings and Bites	156	Shock	186		
		Shoulder Dislocation	187		
Internal Bleeding	168	Skin Allergy	188		
Ipecac	168	Skull, Fractured	189		
Jellyfish Stings	159	Sleep Apnea	190		

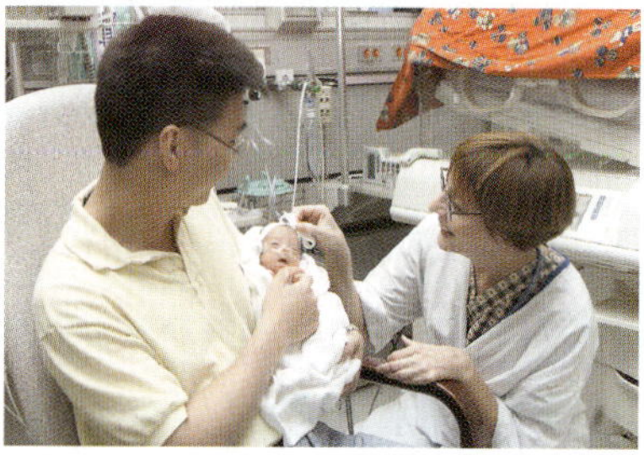
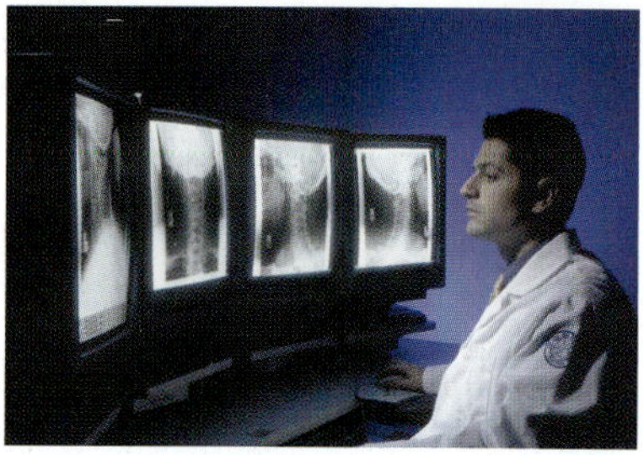
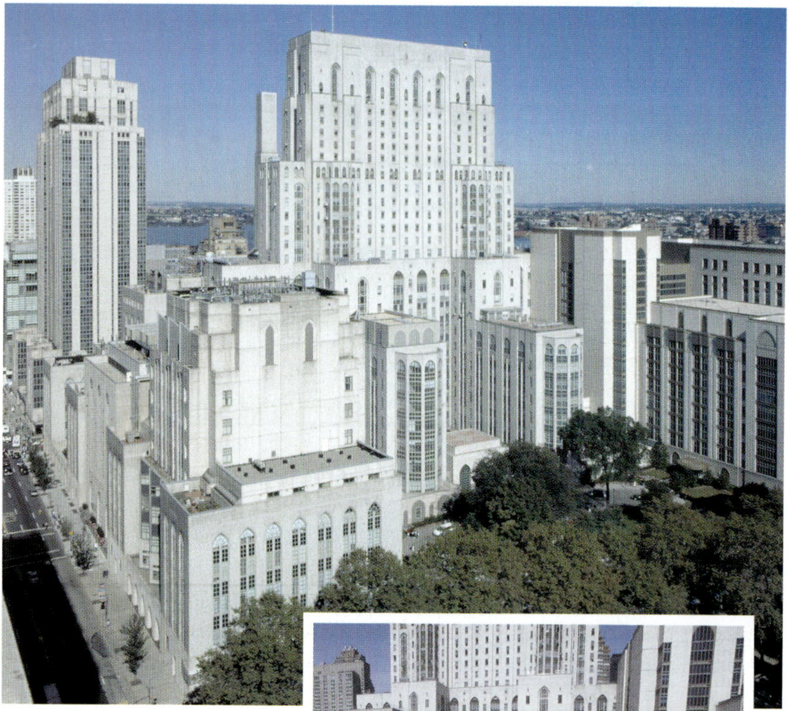
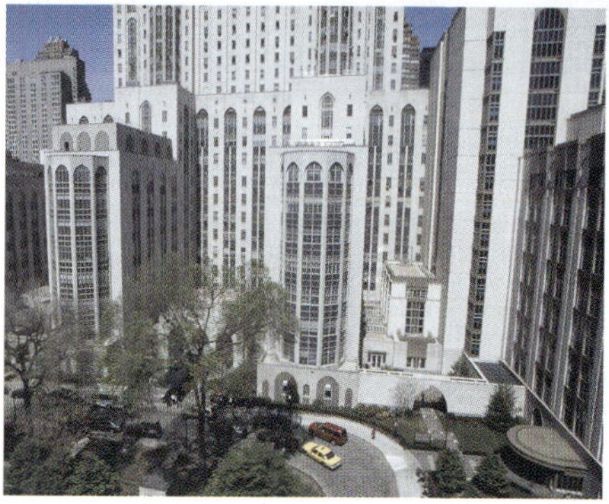

Introduction

Caring in a Time of Crisis

When faced with an emergency situation, the one piece of advice one always hears is how important it is to maintain one's composure, to remain calm and assess the situation with cool detachment. Decision-making is done best, it is said, in a quiet, unhurried, collected atmosphere, one without the shrill sirens (figuratively or literally) of emergency. In practice, however, this is not always easy to do: seconds can often mean the difference between surviving or succumbing, and speed and a sense of urgency are necessary if the patient is going to make it through the crisis. This is the paradoxical nature of emergency medicine—it something that has to be done (like Casey Stengel described turning a double-play) slow, but fast.

Those who work in emergency medicine and attend to the injured and the urgently ill know this paradox all too well, and grapple with it virtually on a daily basis. Act too quickly and something important will be overlooked; take the time to deliberate and the help arrives too late to save the patient from death or permanent damage. This is why preparation—physical, mental, and emotional—are critical in emergency care. Being ready to handle emergencies, foreseeable and unforeseeable, is critical in providing medical care when the emergency happens.

For a community, being ready means (a) having the necessary facilities, equipment, and trained personnel to handle whatever situation arises; (b) having clear procedures in place to handle a wide variety of trauma, injury, and emergency medical situations; (c) having a strong bond of trust and caring between the community and all its emergency, police and firefighters, and medical personnel and institutions.

Introduction

When the calamitous events of September 11, 2001, occurred, emergency personnel across the city reponded and the subsequent care and efforts of thousands of people made the aftermath of the tragedy some of our nation's finest hours. That was because there was readiness in all three areas: the city's response mechanism acted quickly and the casualties, horrendous as they were, were much less than they could have been; the procedures of evacuation, triage, and emergency care were in place and at the ready to treat the wounded and the survivors; and the bond between the people of New York—the Mayor, the police and firefighters, the rescue workers and the people evacuating the World Trade Center—was demonstably a strong one, strong enough to make the rescue and evacuation efforts a heroic chapter in the city's history.

For individuals, this level of readiness in all three areas—physical, mental, emotional—is no less important. Being prepared physically means having some of the necessary equipment available on hand that might be useful in the event of an emergency: a flashlight, bandages, some antiseptic ointment, water, etc. Being prepared mentally means knowing where your local emergency rooms are located, and having the numbers of your doctor and local hospital—and perhaps this book—in a location you can access easily and quickly. Being prepared emotionally means being aware of the times you live in and of the possible dangers and emergencies you might face, and being ready to reach out and help if others are in need of emergency assistance, and to let others provide such assistance and care to you if you are the one in dire medical circumstances. The key to care in a time of emergency, in our view, is establishing a community of caring in all times that covers everyone in all circumstances, emergency or not.

We end by hoping for something few authors and editors of a book ever hope for—that this book never be needed, that it turns out to be a superfluous artifact of a difficult and traumatic episode in the history of mankind, and not a part of history's blueprint for our species.

New York City
October 2001

Abdominal Pain

Discomfort in the abdominal region.

Abdominal pain consists of irritation, soreness, tenderness, or cramping in the abdominal and pelvic cavities, which are located below the ribcage (the thoracic cavity) and above the thighs. The thoracic cavity is separated from the abdominal cavity by the diaphragm muscle. However, no structure separates the abdominal cavity from the pelvic cavity. The abdominal cavity and its organs are covered by a thin membrane known as the peritoneum.

CAUSES

Abdominal pain may have numerous causes, ranging from harmless to quite serious. Perhaps the simplest and most common causes of abdominal pain arise from an individual's lifestyle. An excess of alcohol, spicy or fried foods, or foods high in fat, as well as late, heavy meals, may cause pain or nausea. Stress, anxiety, and tension can cause abdominal pain in both adults and children.

Abdominal pain may also be caused by a number of underlying physical conditions, which may require medical attention. These may include:

- injury to any abdominal organs;
- food allergy, intolerance, or poisoning;
- menstrual cramps;
- colic in infants;
- stomach flu;
- urinary tract infection (cystitis);
- ulcer;
- ruptured esophagus;
- gallstones;
- appendicitis;
- irritable bowel syndrome;
- hernia;
- pelvic inflammatory disease (PID);
- uterine fibroids;
- ovarian cysts;
- a fetus developing outside the uterus (ectopic pregnancy);
- diverticulitis;
- bowel obstruction;
- cancer of the stomach or colon;

Abdominal Pain

> **ALERT   ALERT   ALERT**
>
> ### EMERGENCY ABDOMINAL PAIN
>
> You may have a medical emergency and should contact your physician immediately if you experience acute abdominal pain with fever and nausea. This may indicate appendicitis, a bowel obstruction, or complications of diverticulitis, a disease in which small pouches form in the lining of the intestines, become inflamed, and may bleed. A rigid abdomen may indicate peritonitis. Blood in stools or vomit can be a symptom of gastrointestinal bleeding and requires immediate attention.
>
> If abdominal pain is accompanied by chest, back, or jaw pain; excessive sweating; anxiety; or a sense of impending doom, it may indicate a heart attack. Immediate emergency medical care is required.

TYPES OF ABDOMINAL PAIN

Based on the patient's description of the severity, type, and location of the pain, as well as any correlations between the pain and eating, urinating, and bowel movements, a physician can determine if the pain is likely to indicate a serious condition and if it requires further testing or treatment.

- **Gas pain** (flatulence) is a bloated, distended feeling in the lower abdomen. It can usually be controlled with lifestyle changes, such as a healthy diet, maintenance of a healthy weight, and exercise.
- **Heartburn** is a burning sensation in the upper abdominal area. It is usually harmless and can be controlled with changes in lifestyle and eating habits.
- **Menstrual Pain.** In women, cramp-like abdominal pain that occurs just before or during menstruation, or that occurs during ovulation, is usually normal and requires no special treatment other than possibly over-the-counter pain-relievers.
- **Peptic ulcer pain** is felt in the breastbone at the point where the ribs meet (the sternum). It may be eased temporarily with antacid medication and food. A doctor may prescribe a course of medication, possibly including antibiotics and antacids.
- **Kidney pain** is recurring and intermittent. It may begin below the rib cage and travel to the groin area, and is generally felt towards the back. Further testing is usually done to determine the underlying cause.
- **Pelvic organ inflammation** is a less centrally-located pain. It can spread to the entire abdominal region. There may be a vaginal discharge. Further testing is usually needed to determine the exact cause.

Accidents

- **Appendicitis pain** is a sharp pain that may begin at the navel and travel to the lower right side of the body. Acute appendicitis requires immediate surgery.
- **Gallbladder pain** is a constant, cramp-like pain that begins below the right set of ribs. It may be accompanied by fever and vomiting. Gallstones can be surgically or nonsurgically removed.

Abdominal Pain in Children

More than 10 percent of school-aged children develop abdominal pain. In 90 percent of the cases, the discomfort is caused by stress and anxiety. Children who are depressed or exhibit mental health problems should see a mental health professional, such as a social worker or psychologist. The closer the pain is to the navel, the more likely it is that the pain is caused by a physical disorder. Children with abdominal pain should be examined for signs of hepatitis, parasite infestation, sickle cell anemia, and lead poisoning.

When to Contact a Physician

Contact your physician if:
- You experience severe pain.
- You have had an abdominal injury within the last 72 hours.
- Pain occurs during pregnancy.
- Pain is prolonged and persistent.
- High fever and nausea, sometimes in conjunction with constipation and bloating, accompany the pain.
- You cannot keep food or liquid down for a period of more than 72 hours.
- Pain is accompanied by bloody stools or vomit.

Accidents

Unexpected and undesirable events, often resulting in injury.

Many accidents are preventable. For instance, protective equipment is available for activities from biking to woodworking. Utilizing safety measures that can be easily implemented while driving, in the workplace, and at home can prevent accidents.

Accidents

Questions to Ask

Some general questions important in assessing the severity of an accident include:

- **Is the victim breathing?** Are the air passages clear? If a victim is not breathing, artificial respiration may be necessary.
- **Is the victim's heart beating?** Is there a pulse in the carotid artery? If no heartbeat or pulse is detected, cardiopulmonary resuscitation (CPR) should be performed, preferably by someone trained in CPR.
- **Is the victim bleeding?** A pressure pad on the site of the bleeding—not a tourniquet above it—should be used to control blood loss. In cases involving a broken bone or a foreign object embedded in the wound, pressure may not be advisable.
- **Is the victim fully conscious?** Are there obvious causes for loss of consciousness, such as injury or drug overdose?

In the case of a serious accident, trained emergency personnel should be called immediately. If the victim appears to be suffering from shock, the best course is generally to try to keep the person warm, without attempting to move the victim.

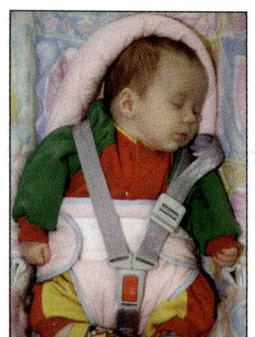

Safety Devices. Adults must be certain that children under their supervision are protected from injury by such measures as guard rails for stairs (above left); car seats for travel in cars or any other conveyance (above middle); and life jackets for swimming, boating, or any activity near water (above right).

Types of Accidents

Burns. Fire, hot water, chemicals, and electricity can all cause burns. Second- and third-degree burns must be treated by medical personnel. Minor burns with unbroken skin should be immersed in cool water, then cleaned carefully with soap and warm water, and covered lightly by gauze. If the skin is blistered and broken, contact a physician immediately.

Accidents

Electrical Injuries. It is crucial to disconnect the source of electricity without endangering the rescuer. Use a non conductive material, such as wood or plastic, to separate the current-carrying conductor from the victim. Treat as for burn or shock. Perform CPR as necessary.

Drowning. Water damage to the lungs and lack of oxygen are two of the most serious dangers in drowning. Time underwater, the temperature of the water, whether the water is salt or fresh, and the age of the victim all may affect the likelihood of recovery. CPR may be necessary.

Poisoning. A general approach, coupled with identifying the toxic substance, is the best approach for successful treatment. Do not induce vomiting without advice from a physician or assistance from a local or national poison control center.

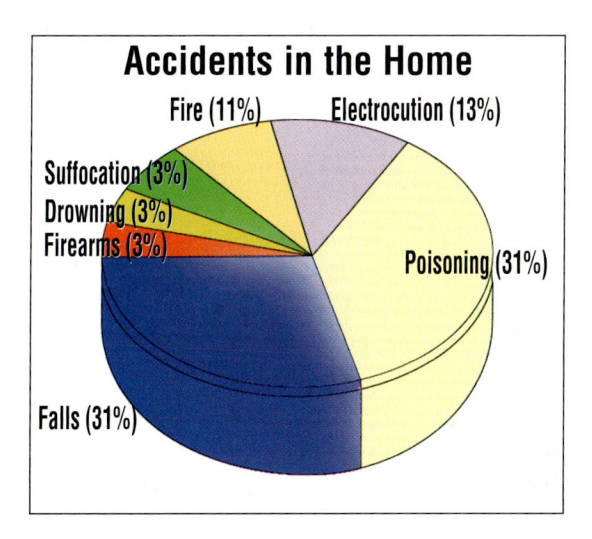

Accidents in the Home

- Fire (11%)
- Electrocution (13%)
- Suffocation (3%)
- Drowning (3%)
- Firearms (3%)
- Poisoning (31%)
- Falls (31%)

KEEPING CHILDREN SAFE

In the home. Store all cleaners, chemicals, medicines, appliances, and matches out of children's reach or in locked cabinets. Cap or tape over unused electrical outlets. Use only shatterproof glass for doors or tabletops and safety locks on windows. Install safety gates in front of stairways.

In the car. Use weight-specific child car seats; never acquire one second-hand. Never put a child in a seat with an airbag. Keep windows closed.

Outdoors. Children should cross streets with adults. Never leave a child alone near water; warn them against eating berries; teach them not to talk to strangers and help them memorize their address and telephone number.

Acting Out

> Expressing a feeling, wish, fantasy, or memory through behavior rather than conscious acknowledgement.

Older children and teenagers may act out for reasons ranging from seeking independence to responding to abuse.

In the context of psychotherapy, acting out refers to a situation in which a patient's behavior is used to express feelings, memories, or conflicts that cannot be acknowledged or put into words.

In its broadest sense, acting out refers to any situation in which a person's behavior serves to express unconscious feelings, memories, or fantasies, and may be self-destructive.

A person who continuously quits jobs or leaves relationships may be using behaviors to express unconscious fears of success or inadequacy. The most serious forms of acting out include substance abuse, delinquency, and self-mutilation.

Examining these behaviors in therapy may provide valuable information about the patient's inner life.

AIDS

Acronym for Acquired Immune Deficiency Syndrome

> A disease that destroys the immune system, caused by a virus known as Human Immunodeficiency Virus (HIV).

Two main strains of the HIV virus, HIV-1 and HIV-2, cause AIDS. HIV-1 is more common in the Western Hemisphere, Europe, Asia, and most of Africa. HIV-2 is more prevalent in West Africa; it is transmitted less easily and progresses less quickly to AIDS than HIV-1. In both strains, the virus may persist at low levels for years in a host without causing disease. The only sign of infection will be the presence of antibodies against the virus. Once immunodeficiency occurs, if left untreated, death usually follows within two to three years of the first onset of symptoms.

The HIV virus itself does not kill the patient. Instead, it destroys the immune system, leaving the patient susceptible to other diseases, especially certain types of cancers and pneumonia. These diseases are the immediate causes of death.

AIDS

The Course of the Disease

HIV infects a specific type of white blood cells (lymphocyte) called a T helper cell. More specifically, it attacks T helper cells that have a protein known as CD4 on the outer membrane. This kind of cell is essential in triggering the immune response to infection or other foreign materials. The HIV virus invades CD4 cells and inserts its own genetic material into them. There it uses the cell's resources to create more copies of the virus and eventually kills the CD4 cell. After enough CD4 cells are destroyed, the body is no longer able to fight off infection or destroy cancerous cells.

Because symptoms appear only after CD4 levels are very low, the progress of HIV infection is followed not by tracking symptoms, but by CD4 levels. The normal range is 800-1,300 per microliter of blood. In the first few months following infection, the count decreases by 50 percent. The immune system forms antibodies against the virus and continues to fight it but is unable to rid itself of the infection permanently. Within six months of the initial infection, the amount of virus in the blood (viral load) stabilizes. However, the CD4 cells continue to be affected. Symptoms of AIDS may not occur for another few years, but by then there will be high viral levels and CD4 counts of below 200.

The blood test for AIDS identifies the presence of antibodies against HIV. However, it is important to note that there is a time lapse of a few months between infection and antibody formation. During this time, viral particles are in circulation, and a person can unwittingly pass the infection on to others.

Symptoms

The earliest symptoms of HIV infection include a low-grade, intermittent fever, a rash, swollen lymph nodes, weight loss (wasting), and fatigue. After initial infection, several years may pass without symptoms.

As the immune system is affected and CD4 levels fall, the body becomes prey to various diseases, referred to as opportunistic diseases.

Opportunistic Diseases. AIDS patients often see other illness manifest with their weakened immune systems: a type of skin cancer called Kaposi's sarcoma; a fungal infection called thrush, caused by the fungus *Candida albicans*; a fungal infection in the lungs, caused by *Pneumocystis carinii*; tuberculosis or atypical mycobacterial infections; cryptosporidium, a gastrointestinal infection; a viral infection in the brain called progressive multifocal leukoencephalopathy; a virus, cytomegalovirus, that affects the retina and causes blindness; and, in women, cervical cancer.

AIDS

Treatment

Various drugs have been developed to fight the AIDS virus. The oldest of these drugs is AZT. Another medication is called ddI (didanosine). These drugs work by attempting to disrupt key chemical reactions in HIV's metabolic cycle, including those controlling its reproduction. However, the virus mutates rapidly, and the drugs lose their effectiveness after a while.

Recently, newer and more effective drugs have been developed in the fight against AIDS. The most promising new medications include a class of drugs known as protease inhibitors. These include the drugs called saquinavir, ritonavir, and indinavir. Protease inhibitors prevent the virus from being able to break down proteins in the host cells, which it needs to do in order to make new, properly developed copies. Protease inhibitors can reduce viral loads to undetectable levels, enabling patients to live normal lives. However, patients must continue to take these drugs indefinitely. The regimen is complicated, and the medications are expensive. There are some unpleasant side effects associated with their use and some indication that the drugs may lose their effectiveness after an extended period of time. Nonetheless, protease inhibitors go a long way in converting AIDS from a fatal disease to a chronic condition.

Recently, clinical trials have been initiated exploring immune-based therapies (IBTs), designed to augment the immune system reaction to HIV. Agents such as interleukin 2 (IL-2) are being tested to boost immunity to HIV.

Prevention

The transmission of HIV can be sharply reduced or eliminated entirely by a few basic practices. Intravenous needles should be safely disposed after each use and should not be shared; safe sex should be practiced in which there is no exchange of bodily fluids; and every sexual partner's history should be determined. The chances of contracting AIDS from a blood transfusion has been minimized, as blood products are routinely tested for HIV before use. (Donated blood is screened for other viral antibodies as well, including those for hepatitis.) It has been found that taking the drug AZT (zidovudine) during pregnancy reduces the chances of passing HIV to the fetus to just 25 percent.

Airway Obstruction

Blockage of the respiratory passages resulting in difficulty or cessation of breathing.

Most deaths caused by a foreign body in the air passages occur in children under the age of five, two-thirds of whom are infants. Adults are acutely aware of a foreign body in the airways, but children may show no symptoms unless the air passages are largely obstructed. The Heimlich maneuver for children over the age of one is the same as that for adults, except that the compression should be gentler. Do not use the Heimlich maneuver for children under the age of one. Instead, lay the infant face down with the chest on one open hand and tap firmly between the shoulder blades with the heel of the other hand.

Alcohol Dependence

A disease in which a person is unable to control his or her intake of alcohol.

Alcohol dependence is characterized by a craving for alcohol, inability to moderate the amount of drinking, physical dependence on and tolerance for alcohol, and withdrawal symptoms when drinking stops.

While over half of all Americans drink socially, about 15 million are dependent on or abuse alcohol. This impacts more than half of Americans, either through their own dependence or abuse or that of immediate family members. Alcoholism is more common in families in which other members are also addicts. It is most likely a combination of both genetic or environmental causes.

Development of Dependence. Early in use, cravings for alcohol tend to be psychological in origin. They may result from the sedative effect that alcohol provides: numbness and relief from uncomfortable feelings.

Over time, the dependence becomes physical. An individual develops a tolerance, and it becomes necessary to increase consumption to achieve the same "high."

Drinking increasing amounts of alcohol on a daily basis results in physical addiction. Alcohol builds up in the bloodstream, and if intake suddenly stops, blood pressure rapidly decreases and withdrawal oc-

Alcohol Dependence

curs. Symptoms of withdrawal include insomnia, sweating, anxiety, rapid pulse, nausea, and vomiting. In severe cases, withdrawal includes delirium trements, which involves delusions, hallucinations, and extreme agitation; severe withdrawal can be life threatening. Withdrawal from alcohol takes three to five days and should be supervised by a physician or within an alcohol treatment program.

TREATMENT

The only treatment known to be effective is complete abstinence. Moderate drinking is not possible after a person has developed alcohol dependence. Recovery can only begin when a person recognizes his or her dependence and is motivated to change; help from a treatment professional vastly improves chances of recovery.

There are a number of treatment options, and it is often best to use a combination of methods. Treatment may be provided on an outpatient basis, in a hospital, or in a residential treatment center. Association with a support group, such as Alcoholics Anonymous, may supplement it.

Allergic Reaction

The immune system's reaction to a foreign particle or substance as if it were a disease-causing agent.

Anaphylactic shock is a severe and often life-threatening allergic reaction. It can be triggered by bee or other insect stings or bites, certain drugs or foods, dyes used in diagnostic tests, or even a blood transfusion. Shock occurs when the allergic reaction triggers the blood vessels to dilate, causing circulatory failure and a drastic drop in blood pressure. Swelling of tissues in the throat may result in a blocked air passageway. Loss of consciousness may follow. Like other allergic reactions, anaphylaxis does not occur upon the first exposure to an allergen but only after prior sensitization.

If a person appears to be entering into anaphylactic shock, seek medical help immediately. Individuals who have a known allergy that can induce anaphylactic shock should carry an emergency kit that contains injectable epinephrine.

Asthma is a disorder in which certain situations trigger the airways to close up and mucus production to increase, resulting in partial or total impairment of breathing. Triggering conditions vary from person to person but include exposure to allergens as well as respiratory infections, exposure to cold, stress, and other situations. Asthma attacks range from fairly mild to life-threatening. People with asthma usually carry inhalers to limit the symptoms of an attack, but an asthma attack can be an emergency that requires immediate medical attention.

Altitude Sickness

A condition caused by insufficient intake of oxygen at high altitudes.

Altitude sickness is a common problem among climbers who ascend rapidly to high altitudes. Decrease in air pressure as altitude increases can cause altitude sickness. The concentration of oxygen is 21 percent at sea level and higher altitudes, but air pressure decreases as elevation increases, resulting in less total air inhaled with each breath. Thus, there is less oxygen available from each breath. This lack of oxygen can impair the functioning of the lungs, muscles, heart, and nervous system.

SYMPTOMS

At altitudes above 8,000 feet, over 20 percent of people report symptoms such as dizziness, fatigue, shortness of breath, nausea, and headaches. More severe symptoms include pronounced shortness of breath, mental disorientation, and disturbed balance.

In the most severe form, fluid builds up in the lungs (pulmonary edema) and the brain swells, which may lead to coma.

TREATMENT AND PREVENTION

The simplest treatment is returning to a lower altitude. If symptoms of altitude sickness persist and are severe, the individual may benefit from the prescription medication Diamox, which promotes faster, deeper breathing, and helps more oxygen to the bloodstream.

To prevent altitude sickness, climbers should progress slowly to higher altitudes. Mountain climbers should rest for a day or two after reaching an altitude of 8,000 feet and rest for a day or two for every 2,000 feet thereafter. At altitudes of over 10,000 feet, supplemental oxygen may be needed. Climbers should drink plenty of fluids, eat foods high in carbohydrates, and avoid alcohol or any drugs that interfere with respiration, such as sleeping medications. Good cardiovascular health also reduces the likelihood of altitude sickness.

Ambulance

A | Ambulance

> Vehicle carrying life-support equipment designed to transport victims of illness or accident.

Ambulances are far more varied in function, design, and staffing than most people realize. In a simple emergency, emergency medical technicians (EMTs) trained in basic life support (BLS) are dispatched. In a severe emergency that requires highly trained personnel and sophisticated equipment, skilled paramedics trained in advanced life support (ALS) are sent.

Equipment. Some ambulances contain stretchers with collapsible legs so that a victim can be transported from the home or an accident site to an emergency treatment center. A fully equipped advanced life support emergency ambulance will have a cardiac monitor and defibrillator, oxygen and oxygen monitoring equipment, as well as intravenous fluids and medications that may be needed in medical emergencies.

In addition to the typical emergency ambulances described above, there are also various types of non-emergency ambulances, which are used primarily for transport. These can include medicars and vans that deliver people to hospitals and day-care clinics. Chair cars are non-emergency ambulances that are designed to lift a wheelchair and hold it firmly in place.

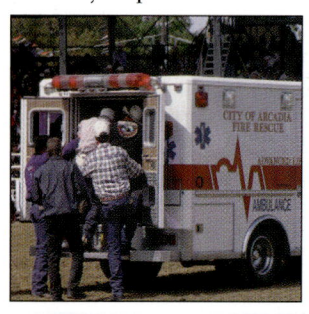

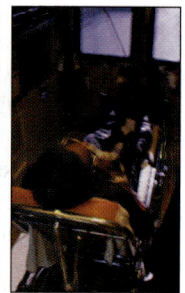

Ambulance. Frequently, the most important element in a medical response to an accident or an emergency is the ambulance service. Getting patients to medical facilities quickly and administering initial emergency procedure en route, above right, can make an enormous difference in the outcome. Above, left, a larger ambulance may have more room for equipment, but a smaller vehicle, above middle, may be better able to negotiate urban traffic.

Amputation

> Surgical removal of part or all of a limb or appendage, usually to prevent the spread of gangrene.

Body parts that may be amputated include arms, legs, hands, feet, fingers, toes, and, on rare occasion, penises. An amputation may also occur accidentally (traumatic amputation), or a limb may be missing from birth (congenital amputation).

Reasons for Surgical Amputations. The primary reason for most amputations is an interrupted blood supply to the body part, which results in tissue death (gangrene). The interruption can be caused by injury to blood vessels or by impaired blood circulation due to diabetes mellitus, atherosclerosis, obstructions in the arteries, and other circulatory disorders. Severe infections, frostbite, malignant tumors, and bone cancer may also require amputation.

Complications from diabetes are easily the largest single cause of amputations. High levels of blood sugar can cause the walls of small blood vessels to thicken (in a process called arteriosclerosis), which can impair circulation in the legs and feet, and subsequently cause gangrene. About 800,000 diabetic patients in the United States develop chronic foot ulcers, which lead to approximately 55,000 limb amputations each year.

Procedure. The site of amputation must contain healthy tissues and be above the site of the gangrene in order to ensure proper healing. A circular incision is made around the part to be amputated; skin and muscle are cut below the level at which the bone is cut in order to create flaps that will later provide a stump. Tissue, muscles, blood vessels, and nerves are severed. The surgeon makes an effort to sever the nerves above the stump in order to minimize pressure pain when the patient is eventually fitted with a prosthesis. The blood vessels are tied off, and the bone is severed, rounded off, and covered with connective tissue. The muscles and skin flaps are then sutured. Tubes are inserted in each side of the wound to allow for drainage.

Recovery. The average hospital stay following amputation lasts from two to seven days. The recovery period is approximately six weeks, during which physical therapy begins and after which a prosthesis is fitted. Recent innovations in prosthetics are so effective that most patients can resume quite normal lives and participate in sports and other activities after an amputation.

Anaphylactic Shock

A | Anaphylactic Shock

A severe, often life-threatening, allergic reaction.

Anaphylactic shock can be triggered by an allergic reaction to bee or other insect stings or bites, certain drugs or foods, dyes used in diagnostic tests, or even a blood transfusion. Shock occurs when the allergic reaction is so severe that it triggers the blood vessels to dilate, causing a sudden drop in blood pressure and circulatory failure. The allergic reaction may also trigger swelling of tissues in the throat, which can result in blocked air passageways. Loss of consciousness may follow.

Symptoms. Symptoms of anaphylactic shock may occur at any time within two hours of exposure to the specific allergen. They include a rapid pulse; difficulty breathing; pallor; cold, clammy skin; very low blood pressure; nausea and vomiting; and convulsions. If left untreated, the patient will lapse into a coma.

Treatment. Anaphylactic shock necessitates immediate medical intervention. If the patient's breathing ceases, mouth-to-mouth resuscitation should be performed immediately.

ALERT   ALERT   ALERT

TREATMENT FOR ANAPHYLACTIC SHOCK

In cases of anaphylactic shock, emergency services (911) should be called immediately. Lay the victim down and elevate the legs. Persons with a history of anaphylactic shock may carry a syringe of epinephrine; this should be injected. If the victim possesses a device called an "EpiPen," remove the cap and firmly strike the victim's thigh. If the victim stops breathing, it is important to perform CPR until medical help arrives.

Aneurysm

The ballooning of the wall of an artery, caused by disease, injury, or a congenital weakness of the blood vessel.

There are two major kinds of aneurysm: degenerative and dissecting. A degenerative aneurysm occurs when the middle wall of the artery, the tunica media, has been weakened and the force of blood pressure causes the artery to become distended. A dissecting aneurysm occurs

Aneurysm

when a split develops in the artery wall, allowing blood to enter. This split can be caused by inflammation, disease, or a congenital defect. The split can grow and damage more extensive regions of the artery.

Less common causes of aneurysms include diseases, such as Marfan's syndrome or inflammation of blood vessels. More than 20 percent of persons with Marfan's syndrome develop dissecting aneurysms. A special kind of aneurysm, congenital bicuspid aortic valve, is a congenital condition that results in the weakening of a heart valve.

Degenerative aneurysms are often the result of atherosclerosis—the thickening and narrowing of arteries caused by increasing deposits of plaque along the blood vessels. Dissecting aneurysms often are associated with hypertension, because abnormally high blood pressure can weaken the artery wall over time. Cigarette smoking can also result in aneurysms.

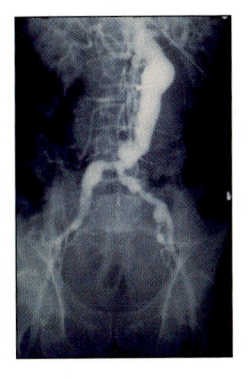

Aneurysm.
Left, ballooning of an artery, called an aneurysm, can be seen with an angiogram, an x-ray image of the arteries. Before the angiogram is taken, a contrast dye is injected into the artery to be studied through a catheter, making the artery and the aneurysm visible on the x-ray.

Treatment. Aneurysms can grow and possibly rupture, creating a condition that can be life-threatening if it occurs in the aorta, the heart wall, or the brain. When an aneurysm is two to three inches in size, surgery may be performed to remove the damaged part of the artery. When the ballooning region is cut out, it is replaced by a patch or artificial graft. If the aneurysm is close to the aortic valve, which controls blood out of the heart, the valve may be replaced by a mechanical valve or one made of animal or human tissue. Open-heart surgery may be needed to repair an aneurysm in the chest.

Outlook. Statistics show that the five-year death rate for persons who undergo surgery for an aneurysm is about 40 percent, while it is 80 percent for those who do not undergo surgery. The mortality rate is higher for emergency surgery when an aneurysm ruptures in the aorta or heart wall, but the risk of death or serious damage without surgical intervention is much higher.

Angina Pectoris

Angina Pectoris

A pain or pressure in the chest that lasts for several minutes and can radiate into the neck or arm.

Angina pectoris results from a decreased supply of oxygen to the heart muscle. It is caused most often by coronary artery disease—the narrowing of the arteries of the heart that results from atherosclerosis (the buildup of fatty deposits in those blood vessels). Angina may also be triggered by a coronary artery spasm, the sudden temporary narrowing of the coronary arteries; by aortic stenosis, the narrowing of the aortic valve through which blood flows from the heart; or by an arrhythmia, an abnormal heart rhythm.

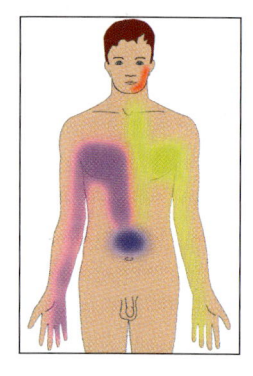

Angina Pectoris. Left, angina pectoris is a pain or pressure that is felt in the chest and sometimes in the arm or neck as well. Angina results from a decrease in the amount of oxygen supplied to the heart.

Angina pectoris generally occurs in times of physical exertion or emotional stress, although there is a variant form, Prinzmetal's angina, that usually occurs while a person is at rest. Angina can occur in men in their 30s, but it usually does not make itself evident until individuals reach their 50s. It starts later in life in women. It is often accompanied by feelings of suffocation and impending death, as well as pain radiating into the left arm.

Treatment. After angina is diagnosed, the initial goal of treatment is to remove any underlying cause of the condition. An obese patient should lose weight to reduce the workload of the heart. A smoker should stop smoking, since the nicotine and carbon monoxide in cigarette smoke accelerate the progression of heart disease. If the patient has hypertension, a drug can be prescribed to lower the blood pressure. Medications can be prescribed for arrhythmia or for high blood-cholesterol levels. Attacks of angina can be prevented or treated with nitrate medications, such as nitroglycerin, or with other medications that increase the flow of blood. Examples of such drugs include beta-

Anoxia

blockers, angiotensin-converting enzyme (ACE) inhibitors, and calcium channel blockers.

Long-Term Treatment. Weight reduction, diet, and drug treatment may reduce and control the symptoms of angina in many cases, but cannot cure the disorder. The cardiologist will monitor an angina patient closely to determine if the attacks occur more often, are more severe, or last longer. These signs indicate a worsening condition called unstable angina, which increases the risk for a heart attack. An individual with unstable angina may be hospitalized, often in a coronary intensive care unit, and treated with heparin and aspirin to improve bloodflow while further treatments for the angina are determined.

In some cases, narrowing of the arteries can be determined to be the cause of unstable angina. If this narrowing is not widespread, it can be treated by balloon angioplasty, a procedure in which a balloon is inserted into a narrowed area of a blood vessel to widen it, improving bloodflow. A tube called a stent may be implanted to help keep the blood vessel open. When artery disease is widespread, a coronary artery bypass operation, which is performed under general anesthesia, is required. In this operation, a segment of a vein is removed from the leg and is attached to the artery or arteries where blockages are found, looping around the narrowed areas to restore better bloodflow.

Anoxia

A condition in which the tissues of the body receive too little oxygen.

Anoxia is a term used to describe the absence of oxygen in body tissue. This condition is often the consequence of cardiac arrest, smoke or carbon monoxide inhalation, reduced oxygen levels, or strangulation. Anoxia commonly results in muscle spasms, seizures, or coma. It is a life-threatening emergency. If anoxia persists for more than four to six minutes, permanent brain damage or death is likely.

Anoxia is marked by a total lack of oxygen to body tissues. It is a severe condition and is very rare. In contrast, hypoxia is a deficiency of oxygen. It is more common than anoxia, and often occurs at higher altitudes among people who have climbed too quickly to become accustomed to reduced levels of oxygen.

If anoxia is not caused by cardiac arrest, treatment is to make sure air passages are open to oxygen administration, possibly followed by respiratory assistance and supplemental oxygen, if available.

Antepartum Hemorrhage

Antepartum Hemorrhage

Any bleeding during the second half of pregnancy.

There are several possible causes of antepartum hemorrhage, including a low placenta and premature separation of the placenta from the uterine wall. Bleeding may be light or heavy and may also be accompanied by abdominal pain. Both the source and the amount of blood are important in determining if there is a threat to the pregnancy.

Mild bleeding may cease on its own, but a doctor should be notified immediately about *any* prenatal bleeding. Heavier bleeding can be particularly dangerous, and requires immediate intervention. Treatment may include close monitoring and bed rest in an attempt to postpone labor; hospitalization may be necessary. When the hemorrhage poses a major threat to the health of the mother or the fetus, medical professionals may decide to induce labor or to perform a Cesarean section.

Anthrax

A disease caused by *Bacillus anthracis*, a spore-forming bacterium that infects the skin, lungs, and gastrointestinal tract.

Cause. Anthrax is a highly contagious disease that is usually transmitted to humans from animals. The spores can lie dormant in the earth for many years and then infect animals or humans when inhaled, ingested, or exposed to an open wound. Anthrax is considered a possible bioterrorism agent.

Symptoms. Symptoms of anthrax become evident between 12 hours and a week after exposure to the bacteria, depending on the location of the infection. When the bacteria invades the skin, the first symptom is a bump that resembles an insect bite. The bump ruptures, leaving an ulcer and then a black, hardened center of dead tissue with swelling around it. If left untreated, the infection may spread to the lymph nodes. When anthrax is inhaled, the lungs are infected, bringing on symptoms similar to those of influenza. Fever rises and difficulties in breathing soon lead to shock and possibly death. Gastrointestinal anthrax produces inflammation of the gastrointestinal tract, abdominal pain, vomiting of blood, and severe diarrhea. This infection can spread to the blood and result in death.

Prevention and Treatment. Those who are exposed to animals or

Antiseptics

animal products on a daily basis can be vaccinated for anthrax. Skin infections related to anthrax are treated with penicillin injections or oral antibiotics, such as doxycycline or ciprofloxacin ("cipro"). Intravenous antibiotics are required to treat lung infections caused by the disease.

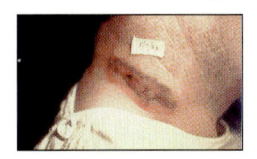

Anthrax. One of the first symptoms of cutaneous (skin) anthrax is often a lesion, as seen at left. As the disease progresses, the lymph and respiratory systems are also eventually affected.

Antifreeze Poisoning

Adverse physical effects resulting from the ingestion of antifreeze.

Antifreeze is usually made of a type of alcohol, either methanol or ethylene glycol. Both are extremely toxic if ingested, and only a few swallows can be lethal.

Symptoms of poisoning include cramps, headache, depressed breathing, and convulsions. Methanol has the potential to damage the optic nerves and cause permanent blindness; ethylene glycol can result in kidney failure.

Both of these alcohols are processed (metabolized) by the kidneys into highly toxic substances. Therefore, a rapid response is essential in treating antifreeze poisoning. The slightest suspicion of antifreeze poisoning is cause for seeking immediate medical help.

Antiseptics

Preparations used to cleanse and disinfect minor wounds or scrapes.

Antiseptics are used to prevent or stop the growth of the bacteria that invade an open wound, thus preventing infection. Antiseptics are intended for application to the skin or mucous membranes of the area around the victim's wound; they are therefore milder than disinfectants, which are intended for the disinfection of inanimate objects, such as knives or medical instruments. In hospitals or nursing homes the preferred antiseptics are chlorhexidine for general skin application and iodophor for genital areas.

Hexachlorophene and iodine are not recommended for use as antiseptics. Hydrogen peroxide is not particularly effective as an antiseptic either.

Aortic Aneurysm

Aortic Aneurysm

A widening or bulging of the main blood vessel that carries blood from the heart.

An aneurysm is a bulge in a blood vessel, similar to a bulge in an overinflated inner tube. An aortic aneurysm affects the aorta—the main artery leading away from the heart. An aneurysm may burst, severely disrupting the circulation of blood.

Causes. In many cases, the cause of an aortic aneurysm is arteriosclerosis—a hardening of the arteries. The condition may also be caused by an inherited disease such as Marfan's syndrome—a rare genetic disorder that affects connective tissues.

Diagnosis. An aortic aneurysm can be detected by x-ray, or it can be detected by imaging techniques, such as magnetic resonance imaging (MRI).

Treatment. Aortic aneurysms are generally repaired surgically. If the surgery fixes the aneurysm before it breaks, 80 percent to 90 percent of patients survive. If the aneurysm is distended or has burst, emergency surgery is always necessary, and the outlook is poor.

Apnea

An involuntary, temporary stoppage of breathing.

Apnea can result from any disorder affecting the nerve center in the brain stem that controls breathing. .

One common form of apnea, sleep apnea, causes brief interruptions of breathing during sleep, waking the affected individual repeatedly throughout the night. Sleep apnea can disrupt normal living by causing extreme sleepiness during the day.

More dangerous forms of apnea result from damage to the brainstem respiratory center, head injury, and temporary or permanent interruption of bloodflow to the brain (known as transient ischemic attack and stroke, respectively). Prolonged apnea is the cessation of breathing long enough to be life-threatening. Blockage of the airways by a foreign object is another cause of prolonged apnea.

The treatment of apnea depends on the underlying cause, such as removal of any object that obstructs the airway. In cases where the nerve center in the brain stem that controls breathing is affected, medications that stimulate breathing (analeptic drugs) may be prescribed.

Appendicitis

The infection and inflammation of the appendix.

The appendix is a small, worm-shaped structure attached to the cecum, where the small and large intestines meet. It has no known function. It can become infected as a result of blockage by a piece of feces or other foreign body, or by a tumor. Often, however, the cause of the infection is unknown. Appendicitis most commonly occurs in individuals between the ages of 10 and 30, although it can occur at any age.

Symptoms. The classic symptoms of appendicitis are a cramp-like abdominal pain beginning around the navel and migrating to the lower right side. The pain may be accompanied by severe nausea and vomiting, as well as a low-grade fever. If the appendix ruptures, the pain may disappear for a time. The abdominal lining becomes infected, however, and pain and progressive illness return.

Diagnosis. Diagnosis of appendicitis follows from an abdominal exam, which may reveal tenderness. A blood test will show an increased white blood cell count in response to the infection. Computed tomography (CT) scans are often performed to confirm a diagnosis postoperatively (after surgery).

Treatment. Appendicitis is treated by the surgical removal of the appendix. In the case of a burst appendix, intravenous antibiotics are administered to prevent peritonitis—an infection of the abdominal cavity lining.

Arrhythmia, Cardiac

An abnormality of the heart rate or rhythm.

Arrhythmias are caused by interference with the generation or transmission of the electrical impulses that govern the heartbeat. These impulses originate in the sinoatrial node, located in the right atrium—an upper chamber of the heart. From there, they are conducted to the atrioventricular node, a transmission center in the middle of the heart. After a brief delay during which the two atria contract, an impulse goes to the bundle of His and Purkinje fibers, a group of fibers that travel to both ventricles. When the muscle cells of the ventricle receive an impulse, they contract to cause a heartbeat.

Asthma Attack

An attack of breathlessness and wheezing caused by the respiratory disorder asthma.

Asthma can occur at any age, but about half of all cases strike children under the age of ten. Childhood cases often become less severe or clear up entirely with age. There appears to be a genetic factor—overall incidence in the American population is about five percent, but someone with a child or parent who has asthma runs a 20-25 percent risk of developing the disorder.

Asthma attacks are unpredictable. They can occur often or seldom, with variations in severity, and can happen at any time, although they are slightly more likely to take place at night. In addition to breathlessness and wheezing, asthma attacks can cause coughing and tightness in the chest.

ALERT   ALERT   ALERT

PREVENTING ASTHMA ATTACKS

It is possible to prevent asthma attacks by testing for and avoiding the allergens that cause them. For instance, parks and the countryside may be avoided because of pollen; mattresses can be wrapped in plastic, and the house kept dust free to minimize dustmites. Cromolyn sodium and corticosteroid drugs can prevent asthma attacks; they are most effective when inhaled many times a day. It is often not possible to build up immunity through injections of an allergen, as can be done with some other allergies.

Causes. In about five out of six asthmatics, the attacks are triggered by an allergic response to something in the air. When a substance capable of causing an allergic reaction (antigen) is breathed in, it is recognized by the immune system. An immune system molecule (immunoglobulin E—abbreviated IgE) and an immune system cell (mast cell) work together against infection. The presence of an antigen causes the mast cell to release a number of substances that act on the smooth muscles lining the airway and lungs. These substances (histamine, leukotrienes, and prostaglandins) cause the muscles to contract. They also cause the lining of the airway to become inflamed, and thick mucus that blocks the airway is released. The combination of inflamed, narrowed airways and clogging mucus makes breathing more difficult. Breathing difficulties may continue for hours after the initial attack. Antigens that can cause this reaction differ from person to person and include natural substances such as pollen, insect droppings, animal dander, and fragments of hair and skin.

Asthma Attack

For a minority of patients, asthma attacks are triggered by something other than an allergic reaction. Cigarette smoke can cause an attack and can increase the severity and frequency of asthma episodes resulting from other causes. Air pollution can set off an attack, and so can the fumes of kerosene, natural gas, or a wood fire. A common cold or other viral respiratory infections can have the same effect.

Some drugs can initiate an asthma attack for individuals who are sensitive to aspirin or nonsteroidal anti-inflammatory drugs. A drug-related asthma attack can be severe enough to cause respiratory failure.

Physical activity can also set off an attack by causing a bronchospasm, a contraction of the muscles that line the airways of the lung. Such an asthma attack is more likely to occur on a cold day. But exercise is not forbidden for people with asthma. The kind of exercise, the amount of exercise, and where it is done must be chosen with care. For example, running outdoors on a winter day may set off an attack, but swimming in a heated pool may not, since warm, moist air has a beneficial effect. Sometimes anxiety or stress can also set off an attack.

Treatment. Treatment of an asthma attack starts with the earliest possible detection of the onset of the attack. In most cases, warning signs begin hours before the onset of symptoms. Deterioration of breathing that signals an oncoming attack can be monitored by a device called a peak flow meter, which indicates the efficiency of breathing. A reading below 80 percent of maximum effectiveness is an indication that preventive measures should be taken, such as increasing the dose of asthma medications. A reading below 50 percent is a clear sign of trouble needing medical attention. The symptoms of an asthma emergency include severe breathing difficulty, blue-tinted lips because of a shortage of oxygen, and an abnormally fast heartbeat.

Most asthma attacks do not require emergency measures. Their severity can be reduced by bronchodilators, medications that widen the airways by relaxing the muscles around them. In addition, medications can be taken on a daily basis to reduce the inflammation that causes asthma attacks. Among these medications are cromolyn sodium and corticosteroids. Medications that treat asthma may be taken in pill or liquid form, or by an inhaler or nebulizer.

Living with Asthma. Asthma is a highly personal condition. Asthmatic patients should work closely with doctors to develop the most effective measures of preventing attacks and minimizing their effects when they occur. For the great majority of patients, asthma can be kept under control well enough to permit near-normal living.

Atelectasis

A slow or sudden collapse of a segment of a lung.

Atelectasis occurs when the clusters of tiny air sacs of the lung (alveoli) become filled with fluid or collapse, usually because the airways of the lung become obstructed. Most commonly, the obstruction is caused by a plug of mucus, although a tumor, an enlarged lymph gland, or an inhaled object may be responsible. Persons who are most vulnerable to atelectasis include heavy smokers and people with cystic fibrosis disease. In children, the condition can occur at birth or be caused by whooping cough in an older child.

Symptoms. A collapsed lung can no longer supply the blood with oxygen and remove carbon dioxide from the blood. The major symptom of atelectasis is difficulty breathing, sometimes accompanied by coughing and chest pain.

Atelectasis usually is not a life-threatening condition for adults, since the uncollapsed part of the affected lung may retain enough function to meet the body's needs. Even if an entire lung is obstructed, the other lung can function well enough to compensate for the damage. Atelectasis in a child can be a much more serious matter.

Diagnosis. A chest x-ray can detect atelectasis and the cause of the blockage. If only a small part of a lung is affected, the x-ray will show horizontal lines in that area. A larger affected area will appear as a dense shadow on an x-ray.

Treatment. Frequent coughing, deep breathing, postural drainage, and chest percussion often are effective as treatment for atelectasis. For postural drainage, the patient lies on a bed with his or her head and chest hanging over the edge, so that gravity will drain the mucus into the upper part of the lung, where it can be coughed out. In chest percussion, the chest is tapped to loosen the mucus. Surgery may be required if a cancerous growth is responsible for the blockage. Once the flow of air is restored, the lung may gradually return to normal function, although some part of the lung may suffer permanent damage or scarring.

Atrial Fibrillation

An irregular heartbeat in which the upper chambers of the heart—the atria—beat very rapidly, up to 300 to 500 times a minute.

When atrial fibrillation occurs, the atrioventricular node, a structure that conducts impulses between the atria and the lower chambers of the heart (ventricles), cannot respond to every atrial beat. It will often block one out of every two atrial beats so that the ventricles contract less frequently than the atria—only 125 to 175 times a minute.

Causes. Atrial fibrillation usually occurs when the left atrium is enlarged, commonly because of chronic heart disease, such as rheumatic heart disease or atherosclerosis; however, it can also occur in the absence of heart disease. The conditions that can bring on atrial fibrillation include overactivity of the thyroid gland, lung disease, and pericarditis—inflammation of the membrane that covers the heart (the pericardium). Excessive consumption of alcohol or caffeine, or the use of street drugs, such as cocaine, are also associated with an increased risk of atrial fibrillation.

Symptoms. As the atria fail to pump blood effectively, the symptoms can include palpitations and chest pain caused by a reduced blood supply (angina). Atrial fibrillation can cause the ventricles to lose 20 to 30 percent of their ability to pump blood to the lungs and the rest of the body, but the pumping capacity usually remains sufficient for the body's needs.

Diagnosis. Atrial fibrillation is diagnosed when the pulse rate is irregular and does not keep time with the heart rate, since many of the beats that can be heard through the stethoscope do not push blood out to the wrist, where the pulse is measured. Diagnosis is confirmed by an electrocardiogram, which records the electrical activity of the heart.

Treatment. Drugs such as digitalis and beta-blockers can be prescribed to lower the heart rate, with anticoagulants or aspirin given to prevent formation of blood clots.

ATRIAL FIBRILLATION: VISITING THE DOCTOR

Any fatigue, chest pain, ankle swelling, faintness, sudden limb weakness, or vision or speech loss should be reported to a doctor. The physician may examine the heart rate, breathing, pulse, blood pressure, and veins in the neck, ankles, and legs. Tests may include thyroid function tests; tests of blood levels of digoxin, potassium, and magnesium; tests of the kidneys; prothrombin time tests, if warfarin is being taken for blood-thinning; an electrocardiogram; and a Holter or an event monitor, if the atrial fibrillation is periodic.

Avulsion

Avulsion

Tearing of body tissue from its normal attachment.

An avulsion is usually caused by injury, but it may also be intentionally performed during a surgical procedure. The term is most commonly used when describing an avulsion fracture, which is the tearing away of an overstretched ligament from bone. The tear may be small or quite large, depending on the severity of the injury and the size of the affected bones or joints.

Treatment. Elevation of the damaged area or the use of a splint to hold the torn area together in its natural position are common treatments. In less severe cases, a compress may suffice to treat the injury.

Back Spasms

Uncontrolled movements of the muscles in the back, causing pain and discomfort.

Many people suffer from back pain or spasms at some point in their lifetimes. In the majority of these cases, the cause cannot be determined, and the spasms will subside with pain-killers and rest. These types of spasms are labeled "nonspecific."

Causes. Nonspecific back spasms are very common, and account for much of the work time that is lost in the United States each year. Individuals most likely to suffer this type of injury are those with jobs that require lifting and carrying of heavy objects, or those who spend long periods of time sitting or standing in awkward positions. Overweight and obese people are also more likely to suffer back spasms because of the additional weight placed on their backs, coupled with the comparative weakness of their abdominal muscles.

Spasms of the back muscles can result from ligament strains, muscle tears, or damage to one or more vertebrae. These spasms can cause tenderness over a wider area than that which is affected by the injury, and may also cause temporary scoliosis (curvature of the spine).

Diagnosis. The cause of back spasms can often be determined by various types of imaging of the affected area. X-rays can reveal abnormalities of the spine, such as fractures or compression. To determine if there is ligament, muscle, or joint damage, CAT or MRI scans may also be needed.

Treatment. If the cause of the back spasms can be diagnosed, it is treated accordingly. General treatment for back spasms of an undetermined cause includes rest and the administration of analgesic (pain-killing) medications. Back spasms that are chronic (occur over an extended period of time) are more difficult to treat. Anti-inflammatory drugs, muscle relaxants, moderate exercise, or acupuncture may help to alleviate some of the pain, or surgery may be required.

Prevention. Reducing strain placed on the back is a simple way to prevent back spasms. Heavy objects should not be pushed from the front with the arms straight, but should instead be pushed while leaning backwards, placing the strain on the legs instead of the back. When heavy objects must be lifted, it is important not to bend over with straight legs, as this can strain the lower back; the knees should be bent while the back is kept straight. Proper posture—sitting up straight in a chair rather than slouching—can also reduce back strain.

Bandage

B Bandage

A gauze or adhesive covering used to protect a wound or control bleeding.

Bandages are an essential element of any health-care device or institution, from the family first aid-kit to the local hospital. For minor cuts or bruises, strips of adhesive tape with a folder of sterile gauze in the center protect a wound from infection and permit the blood to clot.

If the wound is bleeding profusely, a gauze pad must be pressed firmly against the would in order to control the bleeding. Adhesive bandages come in many sizes, and a variety should be kept on hand for minor emergencies.

The bandage should be removed no more than one or two days later so that the wound can be examined for any signs of infection, such as redness, swelling, or the presence of pus. A fresh bandage can then be applied, if necessary.

Joint sprains and strains are often treated with elastic bandages that restrain movement and provide some support.

Triangular bandages should be kept in every first-aid kit so that temporary splints can be made or injuries can be wrapped.

Plaster casts, another sort of bandage, can be put in place only by a health-care professional. They treat broken bones that have been set back into place. Fiberglass bandages, which set faster, weigh less, and resist water, are also coming into regular use. *See also* BLEEDING *and* SPRAIN.

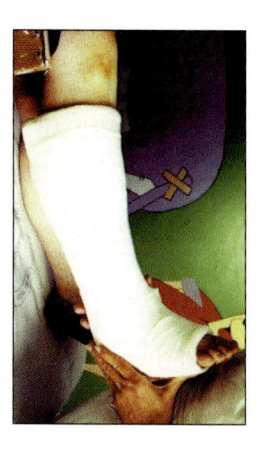

Types of Bandages. Left, a plaster cast is a type of bandage used to set broken bones so that they heal in the proper position. Plaster casts limit motion at the joints adjacent to the break facilitating the healing process. Right, a drawing of a wrist that is bandaged firmly but not too tightly; this type of bandage would be effective to treat a sprain or a strain. Near the wrist, this bandage is wrapped as a spiral; the cross-over pattern that lines the forearm is called a reverse spiral.

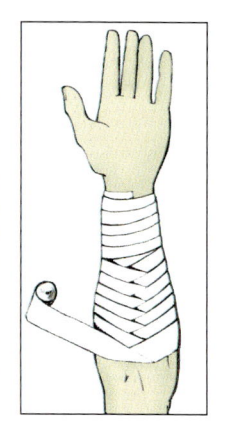

Barbiturate Drugs

Any of a group of organic compounds that come from barbituric acid; they are potentially addictive sedative-hypnotic drugs that are used occasionally as a sleep aid and an anticonvulsant.

Barbiturates, which include such drugs as amobarbital (Amytal), secobarbital (Seconal), and phenobarbitol (Nembutal), are depressants that act on the central nervous system and the respiratory system. Barbiturate use will affect the heart rate, blood pressure, and body temperature, as these drugs cause a feeling of relaxation, calm, and sleepiness that may relieve strong tension, intense anxiety, or temporary insomnia. Barbiturate drugs, such as secobarbital, will also slow signals in the brain and thus may prevent seizures.

ALERT ALERT ALERT

BARBITURATE OVERDOSE

An overdose of barbiturates may be fatal, so it must be treated as quickly as possible. Symptoms of an overdose include an unnatural sleep, slow breathing, a weak pulse, and a bodily state that resembles catatonic drunkenness. If the victim is awake, then he or she may have a headache, be confused, or show signs of delirium. Overdose victims should be forced to vomit when they are awake, when they are not, professionals should be called in immediately.

If an emergency rescue line is called, be sure to know the victim's age and weight while describing the current condition; if it is possible, also tell the emergency technician the name and the strength of the product ingested, when it was taken, how much of it was taken, and whether or not the victim had a prescription for the drug.

Prolonged use of barbiturates may lead to an addiction or to an increased tolerance, in which an individual needs an increasingly larger dose in order to achieve a similar effect. When used in conjunction with alcohol or other sedatives, barbiturate drugs can render a person unconscious, cause a coma, or even be fatal.

Barbiturates are particularly dangerous for senior citizens. The side effects are likely to be more severe, and there is a possible interaction with other drugs. The elderly should avoid barbiturates except when prescribed to control seizures.

Pentothal sodium may be used as an intravenous anesthetic for brief operations. Its reputation as a "truth serum," however, has been exaggerated. Barbiturates may cause drug habits; a doctor's prescription and advice must always be followed closely.

Bends, The

Bends, The

Also known as decompression sickness

A life-threatening condition in which nitrogen bubbles form in the blood and body tissues, obstructing circulation.

The bends is a painful, sometimes life-threatening, condition. It is caused by the formation of nitrogen bubbles in the bloodstream and body tissues, resulting from a rapid reduction in the pressure of the air surrounding the body. It is most often experienced by scuba divers who return too quickly to the surface of the water.

Causes and Symptoms. When the pressure outside the body decreases rapidly, nitrogen and other gases collect in bubbles in the blood vessels. These bubbles block the blood vessels and deprive the body of essential nutrients. As a result, during the 24-hour period following the dive, the individual may experience a tingling of the skin and alternating hot and cold sensations, followed by a loss of muscular control and pain that begins in the joints and spreads to other body areas. If the illness is sufficiently severe, the bends can lead to unconsciousness and even death. The condition may also lead to brain damage and possibly to bone destruction.

Treatment and Prevention. Apart from the most severe cases, the bends will subside if the affected person returns to a higher-pressure, lower-altitude environment. If necessary, a person can be treated with recompression in a sealed pressure chamber. The pressure in the chamber is raised and then lowered slowly, allowing the person to adjust to the reduction in air pressure. To avoid the bends, scuba divers will sometimes breathe pure oxygen before and during their ascent.

Beta-Blocker Drugs

A family of drugs that block adrenaline effects.

Beta-blockers reduce the impact of adrenaline, which responds to stress by narrowing blood vessels and increasing the heart rate. These drugs prevent the narrowing of the blood vessels and reduce the demands on the heart, lowering blood pressure. Beta-blockers control migraine headaches, angina, the effects of anxiety, irregular or rapid heartbeat, and high blood pressure.

Betamethasone

These drugs are not addictive, but do need to be taken for relatively long periods of time before they are effective. In addition, since high blood pressure does not produce symptoms, the effect of beta-blockers in lowering blood pressure may not be noticed. These drugs are very effective in reducing the incidence of repeat heart attacks.

ALERT   ALERT   ALERT

A DANGEROUS COMBINATION

The combination of beta-blockers and injections of epinephrine can be extremely dangerous, since it may raise the blood pressure to very high levels. Also, nonsteroidal anti-inflammatory drugs like acetaminophen or aspirin can negate the effects of beta-blockers. Do not stop taking beta-blockers abruptly, since that can cause a spike in blood pressure and result in a heart attack or a stroke.

Side Effects. There are few side effects, but they vary from patient to patient. They include nausea and vomiting, dizziness and light headedness, diarrhea, lowered libido, slowed heart rate, low blood pressure, cold hands or feet, depression, fatigue or weakness, sleep disturbances, and dizziness if the person rises from a prone position too rapidly. Less frequently, blurred vision and difficulty in breathing have been reported. People with asthma, slow heart rates, congestive heart failure or certain cases of diabetes should not use beta-blockers.

Since beta-blockers lower blood pressure and induce weakness and fatigue, those over the age of 50 may find it hard to maintain exercise routines. If this last side effect occurs, exercise levels should be adjusted accordingly.

Betamethasone

A synthetic corticosteroid used to treat swelling allergic reactions, asthma, and arthritis.

Corticosteroids are hormones produced in the adrenal glands that control inflammation, maintain blood-sugar levels, and control blood pressure and water balance in the circulatory system. Synthetic corticosteroids, such as betamethasone, are prescribed to replace corticosteroids that the body is not producing, to prevent rejection of transplanted organs, or to treat some inflammatory diseases. This drug can be taken orally as a pill or a liquid; it is also available as a lotion.

Biliary Colic

> **Pain resulting from an obstructed flow of bile from the gallbladder.**

Biliary colic may be caused by gallstones or inflammation. The pain may be intermittent, rising and then subsiding. Attacks usually begin 30 to 60 minutes after a meal, especially a meal high in fat content. The location of the pain may vary, but it is felt most often in the central upper abdomen. The pain may extend to the right shoulder blade. Other symptoms may include nausea, vomiting, chills, fever, and jaundice. Treatment involves the removal of the obstruction, or of the gallbladder itself.

Birth Defects

> **Also known as congenital abnormalities**
> Disorders that are apparent at or before birth, or that develop shortly afterwards.

Birth defects usually occur as a result of developmental "errors" during pregnancy. Approximately three percent of newborns have a major birth defect. The severity of birth defects ranges from relatively minor to quite serious. Very severe defects often result in a stillborn delivery or the death of a baby within a few days of birth. Of the remaining abnormalities, many conditions are correctable surgically or in some cases will resolve on their own.

Causes. The cause of most birth defects is unknown, but the following factors have been shown to play a role in increasing the risk of birth defects: lack of proper maternal nutrition, exposure to caustic levels of radiation, consumption of certain drugs and alcohol, infection, trauma, and inherited conditions.

Heart defects include:
- Aortic valve stenosis—a narrowing of the aortic valve, obstructing bloodflow;
- Pulmonary valve stenosis—a narrowing of the pulmonary valve that obstructs bloodflow;
- Underdeveloped left ventricle syndrome—also called hypoplastic left heart syndrome, the left side of the

Bites

heart is severely underdeveloped or absent. This condition is usually fatal;
Bone and muscle defects commonly affect the skull, spine, hips, and feet. Most of these are correctable surgically.
- Missing limb—either part or an entire arm or leg are missing at birth.
- Osteogenesis imperfecta—abnormally fragile bones which break easily;

Brain and spinal cord defects, many of which are detected before birth, include:
- Anencephaly—most of the brain fails to develop. This condition is fatal;
- Spina bifida—one or more of the vertebrae fail to develop properly, leaving a portion of the spinal cord exposed.

Urogenital abnormalities often include ambiguous genitals. In hermaphrodism, a baby is born with both ovaries and testicles. After doctors study the infant's chromosomes, it is "assigned" gender based on the results, and surgery is performed for cosmetic purposes.

Bites

The wounding, piercing or stinging of the flesh by an animal, insect or another person.

Animal Bites. Depending on the region of the world, some animal bites are more likely than others. In Pacific coastal areas, attacks from sharks, jellyfish, and other aquatic creatures are not uncommon. In regions of Central and South America, crocodile attacks are serious. Bites from cattle, horses, and pigs can also be fatal. By far, the greatest number of animal attacks worldwide come from dogs.

Any bite from an animal that breaks the skin presents a danger of infection. The mouth of an animal contains a large array of bacteria and viruses, all of which can cause severe infection. The possibility of rabies adds a further risk. Minor bites and scratches can be treated in the same way as minor wounds. In the case of severe bites, professional treatment must be sought.

Treatment. Medical treatment of a severe animal bite begins with a cleaning and examination of the wound. Instead of being stitched, the wound is bandaged (dressed) to avoid closing bacteria from the bite in

Black Eye

B the wound. To reduce infection, a course of antibiotics and an antitetanus injection will also be administered as a preventive measure. An antirabies vaccine may also be given.

Emergency rooms report far more human bites than most of us may expect. The human mouth harbors numerous bacteria and viruses that can infect a wound. Human bites rarely cause significant tissue damage.

Most human bites can be treated by washing the area with soap and warm water and applying a cold compress to reduce swelling and pain. In terms of infection, the human mouth contains as many bacteria and viruses as animal mouths. Humans even occasionally transmit rabies. Thus, treatment of a human bite is the same as for an animal bite.

Black Eye

> The bruised, darkened appearance of the skin around the eye following an injury.

A direct blow to the eye causes damage to the small blood vessels under the skin, causing blood to collect in the injured area. Because the skin around the eye is loose and relatively transparent, bruising is relatively darker in this area than in other body parts. This bleeding is usually minor. A cold compress held over the eye reduces inflammation and relieves pain.

Bleeding

> Losing blood from the circulatory system when blood vessels are torn, cut, or damaged.

The body has an elaborate system of safeguards to control bleeding and repair injury. The basic system of repair is based on the platelets in the blood. These are small, round disks that stick to each other and clog the opening in the blood vessel to limit blood loss. On the other hand, blood clots in the circulatory system are extremely dangerous if they clog blood flow. They can cause heart attack, if the blood cannot reach the heart, or stroke, if it cannot reach the brain.

The fluid (known as plasma) that carries red blood cells, white blood cells, and platelets also contains proteins called procoagulants,

Bleeding, Treatment of

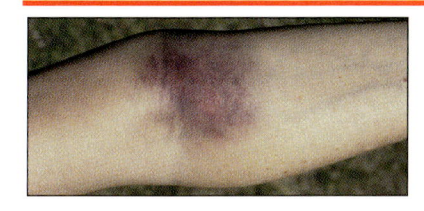

Bleeding. Blood from injured tissue accumulates near the skin's surface, causing bruising such as that seen at left on the inside of the forearm.

which promote coagulation, and anticoagulants, which inhibit coagulation. It is the balance among the factors that determines whether the blood starts the coagulation process and whether the clots dissolve after healing has taken place.

The life span of platelets is about ten days, so new platelets must be produced in the bone marrow to replace those that are dead or in use. This is an ongoing process in healthy bone marrow; if it is interfered with by disease or poor nutrition, a major health risk can be present. See also BLEEDING, TREATMENT OF; BRUISE; EMERGENCY MEDICINE; and TRAUMA.

ALERT   ALERT   ALERT

THE DANGER OF INTERNAL BLEEDING

It often takes several days or weeks for the symptoms of internal bleeding to show up in a patient, if they appear at all. If there is blood coming from any bodily opening—if an individual is coughing, vomiting, urinating or defecating blood—that is a sign of internal bleeding. If any of these conditions is present, medical help should be sought immediately. Visit a health care professional after any traumatic injury, no matter how insignificant it may seem. Someone who is bleeding internally may also react with a tense or a spasming abdominal muscle to the touch, or the abdominal region may just be tender in general. Internal bleeding is potentially life-threatening and professional care must be sought as soon as possible.

Bleeding, Treatment of

Measures used to stop bleeding. These vary according to the nature and severity of the wound.

Oxygenated blood flows under pressure from the heart through the arteries to all the organs and tissues of the body. It returns to the heart through the veins, which are closer to the surface. Blood pressure in the veins is lower than that in the arteries. Bleeding from the veins tends to be slow and steady while bleeding from the arteries may be copious and pulsating. Any bleeding should be controlled as quickly as

Bleeding, Treatment of

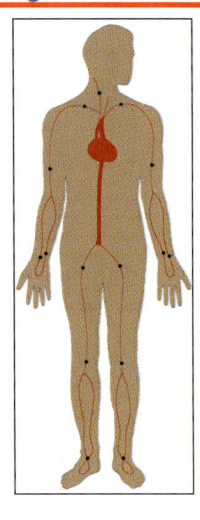

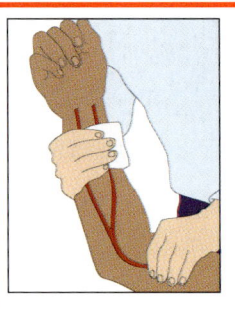

Treating Bleeding. Pressure points are marked with black dots (left). Pressure should be applied at these points to manage rapid bleeding. Even though these points may be a distance from the bleeding itself, the arteries bringing blood to the wound are supplied from blood vessels at these points; thus, pressure will slow the bleeding. Above, pressure applied at points distant from the trauma site will also slow bleeding. Whenever possible, the injury should be elevated.

Pressure Points & Severe Bleeding

Besides direct pressure, indirect pressure should be applied to the most severe wounds and to wounds that have foreign objects embedded in them. There are several specific arterial pressure points throughout the body that will slow the supply of blood to the wound. They are located at the ankles, behind the knees, at the point where the thigh meets the trunk, on the inside of the arm just below the shoulder, below the wrist, and just above the collarbone. After finding the arterial pressure point nearest the wound, hold it tightly with two or three fingers. Pressure should only be maintained long enough to control the bleeding. If direct pressure is also being applied to the wound, then it should be maintained for the duration or until medical professionals arrive.

possible, but bleeding from the arteries is particularly dangerous.

Ascertaining the Severity of the Wound. The amount of blood lost is not a good indicator of the seriousness or severity of the trauma. Bleeding from head wounds can be heavy from minor cuts or scrapes, because the blood vessels are close to the surface. Bleeding from a deeper wound elsewhere on the body might seem less dangerous, while a large share of the bleeding is internal.

It is best not to come into direct contact with the blood, since this is one of the most direct ways of getting AIDS or other infectious diseases. Immediately after treating a bleeding wound, a person should wash her or his hands in hot, soapy water.

Home Treatment. The first rule in bleeding treatment is to put pressure on the wound and hold it until the bleeding stops or more specific remedies can be applied. However, this is not true if there is a

Bleeding, Treatment of

possible skull fracture or some other broken bone near the wound, or if there is an object embedded in the wound. If the wound is to one or both eyes, a light clean dressing must be applied to both eyes, since eye movements may damage the wounded eye. If the wound is to the nose and it is unbroken, a cold compress should be applied and the nostrils should be held firmly for a few minutes.

Tourniquets. Once, a common treatment, tourniquets are now considered a dangerous means of stoping bleeding. Wrapped tourniquets can cause gangrene, making an injury worse. The only time a tourniquet can even be considered is when an extremity has been amputated in an accident. Tourniquets are made of straps or fabric folded to about two inches wide, wrapped just above the wound, and knotted at the pressure point; a belt or strap of fabric is best. A bandage and properly applied pressure is preferred.

TYPES OF INJURIES

Bruises are the result of blows that do not break the skin. They may cause tissue damage, appearing as discolorations under the skin, as well as internal bleeding if the blow is severe. Internal bleeding should be treated only by a doctor.

Puncture wounds may be as mild as a splinter or as serious as a gunshot wound. The exit wound from a gunshot is more serious than the entry because the bullet expands and distorts during its passage through the body. These wounds will bleed both externally and internally, but the amount of external bleeding is not a good measure of the seriousness of the wound.

ALERT   ALERT   ALERT

SHOCK

The sight of blood can be extremely frightening to some people, so even a minor cut or laceration may cause a person to faint. A serious laceration with considerable loss of blood may cause a person to go into shock. If there is danger of shock and the injury is not to the spine, the injured person should lie flat on his or her back with the feet elevated to reduce blood pressure. The legs should not be raised if the trauma was a venomous bite. The person should be covered and kept warm, and breathing should be checked to see if it is normal. If not, artificial respiration may be necessary.

Any penetrating wound offers serious danger of infection, since the foreign object carries bacteria through the protective layer of skin. Tetanus shots are usually recommended if the puncture wound is relatively deep, since the bacteria that cause tetanus are likely to have contaminated most puncturing objects.

Blister

Blister

Also known as a bulla (large) or vesicle (small)

A raised fluid-filled bump just under the outer layer of the skin.

Blisters can be caused by burns or by friction, such as with a shoe, against the skin. Blisters can also be caused by certain viral infections. Herpes simplex type I invades the mouth and causes blisters. One out of 1000 people may be infected with this form of the virus. Most people come into contact with it at before age 20. Herpes simplex type II causes genital herpes and infections in babies. Other viruses and certain bacteria can also cause blisters.

Both types of the herpes virus are very contagious. The first symptoms occur about one to two weeks after the initial exposure. Blisters in the mouth usually heal in seven to ten days. The virus then becomes latent, and recurrences are usually less severe. In the case of blisters caused by viral infection, antiviral medications, such as acyclovir, are used to treat the symptoms and help reduce pain. Blisters that are caused by burns or by friction should be allowed to heal on their own, unless they are particularly severe, in which case medical attention should be sought.

Blood Poisoning

Also known as septicemia

A disease caused by bacteria from an infected part of the body entering the bloodstream.

Blood poisoning—or septicemia—occurs when a disease-producing organism (pathogen) enters the bloodstream. It may result in life-threatening septic shock.

Septic shock differs from septicemia because septic shock is not an infection, but is rather the response of the body to the existence of large quantities of bacteria in the bloodstream.

Causes. Blood poisoning occurs as a result of a contaminated blood transfusion or from an infection that is already present in the body. As recently as the 1940s, nearly one-quarter of all transfusion patients contracted blood poisoning, but the introduction of disposable, sterilized containers and effective refrigeration procedures have reduced this occurrence to a virtual rarity. Today, about 90 percent of cases of

Blood Pressure

blood poisoning are caused by infectious bacteria. Almost all others arise from fungal or viral infections.

The bacteria that infect the blood can come from various sources. An open wound can serve as a point of entry or the patient may already be suffering from a disease involving bacteria in the bloodstream, such as listeriosis. Some unpasteurized dairy foods contain the bacteria *Listeria monocytogenes* which causes listeriosis. Septic shock is the major cause of mortality in burn patients because certain bacteria associated with sepsis (bacterial infection) thrive on burned flesh. Septicemia is a risk for hospitalized patients, who may develop infections during the course of their stay. Especially at risk are those who already have a compromised immune system, such as those with cancer or AIDS.

Diagnosis and Treatment. A blood culture can determine the nature and amount of the organisms that have invaded the bloodstream, and what course of treatment to pursue. Patients suffering from septicemia are often given antibiotics.

ALERT   ALERT   ALERT

SEPTIC SHOCK AND BLOOD POISONING

Septic shock is very hard to diagnose because its symptoms are common to those of so many other disorders, including blood poisoning. Symptoms of blood poisoning include fever, chills, diarrhea, nausea, headache, vomiting, and abdominal pain. Septic shock is indicated by: thirst, weakness, lethargy, confusion, dilated pupils, fever, low blood pressure and weak pulse, extreme pallor or bluish skin, rapid or shallow breathing, nausea or vomiting, and loss of consciousness.

If left untreated, multiple organ failure can occur. While sepsis (a bacterial infection) alone can cause death in 30 to 40 percent of cases, if three or more organs fail, septic shock is fatal in over 90 percent of cases. If septic shock is suspected, place the victim in the shock position; lay the victim on his or her back with the feet elevated above the heart. The head should lie flat. A blanket may be used for warmth.

Blood Pressure

The force exerted by the blood against the arteries as the heart beats.

Blood pressure is expressed through the use of two distinct numbers. The first number is for systolic pressure and the second is for diastolic pressure. Systolic pressure is the pressure at which blood is forced out of the heart, and diastolic pressure is the pressure of the blood between heartbeats.

Blood Pressure

B Blood pressure is measured in millimeters of mercury, which is marked as mm Hg. The millimeters-of-mercury measurement is an expression of the height to which a column of mercury is raised in a sphygmomanometer, the standard device for measuring blood pressure.

ALERT ALERT ALERT

HYPERTENSION

Hypertension, or high blood pressure, is a major risk factor for cardiovascular conditions such as heart attack and stroke. It is defined as a blood pressure level of 140/90 or greater that is found in several measurements over a period of time. There are variations among individuals, however. Some persons may have systolic pressure within normal limits but an elevated diastolic pressure of from 110 to 115 mm Hg. Older persons are more likely to have a form of hypertension in which the diastolic reading is below 90 but the systolic reading is abnormally high—160 mm Hg or higher. This systolic hypertension increases the risk of heart attack, stroke, or heart failure.

Normal Levels. A healthy young adult at rest will have a systolic pressure ranging from 100 to 130, with diastolic pressure ranging around 60 to 80. Blood pressure changes with age and with activity.

Risk Factors. Blood pressure can change because of environmental factors affecting the body. For example, caffeine or cigarette smoke can raise pressure, so it is advisable not to smoke cigarettes or drink caffinated beverages before a blood pressure measurement is taken.

Stress, either emotional, physical, or both, also has the potential to raise blood pressure. Anger and fright can cause the adrenal glands to produce epinephrine, which is a hormone known as adrenaline. This hormone will act to make the heart beat more often and harder, causing blood vessels to constrict and increasing blood pressure drastically.

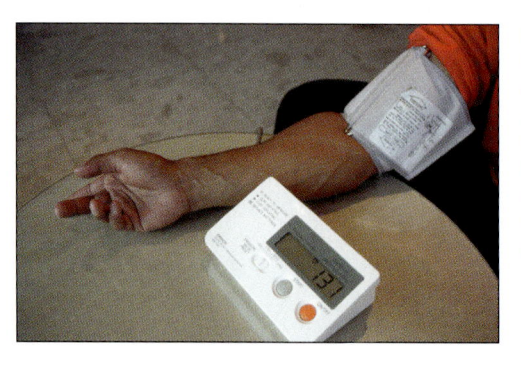

Blood Pressure. At left, a digital blood pressure machine measures both blood pressure and pulse rate. These are useful for home monitoring of blood pressure. Some physicians will recommend this device for patients who wish to monitor their own blood pressure throughout the day.

Boil

Also called furuncle

The result of an infection—usually involving staphylococcus bacteria—that has developed around a blocked hair follicle or oil gland.

Boils are usually caused by a staph infection that enters the body through a break in the skin. Immune problems, diabetes, overuse of corticosteroids, and poor health can cause a predisposition to boils.

A boil is red and tender for about four to seven days, after which pus collects inside, turning the boil white. The pus, a collection of white blood cells, fights the infection. A boil may be painful until the skin breaks and the pus drains.

Treatment. Treatment for boils involves applying hot compresses and, usually, oral antibiotics. If the pain is severe, a doctor can lance the boil. Boils should not be lanced at home, as this can lead to the spread of infection. A boil on the eyelid is called a stye.

Botulism

Rare and potentially fatal food poisoning.

Botulism is an extremely serious and potentially fatal form of food poisoning resulting from a toxin generated by an anaerobic bacillus. *Clostridium botulinum* is usually found in improperly preserved food, although it rarely appears in commercially produced foods. The bacillus also lives in soil and can infect an open wound through contact with the infested soil.

If botulism poisoning is suspected, seek medical help immediately and notify health authorities, especially if the source of infection is thought to be a restaurant or a commercial product.

Symptoms of botulism poisoning can appear between six hours and eight days after eating tainted food, and include blurred or double vision; paralysis of limbs, chest muscles, throat, and eye muscles; dry mouth and difficulty swallowing; breathing difficulty; vomiting; and abdominal pain. Treatment involves administration of an antitoxin as well as rehydration fluids. *See* FOOD POISONING.

Brain Hemorrhage

Brain Hemorrhage

Bleeding in or around the brain.

A hemorrhage can be caused either by injury or by rupture of a blood vessel. Brain hemorrhages account for about one quarter of all strokes; the rest are caused by blockage of a blood vessel. Brain hemorrhages are classified by the site where the bleeding occurs.

An extradural hemorrhage occurs underneath the skull but above a membrane called the dura.

A subdural hemorrhage occurs below the dura but above a second membrane called the arachnoid. Both extradural and subdural hemorrhages are usually the result of injury.

A subarachnoid hemorrhage occurs on the outer surface of the brain below the arachnoid, resulting in a flow of blood into the space between the brain and its lining.

An intracerebral hemorrhage occurs within the brain. The common cause of subarachnoid and intracerebral hemorrhages is a ruptured aneurysm—the blood vessel balloons, weakening the vessel wall.

In brain hemorrhages, brain cells die because they lose their supply of oxygen. Cells also die as blood accumulates in the brain, or between the brain and the skull, putting excess pressure on brain cells. The blood that flows from the ruptured vessel presses against the brain, destroying tissue and disrupting cerebral function. More than 10 percent of all strokes are caused by intracerebral hemorrhages.

Symptoms of an intracerebral hemorrhage include sudden headache, weakness, and confusion. There is often loss of consciousness, and the person collapses to the ground. Symptoms require immediate medical attention.

Diagnosis is made by a physical examination and tests of body and brain functions, such as walking, hearing, vision, reading, and understanding spoken language. The diagnosis can be confirmed by a computerized tomography scan or magnetic resonance imaging, both of which produce an image of the brain.

Treatment generally consists of measures to maintain bodily function, reduce blood pressure, and relieve pressure within the skull. Surgery may be performed to remove a clot that has formed near the surface of the brain. Persons with arteriosclerosis and diabetes are at higher risk for a brain hemorrhage. The prognosis depends on the location and extent of the bleeding.

Breathing Difficulty

An abnormal change in depth and rate of breathing.

Breathing difficulty can be a symptom of many different diseases, or it can be a general physical and lifestyle characteristic. It results from any condition that affects airflow into or out of the lungs, the ability of the lungs to infuse the blood with oxygen, or the ability of the brain stem to regulate breathing.

> **ALERT ALERT ALERT**
>
> **ALLERGY AND SHOCK**
>
> *Persons with allergies can experience extreme breathing difficulty during an unusually strong response—anaphylactic reaction—to an allergy-causing agent, such as peanuts, fish, eggs, bee stings, or medications such as penicillin. The reaction causes a severe drop in blood pressure, constriction of the airways of the lungs, and swelling of the throat or tongue. An anaphylactic reaction requires immediate treatment with epinephrine or other medication and emergency resuscitation. Individuals prone to anaphylactic shock are advised to carry their own medication and wear a medical identification bracelet warning of the potential problem.*

Breathing difficulty can be either labored breathing or pain related to breathing movements. Whether a person is asleep, resting, or exercising, breathing difficulty can occur.

Anemia or a similar blood problem can lead to breathing difficulty. Anemia is a shortage of oxygen-carrying red cells in the blood. The body does not get enough oxygen, so the lungs must work harder. The end result is continued breathlessness.

Anxiety. Times of stress or tension can bring on abnormally rapid or deep breathing (hyperventilation) that causes faintness and a feeling of being unable to breathe adequately, sometimes accompanied by muscle spasms or numbness of the hands and feet. These symptoms are caused by an excess loss of carbon dioxide from the blood and can be lessened by breathing into a paper bag, which helps to restore normal carbon dioxide levels.

Altitude Sickness. Breathing difficulty can occur at high altitudes, where the air is thinner and less oxygen is taken in with each inhalation. It is often experienced by individuals who are unaccustomed to high altitudes and can worsen with activity for those who are less phys-

Breathing Difficulty

B ically fit. As the lungs work harder to supply the body with oxygen, there is a feeling of breathlessness. Eventually, the individual's system becomes accustomed to the thinner air. Problems can be lessened by a reduction in physical activity while this change occurs.

Breathlessness is the inability to breathe at the rate required by the body. It is most commonly associated with exertion (intense exercise) and panic attacks. This is normal for those in good health and is not a cause for concern. Other more serious causes of breathlessness include heart problems, regular or repeated exposure to poor air quality (as in smoky or dusty workplaces), allergies, and smoking. Treatment of these problems will help to remedy the symptom of breathlessness.

OBESITY AND PICKWICKIAN SYNDROME

One form of breathing difficulty that can occur in overweight persons is the Pickwickian syndrome or obstructive sleep apnea. In Pickwickian syndrome, obesity leads to the narrowing of the upper air passageway periodic obstruction of breathing during sleep. The result is repeated episodes of obstructive choking and startled awakening accompanied by gasping. The complications of Pickwickian syndrome include excessive daytime sleepiness, morning headaches, and loss of concentration. The condition can eventually result in serious heart abnormalities such as ventricular tachycardia—an abnormally fast heartbeat.

Circulation Disorders. Chronic heart conditions, such as impaired ability of the heart to pump blood—heart failure—can cause breathing difficulty. Other heart conditions that cause breathing difficulty include a blood clot in the lung (pulmonary embolism) and abnormally high blood pressure in the arteries of the lung (pulmonary hypertension).

Lack of Fitness. Many physically inactive people do not have the heart and lung capacity needed to respond to the body's increased demand for oxygen at times of exertion. The increased demand causes discomfort and pain. The remedy is to cease the physical activity. The long-term solution is regular fitness training.

Lung Damage. Conditions that cause temporary or permanent damage to the lungs inevitably result in breathing difficulty. Emphysema (chronic breathing difficulty) damages the lungs by destroying the sensitive tissue where oxygen enters the blood and carbon dioxide is removed from blood. Breathing difficulty can be due to inflammation of the lungs (pneumonia) or inflammation of the airways of the lung (bronchitis). In these cases, breathing difficulty may be tempo-

Bronchodilator Drugs

rary, easing when the infection that causes the inflammation yields to treatment. Physical damage, such as a collapsed lung (pneumothorax) or excess fluid around the lung (pleural effusion), can also cause breathing difficulty.

> ### SMOKING AND BREATHING
> The damage that smoking does to lung tissue is a major cause of breathing difficulty, and smoking exacerbates the difficulty resulting from any other cause. For someone who smokes, the first step in treating breathing difficulty is to quit smoking. For someone who does not smoke, it is essential not to start.

Obesity. An obese person may have trouble breathing during even mild exertion because of the extra effort required by excess body tissue. In addition, extreme obesity may have an affect on the breathing control center of the brain stem, aggravating the problem. Painful breathing, chest tightness or pain, and wheezing may occur as the result of this condition. Gradual weight loss and regular fitness training can reduce or eliminate any accompanying breathing problems.

Bronchodilator Drugs

A family of drugs that relax the muscles around the air passages to the lungs (bronchi), making it easier to breathe.

Diseases that inflame the bronchial passages make it difficult to breathe and restrict the amount of oxygen provided to the tissues of the body. Some common diseases that bronchodilators are used to treat are asthma, emphysema, and bronchitis. Asthma is usually an allergic reaction, while the vast majority of people with emphysema and chronic bronchitis developed the condition from smoking.

Most bronchodilators relax the passageways to the lungs, while others, such as epinephrine, constrict blood vessels, which can reduce inflammation, slow or stop bleeding, and increase blood pressure. In larger doses, bronchodilators also affect heart function and may be used as a treatment for heart-rhythm problems. When used to treat bronchial diseases, bronchodilators are taken either orally or as an inhalant.

Short-term bronchodilators are intended for fast, temporary relief and are effective for about four hours. The relief should be evident

Bruise

within two or three minutes. These include albuterol, pirbuterol, metaproterenol, terbutalin, and bitolterol, among others. They are administered through an inhaler and take effect within twenty to thirty minutes. Side effects may include quickened heartbeat, nervousness, shakiness, nausea, and dizziness.

> **ALERT ALERT ALERT**
> **CAFFEINE AND BRONCHODILATOR DRUGS**
> Caffeine should be avoided when taking any bronchodilator drugs. If the patient experiences a change in blood pressure or heartbeat, trembling, lightheadedness, chest pain, or vomiting, a physician should be consulted immediately.

Long-acting bronchodilators include beta agonists and methylxanthines, which help people breathe more easily over a long period. The beta-agonists include salmeterol (used in an aerosol inhaler or powder inhaler), albuterol (taken orally), and theophylline (taken orally). Salmeterol is not recommended for use in acute attacks of bronchitis. It is intended for long-term control of asthma symptoms, especially at night. It is usually taken with an anti-inflammatory drug, is longer acting, and has fewer side effects, though the patient may experience nervousness, trembling, dry mouth, and rapid or irregular heartbeat. Theophylline may cause nausea, nervousness, and insomnia. *See also* ASTHMA ATTACK.

Bruise

Injury-related skin discoloration.

Everyone experiences bruises—from minor bumps to sprains—in the course of a normal life. The purple discoloration appears when the blood from small ruptured vessels leaks into tissue and under the skin. Bruising typically occurs from a blow, but it can also result from a twisted ankle, a strained muscle, or a scrape that removes parts of the skin. People who have blood clotting problems bruise easily, because the blood continues to leak into the skin.

Other than applying cold compresses on the bruised area for fifteen minutes every hour to reduce swelling and pain, there is no specific treatment for bruising. Most bruises will eventually heal on their own as the blood is reabsorbed into the body.

Burns

Destruction of the skin or deeper tissues from excessive heat.

Burns result from direct dry heat, fire, wet heat as from scalding, chemicals such as acids, and electric current. Burns are divided into three categories.

First-degree burns damage only the outer surface of the skin. After a burn, the skin becomes red, extremely sensitive to the touch, wet, and swollen.

Second-degree burns are deeper. Blisters form and are filled with a clear, thick liquid. The area is painfully sensitive to touch and is swollen.

Third-degree burns go deeper still. The immediate surface may be charred and leathery or white and soft, so that observers may not realize that a burn has taken place. There may be blistering. The area may be extremely painful to the touch or, if nerve endings have been destroyed, there may be no pain at all.

Inhalation and Chemical Burns. Inhalation burns occur when hot gases enter the mouth, air passages, or lungs. Chemical burns of the throat and esophagus can be the result of drinking acid, alkali, mustard gas, or phosphorus.

Treatment depends on the source and depth of the burn. Extensive second-degree burns and all third-degree burns should be treated by trained medical personnel.

Doctors will first make sure the victim can breathe properly. Oxygen will be supplied if carbon monoxide poisoning is suspected. Lost fluids will be replaced intravenously; this method also serves as a preliminary response to treating shock.

The site will be carefully cleaned of dirt and other debris. If necessary, doctors may administer an anesthetic so that the area can be scrubbed with a soft brush. An antibiotic cream may be applied and the area covered with a loose bandage. The burn area will be vulnerable to infection, so it must be kept clean and covered with sterile bandages.

Skin Grafts. More extensive burns often require a section of skin to be taken from an unburned part of the body, from another person, or even from a pig, since pig skin most resembles human skin. Grafts from the victim will integrate well with the surrounding skin. Grafts from other sources will serve to protect the area for ten days to two weeks; the grafts are sloughed off as the person heals.

Burns

Besides being painful, burns take a long time to heal, can be disfiguring, and require extensive physical therapy. Victims of extensive burns can be depressed and may need psychiatric assistance to see them through.

ALERT ALERT ALERT

FIRST-AID TREATMENT FOR BURNS

FIRST-DEGREE BURNS *are red, mildly painful, and swollen. If treated properly, they will heal in a few days.*
- *Immerse the affected area in cool water or cover with a cold, wet cloth until pain subsides;*
- *Clean with warm, soapy water;*
- *Cover with clean, dry gauze dressing;*
- *Change dressing frequently.*

SECOND-DEGREE BURNS *are blistered, rough on the surface, swollen, and extremely painful. If treated properly, they will heal in a few weeks. If extensive, they should be treated by trained medical personnel.*
- *Immerse the affected area in cool water or cover with a cold, wet cloth;*
- *Clean with warm, soapy water. Do not rub!*
- *Blot gently;*
- *Cover with clean, dry gauze dressing;*
- *Change dressing frequently.*

THIRD-DEGREE BURNS *have a charred or white appearance. They should be treated by trained medical personnel.*
- *Do not remove clothing on or near the burn;*
- *Do not apply cold water or medications to the burn;*
- *Place a clean, dry cloth over the burned area;*
- *If burns are on arms or legs, raise the limbs above the heart;*
- *Check frequently to be sure victim is breathing properly;*
- *Get the victim to an emergency room immediately.*

CHEMICAL BURNS
- *Remove clothing near the burn. Cut it off rather than pull it over the head;*
- *Wash the area thoroughly with large amounts of cool water for at least 20 minutes;*
- *Cover with a sterile gauze dressing;*
- *Get the victim to an emergency room immediately.*

ELECTRICAL BURNS
- *Make sure victim is free of contact with the electrical power source;*
- *Check that the victim is breathing and has a pulse; If not, apply CPR;*
- *Treat as for a third-degree burn;*
- *Get the victim to an emergency room immediately.*

Caffeine

Cadmium Poisoning

Poisoning caused by the inhalation of fumes or dust from cadmium.

Cadmium is a metal widely used in industry; it may be inhaled from cadmium-emitting factories. It may be present in contaminated water, soil, air, and food. Toxic levels may be ingested via contaminated foods or liquids from vending machines soldered with cadmium compounds. Ingestion can cause vomiting, diarrhea, headache, aching muscles, salivation, and chills. At risk for poisoning are painters, welders, ceramic workers, and photographers. Inhalation can result in metal fume fever and, over time, shortness of breath, loss of smell or sensation, cough, weight loss, fatigue, yellow rings on the teeth, bone pain, and kidney damage. Continuous exposure causes accumulation in the body, resulting in kidney failure and lung inflammation, eventually leading to emphysema or death.

Caffeine

Stimulant and diuretic obtained from certain natural substances.

Caffeine is a substance that occurs naturally in coffee beans, tea leaves, cacao trees, and kola nuts. It is added to soft drinks (cola and non-cola) and is a component of many over-the-counter and prescription drugs, including diet pills, stimulants, pain relievers, and allergy medicines.

ALERT ALERT ALERT

WHO SHOULD AVOID CAFFEINE?

A direct link between caffeine consumption and heart disease has not been established, but most physicians advise patients with heart conditions to eliminate or limit caffeine consumption because of the stimulant effect caffeine has on the heart. Those trying to quit smoking should also limit or eliminate caffeine, as it increases cravings for nicotine. Heavy coffee consumption by pregnant women can have negative effects on the child, as caffeine is secreted in breast milk. People with extreme sensitivity to caffeine should never consume it. Insomniacs should not consume caffeine, nor should those afflicted by or with any family history of osteoporosis. High caffeine consumption may exacerbate the conditions of those who suffer from incontinence, dehydration, trembling, gastrointestinal problems, high blood pressure, and anxiety.

Caffeine

Caffeine stimulates the central nervous system. It can be used to increase alertness, and to treat migraine headaches. It also acts as a diuretic. Too much caffeine can result in negative side effects. The amount of caffeine that is "too much" varies from person to person. Possible effects of caffeine toxicity include cardiac arrhythmia, diarrhea, vomiting, heartburn, and convulsions, as well as anxiety, tremors, and insomnia. Chronic consumption may cause agitation, irregular heartbeat, fever, hyperventilation, and respiratory failure.

Under certain conditions, caffeine can be addictive. Withdrawal may occur in heavy coffee drinkers who abruptly stop their intake of caffeine. Symptoms of withdrawal include headaches, tiredness, and irritability. Withdrawal symptoms can be prevented by reducing intake gradually.

Carbon Monoxide

A colorless, odorless, highly toxic gas.

Carbon monoxide is one of the leading causes of death in the United States. All combustion devices, including car engines, heaters, stoves, and furnaces, emit carbon monoxide. Tobacco smoke is another source. Methylene chloride, a paint stripper, is metabolized into carbon monoxide, posing an occupational risk.

Prevention. To prevent exposure to toxic levels of carbon monoxide, heating appliances should be properly vented, with vents and chimneys kept clean and unobstructed. Car engines and exhaust systems should be properly maintained. Cars and other power equipment should never idle in an attached garage. Homes should be equipped with carbon monoxide detectors.

ALERT   ALERT   ALERT

EXPOSURE TO CARBON MONOXIDE

Indications of exposure to carbon monoxide may appear slowly and resemble flu symptoms. A person may also experience headache, shortness of breath, chest pain, nausea, confusion, and fainting. Exposure to higher concentrations may cause drowsiness, unconsciousness, and even death. In chronic cases, it can cause bizarre and hyperactive behavior, and convulsions may occur. Chronic exposure at low levels has been correlated with mental deterioration and hearing loss. Treatment for acute carbon monoxide poisoning involves oxygen therapy.

Cardiac Arrest

The sudden failure of the heart to pump blood.

Cardiac arrest is frequently caused by ventricular fibrillation, a severely irregular rhythm of the heart. Ventricular fibrillation is usually brought on by a heart attack (myocardial infarction). Cardiac arrest can also be caused by asystole, which means the heart has ceased to beat. Cardiac arrest can be related to an underlying cardiovascular condition, such as cardiomyopathy, heart failure, or hypertension. It can also occur in people with severe burns, major injuries that result in the massive loss of blood, severe allergic reactions, drug overdoses, or electric shock.

ALERT ALERT ALERT

IN CASE OF CARDIAC ARREST

If cardiac arrest occurs in a home or public place, emergency cardiopulmonary resuscitation must be administered to restore heart function or to maintain viability until more sophisticated measures and rescue personnel arrive. In CPR, the patient's airway is opened, and the person administering CPR breathes into the mouth while compressing the chest at regular intervals. Emergency medical help should be called while CPR is being performed.

Symptoms. These are swift and devastating and include failure to breathe, loss of consciousness, physical collapse, and absence of the normal pulse. Symptoms usually occur without warning, although the patient may have felt chest pain, shortness of breath, or severe fatigue in the days before cardiac arrest took place.

Treatment. Emergency teams are trained in defibrillation—the delivery of a shock to the heart or administration of medication intended to start it beating properly again. In a hospital, more advanced techniques can be used, and drugs such as lidocaine can be given intravenously to stabilize the heartbeat.

Prognosis. When the heart stops beating, quick treatment is necessary to prevent major damage to the brain can occur from lack of oxygen. Permanent damage can take place in as little as three minutes. Even with treatment, the outcome may not be favorable. About two-thirds of cardiac arrest patients die immediately, and the death rate for survivors in the year following the arrest is high. People at high risk of cardiac arrest should be on the alert for warning signs.

Cardiopulmonary Resuscitation (CPR)

Cardiopulmonary Resuscitation (CPR)

> An emergency method used to restart the heart and initiate breathing when a person's pulse has stopped (cardiac arrest).

Cardiopulmonary resuscitation combines cardiac compression to restart or maintain the heartbeat with, if possible, mouth to mouth resuscitation to supplement or enhance ventilation and oxygen delivery to the lungs. When the heart stops beating, its pumping action ceases, and oxygen-rich blood fails to reach the brain. This can result in permanent brain damage after only three or four minutes and death after eight to ten minutes. It is therefore crucial to begin CPR as quickly as possible.

Ideally, a person performing cardiopulmonary resuscitation should be formally trained. You can locate the nearest CPR class in your area by contacting your local chapter of the American Heart Association or the American Red Cross. Mouth-to-mouth resuscitation can be successfully administered by an untrained individual, but the most effective method of restoring circulation is cardiac compression massage performed by a trained individual. The instructions included here are **not** a substitute for classroom training.

How to Perform CPR

First, it is important to verify that the victim has indeed suffered cardiac arrest and is not merely unconscious. Look in the victim's mouth to make sure that no food or foreign material is obstructing the airway, then with your ear over the victims mouth and nostrils listen for signs of breathing. If a spinal injury is suspected, do not move the head or neck, as that may worsen the injury.

Immediately call for emergency medical help. Have a person not performing CPR make the call. If you are alone, call before starting CPR.

Remember to be gentle when applying pressure to the chest, particularly with children. Be sure to press straight down; do not rock. Count the compressions so that they are evenly spaced. If the victim vomits while CPR is being administered, roll him or her over to the left side until he or she is finished. Clear the air passages and resume CPR if there is still no heartbeat or breathing.

Cardiopulmonary Resuscitation (CPR)

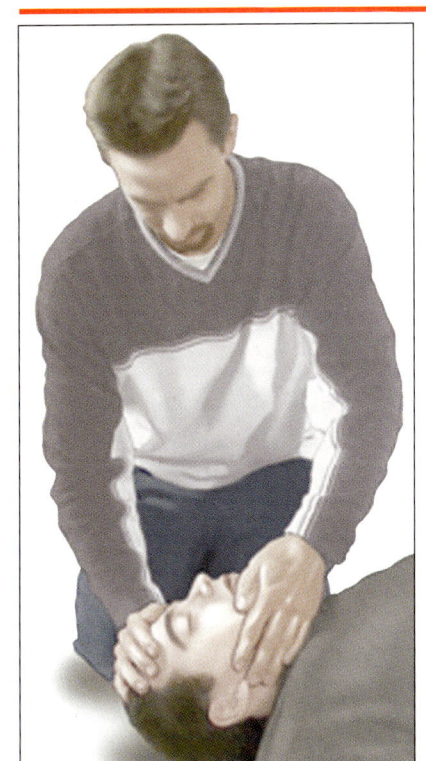

Performing CPR. At left, first check for breathing and open the airway. Below, mouth to mouth resuscitation. Bottom left, chest compressions.

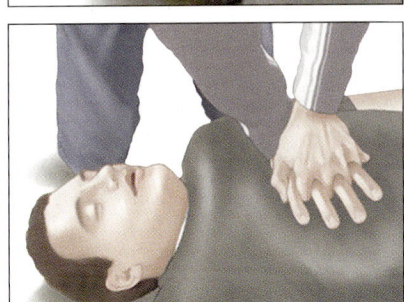

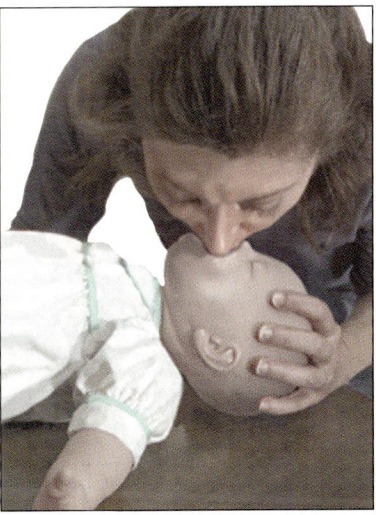

ADULTS

- Place the person on his or her back, tilt the head back, and lift the chin.

- Pinch the nose and make an airtight mouth to mouth seal. Give two full breaths. The victim's chest will rise if he or she is getting enough air.

Cardiopulmonary Resuscitation (CPR)

- If there is no response or pulse, begin chest compressions at about 100 per minute, with two breaths given after every 15 compressions. Place one hand on top of the other and position the hands about two finger-widths above the lowest part of the person's breast bone. Press straight down, about one and one-half to two inches. and release.

- Continue until help arrives, breathing and pulse begin again, or your fatigue becomes overwhelming.

Children Ages One to Eight

- Place the child face up, tilt the head back, and lift the chin.

- Pinch the nose and make an airtight mouth to mouth seal. Give two full breaths. The victim's chest will rise if he or she is getting enough air.

- If there is no pulse, begin chest compressions at a rate of 100 per minute. Place the heel of the hand about two finger-widths above the lowest part of the child's breastbone. Press gently straight down about one to one and one-half inches and then release. After every five compressions, give one breath.

- Continue until help arrives, breathing and pulse begin again, or your fatigue becomes overwhelming.

Infants

- Place the infant on his or her back across your knees, tilt the head back, and lift the chin.

- Create a seal over the mouth and nose of the victim. Give two small puffs. The chest will rise if he or she is getting enough air.

- If there is no pulse, begin quick chest compressions at a rate of 100 to 120 per minute; after every five compressions give one puff of breath. Place two fingers in the middle of the breastbone, between the nipples. Press gently straight down about a one-half inch to one inch and release.

- Continue until help arrives, breathing and pulse begin again, or your fatigue becomes overwhelming.

Cardiovascular Disorders

Disorders of the heart and blood vessels.

Heart disorders are the most common cause of death in the United States and in other industrialized nations.

Disorders that impair blood flow include the major causes of death, such as heart attacks (myocardial infarction). Underlying most of these conditions is deterioration of blood flow through the coronary arteries, which supply blood to the heart muscle. Over time, the coronary arteries can become narrowed and less flexible because of a buildup of fatty deposits in the artery walls (atherosclerosis). As all or part of the heart muscle is deprived of its normal blood supply, it must work harder to maintain blood flow to the rest of the body.

One result can be congestive heart failure, in which the heart cannot supply enough blood to the body. Another can be angina pectoris, pain that occurs at first during exertion and later even at rest. The heart can experience a disturbance of its normal rhythm (arrhythmia), which in extreme cases can lead to a complete loss of rhythm (fibrillation). Also, an artery can become blocked, causing myocardial infarction, the death of part of the heart tissue, which can result in sudden death.

Congenital Disorders. These consist of abnormalities in the structure of the heart or its major blood vessels that are present from birth. They include septal defects, "holes in the heart," and malformations of the heart valves, such as stenosis or prolapse.

Infection. A bacterial, fungal, or viral infection can cause inflammation of the tissue lining the inside of the heart muscle (endocarditis) and often damage the heart valves. The result can be conditions including mitral insufficiency, in which the mitral valve does not close properly, and mitral stenosis, narrowing of the valve opening.

Muscle Disorders. Cardiomyopathies result in a weakening of the heart muscle and reduced blood flow. They can be due to a congenital condition, a vitamin deficiency, overconsumption of alcohol, or an infection. Myocarditis is inflammation of the heart muscle as a result of infection, certain drugs, or radiation therapy.

Injuries. Many highway fatalities are caused by blunt injuries to the heart, as in auto accidents. Mild compression can bruise the heart, but a severe impact may result in fatal rupture of the heart muscle. Seat belts and air bags have reduced the incidence of these injuries.

Cardiovascular Disorders

There is no similar protection against a stab or bullet wound to the heart, which can be fatal unless treatment is given within minutes.

Nutritional Disorders. The most common nutritional disorder affecting the heart is obesity, which leads to high blood pressure, atherosclerosis, and an excessive demand on the heart's pumping ability. A diet low in fat and cholesterol and high in fibers, fruit, and vegetables can slow the progression of atherosclerosis.

Beriberi is a deficiency of vitamin B_1 leading to heart failure. While most Americans get enough vitamin B_1 in their diets, it still is a major problem for alcoholics.

Alcohol. Alcoholism can cause cardiomyopathy, which is reversible if the intake of alcohol is ended.

Drugs. Some anticancer and heart disease drugs, as well as tricyclic antidepressants, can potentially permanently damage the heart.

DISORDERS OF VEINS

Thrombosis. The most common disorder of the veins is venous thrombosis, formation of blood clots in the veins. A blood clot (thrombus) that forms in the deep veins of the legs or the abdomen can break away and float to the lungs, where the blockage it causes can be life-threatening. Thrombosis can also lead to chronic venous insufficiency, in which a blood clot blocks a vessel in a leg and causes swelling and discoloration.

Varicose Veins. These result in swelling and distortion of the blood vessels. Varicosity usually occurs in veins just below the skin of the leg, but they can also affect veins of the anus, esophagus, and scrotum.

DISORDERS OF ARTERIES

Arteriosclerosis. This thickening and loss of elasticity of the artery walls is most often caused by atherosclerosis. The build-up of plaque or the formation of blood clots can reduce bloodflow. Complete blockage of an artery can cause a heart attack or stroke.

Atherosclerosis. This is a build-up of fat deposits that cause artery walls to thicken. It is the most common artery disease and can occur in the legs, heart, and brain. Severely restricted bloodflow in the arteries to the heart muscle leads to symptoms such as chest pain.

Aneurysm. Congenital defects or atherosclerosis may cause artery walls to thin and swell, forming an aneurysm.

Hypertension. High blood pressure can cause arteries to thicken and narrow, increasing a person's susceptibility to heart disease, stroke, and kidney failure.

Carditis

Inflammation of any part of the heart muscle or the tissue that lines it.

Inflammation of the heart muscle (myocarditis) usually results from infection by a virus. Inflammation of the lining of the chambers of the heart and the heart valves, called endocarditis, usually results from a bacterial infection. Inflammation of the outer lining of the heart is called pericarditis and can result from a bacterial infection, a viral infection, or a heart attack (myocardial infarction). Pericarditis is sometimes caused by an autoimmune disease, such as systemic lupus erythematosus or rheumatoid arthritis. Carditis often occurs in patients with Lyme disease, an infection caused by a spirochete, a microbe transmitted by the bite of ticks.

Symptoms of carditis can include a heart murmur, the sound produced by an abnormal backward flow of blood through a damaged heart valve; chest pain that may mimic that of a heart attack; and a number of other discomforts, including fever, chills, and breathlessness.

Treatment of endocarditis starts with antibiotic medication to attack the underlying infection. Pericarditis is treated with anti-inflammatory drugs and occasionally antimicrobial agents as well. Severe cases may require other medications to stabilize the function of the heart and prevent major complications. *See also* HEART ATTACK.

Catastrophic Health Insurance

Also known as major medical insurance

A health insurance policy with an extremely high deductible that covers all costs above the deductible.

Catastrophic health insurance is an insurance policy that has a high deductible and covers health-care expenditures in excess of a predetermined level, often thousands of dollars or more. Individuals pay all the costs for a medical service up to the level of the deductible. In some cases, catastrophic insurance covers only some medical expenses, such as treatment and hospitalization for specific serious illnesses.

Policy holders sometimes supplement basic medical insurance with catastrophic insurance, which is used to cover costs if the policy holder exhausts the basic coverage. *See also* ACCIDENTS.

Cauliflower Ear

Also known as auricular hematoma

A condition in which the shape of the ear becomes distorted due to an accumulation of blood in the cartilage of the outer-ear.

Cauliflower ear is caused by trauma, friction, or infection of the ear. It may result from a single injury but is more common among those whose ears are repeatedly subjected to trauma, such as boxers and other athletes. Cauliflower ear causes swelling and extreme sensitivity to touch.

Prompt treatment can prevent or limit deformity of the ear. The ear is usually drained of excess fluid. Antibiotics may be prescribed to cure an underlying infection. If the condition is left untreated, the ear can become permanently disfigured.

Causalgia

Intense burning pain caused by damage to nerves.

Causalgia is an intense, continuous pain that may follow an injury or disease in a major nerve pathway. It is accompanied by changes in bloodflow. Other symptoms include swelling, sweating, and red and tender skin around the affected area. It is often a result of a gunshot wound in the leg, a fracture, or a deep cut severing a nerve. Physicians may treat patients with a sympathetic nerve block. In extreme cases, a surgical procedure severing the affected nerves (sympathectomy) is performed.

Centers for Disease Control

The agency that heads the federal government's efforts to prevent the spread of disease.

The Centers for Disease Control (CDC), headquartered in Atlanta, Georgia, is part of the Department of Health and Human Services. It works to control the spread of disease, improve the nation's environmental health, and educate the public about disease prevention.

Chest Pain

The CDC has more than 2000 employees who work in its U.S. offices, and more than 100 in its offices overseas. The CDC's activities range from analyzing the epidemiology of infectious diseases to training people in HIV prevention and traveling to foreign locales to help stop outbreaks of infectious diseases.

Chest Pain

Discomfort in the chest region that may vary in severity, type of sensation, and location.

Chest pain comes in many forms, can have many different causes, and can be nothing more than a minor annoyance. But it can also be an urgent signal of a life-threatening condition—it is the second most common symptom of heart disease, ranking just behind shortness of breath.

NONCARDIAC CAUSES

Chest pain that is not caused by a heart disorder may stem from a condition such as a muscle strain or a broken or bruised rib. An infection such as bronchitis or pneumonia can cause chest pain by inflaming the tissue that lines the lungs. Acid indigestion can cause the discomfort behind the breastbone called heartburn, and the viral infection called shingles can cause severe pain in the chest and skin blisters.

CARDIAC CAUSES

Angina Pectoris. The most common chest pain related to heart disease is angina pectoris. It occurs when the heart muscle does not receive enough oxygen because the arteries that carry blood to it become narrowed, usually from a build-up of deposits containing cholesterol.

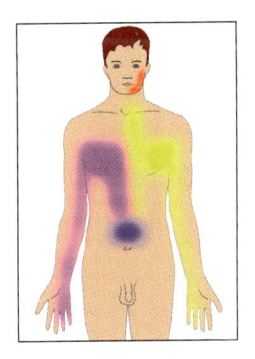

Angina. Left, an image of angina. This is a form of recurring chest pain that affects certain sections of the chest whenever part of the heart is not receiving enough oxygen. It often feels as though another person is pressing on the body or squeezing tightly just below the ribs or breast bone. Angina can usually be treated with simple lifestyle changes that reduce a person's risk of suffering such pains.

Chest Pain

Pericarditis. This is another common cause of chest pain, and it may sometimes cause pain severe enough to mimic a heart attack. The pain is caused by friction when the two membranes that cover the lung and heart become inflamed and rub against each other. Diagnosis of pericarditis can be made by a physician, who listens for the sound of the friction through a stethoscope.

Mitral Valve Prolapse. This is deformation of the valve between chambers of the heart; it can cause sharp pain on the left side of the chest that does not require emergency treatment. It can be diagnosed by the sound, or murmur, caused by backflow of blood through the valve.

Aortic Valve Regurgitation. Chest pain resembling that of angina can be caused by another valve problem, aortic valve regurgitation, due to malformation of, or damage to, the main valve through which blood flows out of the heart.

Arrhythmia. This is an abnormal heartbeat; it can also cause chest pain or pressure that can be mistaken for angina.

Dissection of the Aorta. One cause of chest pain requiring emergency treatment is dissection of the aorta, a disruption of the inner lining of the main artery from the heart. Dissection produces pain that radiates out from the front to the back of the chest, or from between the shoulder blades. This disorder is most common in older people with high blood pressure that has produced an aneurysm, a ballooning out of the wall of the aorta.

ALERT   ALERT   ALERT

WHEN TO TAKE IMMEDIATE ACTION

When acute chest pain occurs, medical authorities say that time should not be wasted in debating its cause. According to the National Institutes of Health, the chance of surviving a heart attack is increased by 40 percent if the patient gets to a hospital or receives emergency care at home within 30 minutes after the symptoms begin. Swift treatment not only improves the chance of survival but also decreases the amount of damage done to the heart.

A sudden, sharp pain that is accompanied by difficulty swallowing and breathing and by coughing up of blood can indicate a pulmonary embolism—blockage of the pulmonary artery, which carries blood from the heart to the lungs, by a blood clot. Pain in the center of the chest, radiating to the left side of the body and down the abdomen, and accompanied by difficulty breathing, can be a symptom of pericarditis—infection of the sac around the heart muscle. A dull, persistent chest pain with breathlessness, dizziness, paleness, and cold, clammy skin can indicate a heart attack (myocardial infarction). Chest pain with sudden loss of coordination and paralysis, numbness, or weakness on one side of the body can indicate a stroke.

Childbirth

The process of giving birth.

Giving birth, which consists of labor and delivery, is the culmination of nine months of pregnancy. A vaginal delivery, in which the baby emerges from the birth canal, propelled by contractions, is the most common. However, some births, for reasons ranging from fetal distress to the baby being too large to pass easily through the birth canal, require surgical intervention in the form of a Cesarean section.

WHEN LABOR BEGINS

Labor is characterized by regular contractions that are from 10 to 20 minutes apart at first and last 45 seconds to one minute. Rupture of the membranes, or "breaking the waters," is a sudden flow of liquid—amnionic fluids—in a gush or slow leak. Rupture of the membrane may occur from shortly before labor to well into labor. Once labor has begun, the mother should not eat any solid food. If anesthesia is administered, a full stomach can cause nausea and complicate delivery.

LABOR

Labor and delivery consist of three stages. The first stage, which lasts the longest, consists of gradually strengthening contractions at increasingly closer intervals. These contractions cause the cervix to start to open and thin out. The contractions gradually intensify and the woman should notify her doctor that labor has begun. This stage is completed when the cervix is at 10 centimeters dilation and is completely effaced.

DELIVERY

The second stage, which lasts about 50 minutes in first mothers and 20 minutes in later pregnancies, consists of pushing out the baby. This stage is reached when the cervix is fully dilated. The mother starts feeling an urge to push, and is encouraged to push with each contraction. Most babies are born head first. The baby has "crowned" when the head is visible from the vaginal opening.

The third stage involves the delivery of the placenta, or afterbirth. The placenta has usually already separated from the uterine wall in response to contractions; the doctor may tug gently on the umbilical cord, taking care not to damage it. In rare circumstances, the placenta may have to be surgically removed. Any retained portions of the placenta can contribute to hemorrhaging.

Chlorate Poisoning

The ingestion of toxic chlorates, which can result in kidney and liver damage.

Symptoms of chlorate poisoning include diarrhea, abdominal pain, and ulceration of the mouth.

Treatment. Skin that has come in contact with chlorates should immediately be washed with soap and water. Eyes should be flushed out with liberal amounts of water. In case of ingestion, medical help should be contacted immediately. Depending on the severity of symptoms and the amount of time elapsed since poisoning, treatment may involve administering oxygen or intravenous fluids, washing the stomach with activated charcoal, or even hemodialysis.

> **ALERT   ALERT   ALERT**
> **HIGHLY TOXIC**
> *Chlorates are highly toxic substance present in defoliant weed killers and fertilizers. Ingestion of chlorates can result in kidney and liver damage, corrosion of the intestine, a chemical change in hemoglobin (methemoglobineria), and depression of the central nervous system. In some cases, ingestion can be fatal.*

Prevention. Pesticides and fertilizers should be kept out of the reach of small children. When assisting a victim of chlorate poisoning, avoid direct contact with clothing that may be contaminated, and use rubber gloves while cleaning the toxins from hair and skin. *See also* ANTIFREEZE POISONING *and* POISONING.

Choking

Partial or complete obstruction of the airway, resulting in coughing, gagging, or wheezing.

Symptoms. A choking victim will not be able to speak. The person who is choking may, occasionally, place both hands around the neck or lean forward in an attempt to dislodge the obstruction. The victim is likely to make wheezing or snorting sounds and may become pale or blue in the face. Sometimes choking victims will faint.

If a person appears to be choking but there is no obstruction, he or she may actually be suffering from anaphylactic shock. This is a severe

Choking

Heimlich Maneuver. A choking victim can be helped by using the Heimlich maneuver. Left, the person helping the victim should go behind the person, wrap their arms around the victim's upper abdomen, and thrust inward near the bottom of the ribcage. Right, choking victims who are alone may use the back of a chair to simulate the thrust another person would give them.

allergic reaction to food, medication, or an insect bite that results in shock and can be fatal in as little as 15 minutes. Accompanying symptoms may include hives, swelling, and redness or blueness of the skin (cyanosis).

Treatment. An object caught in the air passages may be removed by using the Heimlich maneuver (see picture). The Heimlich maneuver should only be performed on a conscious person. Once normal breathing resumes, it is important to determine if any part of the object was inhaled into the lungs, since this can cause subsequent medical problems (pneumonia).

In all cases of blockage, emergency medical help should be sought immediately. If the Heimlich maneuver does not remove a blockage, or if there is no object in the air passages, medical technicians will decide if a surgical procedure on the airway should be used and whether or

ALERT   ALERT   ALERT

PREVENTING CHOKING IN CHILDREN

- Keep chunks of meat or cheese, grapes, hard candy, and other foods that children may choke on, out of their reach. Nuts should not be given to any child under the age of seven.
- Teach older children not to offer foods that may cause choking to younger siblings.
- Cut firmer foods into small pieces before feeding to a small child.
- Teach children to chew well before swallowing.
- Children should never be allowed to run or play with food or drinking straws in their mouths.
- Always keep small toy parts and other household objects out of the reach of small children.

Choking

not the victim should be taken to the hospital. Oxygen deprivation for more than five or six minutes may cause brain damage.

Choking in Children. Children beginning solid food for the first time and children under the age of four who do not chew their food well are at high risk for choking. Nuts, chunks of meat (such as hot dogs, cheese, grapes, hard candy, and popcorn) are the most dangerous foods for small children. Common household items may also pose a potential hazard to a young child's air passages. Rubber or latex balloons, coins, marbles, small parts of toys, pen caps, and button-type batteries are also frequent causes of airway obstructions. *See* ANOXIA; CARDIOPULMONARY RESUSCITATION (CPR); *and* HEIMLICH MANEUVER.

Cold Injury

Tissue injury due to freezing temperatures and outdoor exposure.

The three stages of cold injury are chilling, frostnip, and frostbite. The first stage, chilling, involves a rapid lowering of body temperature. The skin then becomes numb and loses color, marking the second stage, frostnip. At this stage, tissue damage is still reversible. In the last stage, frostbite, normally red skin becomes pale or white, and ice crystals form on the skin's surface. As the skin warms, it will appear blue or purple. Burning, swelling, and chilblains (burning or chilling sensations) may also occur. Chilblains (also known as pernio) are usually experienced in areas of the body that were previously frostbitten.

Warning signs to look for if cold injury is suspected include shivering, a change in skin color (to pale or blue), and numbness. Affected children who have been complaining about the cold may suddenly stop complaining.

Compared to adults, children have a higher ratio of body surface to weight, and thus are more likely to suffer cold injury. Factors that may cause cold injury include low temperature, moist skin subjected to low temperature, wind, and high altitude. Cold injury is treated by warming the affected area (in the case of frostbite, the area must be warmed slowly and carefully). Chilblains usually resist attempts at treatment and can persist for months or even years. *See also* FROSTBITE *and* HYPOTHERMIA.

Coma

A state of deep unconsciousness caused by disease or injury.

Coma is a state similar to deep sleep, but a person cannot be roused from it. A person in a coma does not respond to external stimuli, such as light, touch, sound, or pain. The patient is also unaware of internal sensations, such as an urgency to empty a full bladder. Patients in comas thus need urinary catheters, intravenous feeding, and sometimes even artificial respiration. In a mild coma, the patient may be able to move the limbs in response to pain. In a deep coma, there is no such response.

Causes. Coma results from damage or injury to the cerebrum, brain stem, or other parts of the brain. Coma may be caused by:
- head injury, such as a concussion or bleeding around the brain;
- infections, such as meningitis and encephalitis, that produce high fever;
- oxygen deprivation resulting from cardiac arrest;
- carbon monoxide inhalation;
- extreme high or low body temperature;
- low blood sugar (hypoglycemia); and
- drug and alcohol abuse.

Diagnosis. The severity of a coma can give important information about prognosis and the best choice of treatment, so a physician will test the patient's level of response and functioning of vital signs. To determine the cause of the coma, blood tests check for anemia, infection, and abnormal levels of alcohol, oxygen, or carbon dioxide. Computed tomography (CAT) or magnetic resonance imaging (MRI) can be used to detect possible brain damage.

Treatment. In some instances, the coma can be treated by treating the underlying cause. Otherwise, the patient can only be made as comfortable as possible. A deep coma may last for years, or a person may recover after a shorter period of time. The outlook is better in cases of injury than in cases where the coma is caused by tissue death due to a lack of oxygen.

Complication

Complication

> Negative reaction to, or undesirable side effect of, an illness or surgical procedure.

Complication is a general term covering the full scope of side effects and undesired consequences. A complication can be further damage brought on by an existing condition, or can be caused by the treatment itself. A patient might have a negative reaction to a procedure or to a medication or anesthesia.

Even the most common surgeries have potential complications. A tonsillectomy (a removal of the tonsils) can cause severe bleeding that may be fatal if left untreated. Oral surgery to remove wisdom teeth can lead to facial paralysis. One of the most common sources of surgical complications is the use of general anesthesia. Complications from anesthesia include heart attack, stroke, sore throat, damage to the teeth, blood clots, and allergic reaction.

Compress

> Padded material used either to apply heat, cold, or medication to a part of the body or to stop bleeding from a wound.

A compress is usually applied under pressure to an injury or wound and held in place by a bandage. Compresses can be made of gauze, linen, or plastic envelopes filled with heat- or cold-retaining jelly or ointment. Hot-packs are commonly heated up in warm water, while cold packs are usually chilled in a refrigerator. Fabric compresses are cooled by ice or cold water, or heated by warm water.

Usage. A cold compress can reduce pain, swelling, and bleeding under the skin (bruising) after an injury. A dry compress can stop bleeding or can be used to apply medicated cream to infected skin. *See also* BANDAGE; EMERGENCY, FIRST STEPS; FIRST AID; *and* ICE PACKS.

Concussion

Mild injury to the brain as a result of a blow to or violent motion of the head.

Any blow to the head may force the brain against the bony structure of the skull. Concussion is a form of injury to the brain that is sometimes associated with a brief loss of consciousness.

Symptoms. Beyond a loss of consciousness, symptoms can include loss of memory, dizziness, vomiting, nausea, and headache. Head injury causing unconsciousness should be investigated by a doctor. Recovery generally occurs without treatment and is complete within 24 to 48 hours.

> **ALERT ALERT ALERT**
> CHILDREN AND HEAD INJURY
> Children are at particular risk for brain injury because they are more prone to accidental falls. Also, infants and toddlers are, accidentally or intentionally, easily shaken by adults and can suffer severe brain injury. Any vomiting, paleness, drowsiness, or even a very brief period of unconsciousness following a blow to the head is evidence of brain injury, and the child should be checked by a physician as soon as possible.

Serious symptoms may develop after a period of time, including persistent headaches, amnesia, confusion, and increasing sleepiness and lethargy. Emergency symptoms include persistent unconsciousness, seizures, drowsiness, repeated vomiting, unequal pupil size, confusion, and difficulty walking.

Children and Concussion. Children are particularly at risk for brain injury, because they are more prone to falls. Any fall or blow to the head of a child that results in a loss of consciousness warrants an immediate evaluation by a medical professional.

Contraception

Also known as birth control or family planning

Various methods used to prevent conception.

Barrier methods are designed to prevent sperm from entering the uterus. These include condoms (male and female), diaphragms, cervical caps, sponges and contraceptive creams, foams and jellies. They

Cornell Illustrated Emergency Medicine & First Aid Guide • 79

Contraception

have varying success rates.

The male condom is used to prevent semen from entering the vagina. Made of latex or rubber, it is rolled over the erect penis and contains a reservoir—space in the tip—to hold sperm upon ejaculation. Most condoms also contain spermicide. Condoms are 99 percent effective in preventing pregnancy. A fresh condom must be used for each incident of intercourse.

The female condom, which lines the vagina, is similar in construction to its male counterpart. It is larger than the male condom and is held in place with a ring. The failure rate of the female condom is higher than that of the male condom.

The diaphragm is a dome-shaped rubber cup that fits over the cervix and prevents sperm from entering the uterus. It is filled with a contraceptive cream or jelly that contains a spermicide. The diaphragm, which must be fitted by a medical practitioner, should cover the entire cervix without causing discomfort when positioned properly. The diaphragm must be inserted prior to intercourse and should remain in place for at least eight hours afterwards but not for more than 24 hours.

The diaphragm must be refitted after a woman gives birth, undergoes an abortion or miscarriage, or gains or loses more than 10 pounds. Some doctors recommend refitting after a year, whether or not any of these events have actually taken place. The diaphragm is 80 to 90 percent effective in preventing pregnancy.

The cervical cap is a smaller and more rigid version of the diaphragm. It fits directly over the cervix. It also must be fitted by a healthcare professional. A contraceptive cream or jelly must be used as well. The cap should be inserted before intercourse and left in place for at least eight hours afterwards, but not for longer than 48 hours. Cervical caps are approximately as effective as diaphragms.

Morning-after pills, or high doses of oral contraceptives, are sometimes used to prevent pregnancy after a single act of unprotected sex. This must be taken within 72 hours of intercourse to be effective.

Abortion should not be viewed as a method of birth control, but rather a means to terminate an unwanted pregnancy in cases where contraception has failed or was not used.

Aside from a conventional surgical abortion, there are chemical means of ending a pregnancy in the early stages. Mifepristone, known more widely as RU-486, can be taken in combination with contraction-inducing chemicals known as prostaglandins. This is an effective method of terminating a pregnancy before the ninth week.

Coronary Heart Disease

Coronary Heart Disease

Also known as coronary artery disease

A chronic, progressive condition in which the arteries supplying the heart become narrower and harder, impeding the flow of blood to the heart muscle.

Coronary heart disease is the leading cause of death in the United States, resulting in almost half of deaths.

Causes
While some degree of coronary heart disease occurs in many individuals with age, the risk is raised significantly by lifestyle practices, such as smoking, obesity, lack of exercise, and a diet rich in fat and cholesterol. Medical conditions, such as high blood pressure and diabetes, are also associated with coronary heart disease.

Symptoms
The first symptom of coronary heart disease is often angina. Angina can occur in men as early as their 30s; in women, it generally does not occur until after menopause.

Angina can be felt as a dull pain or pressure in the the chest that extends up the neck or down an arm (most often the left arm). The pain or pressure often occurs after physical exertion, even something as moderate as walking up a hill or a flight of stairs, or after some emotional stress. A variant form of the condition, called vasospasm or Prinzmetal's angina, can progress quickly, when a spasm in an artery blocks blood flow to the heart. Vasospasm is uncommon and usually occurs when a person is at rest, but like the common kind of angina, it indicates the presence of severe coronary heart disease.

ALERT ALERT ALERT
In Case of a Heart Attack

Severe chest pain, fainting, and pain in the middle of the chest spreading to the back or left arm is a medical emergency. Half of all heart attack deaths occur in the first few hours after the onset of symptoms. The sooner the person is treated, the greater the chance of survival. Medical help should be sought immediately by dialing 911.

Treatment
If lifestyle changes cannot stop the progression of coronary heart disease, drug treatment can help to slow the process or control the symp-

Coronary Heart Disease

toms. Medications are chosen on the basis of the degree to which the condition has progressed and the symptoms the patient feels.

Medication. Vasodilators, drugs that cause arteries to relax and widen, may be prescribed for angina pectoris. In angina pectoris, the chest pain or discomfort results when the myocardium, the heart muscle, is no longer receiving an adequate supply of oxygen because of reduced blood flow through the arteries. One of the oldest and most commonly used vasodilators is nitroglycerine, which can have a beneficial effect in a matter of minutes after a pill is dissolved under the tongue or a dose is sprayed into the mouth.

Surgery. If coronary heart disease progresses to the point where blockage of one or more arteries is imminent, one of several techniques can be used to keep the arteries open and blood flowing adequately. A narrowed region of an artery can be widened by balloon angioplasty. In balloon angioplasty, a catheter is inserted to the point of blockage, with a balloon at its end, which is inflated to open the artery. Balloon angioplasty may be followed by implantation of a stent, a metal tube that keeps the artery open. If there is excessive blockage or multiple blockages, coronary bypass surgery may be necessary.

Coughing Up Blood

Also known as hemoptysis

Blood in the sputum.

Any number of medical conditions can result in the presence of blood in the sputum (hemoptysis), including bacterial infections, lung cancer, bleeding disorders such as hemophilia, inflammation of the trachea, heart failure, mitral stenosis, and congestive heart failure. Any of these conditions can result in broken blood vessels in the airways, nose, throat, or another part of the respiratory system. While a simple persistent cough can cause blood in the sputum, such blood is usually a sign of a serious underlying condition that requires immediate medical attention.

Causes. Most often, coughing up blood is the result of a respiratory tract infection such as tuberculosis, bronchitis, or pneumonia. Such an infection can inflame the airways (bronchi) of the lung or the small sacs (alveoli) where air is exchanged in the lung. An infection may also damage a blood vessel of the respiratory tract enough to cause it to rupture.

When the bronchi become enlarged and distorted (bronchiecta-

Coughing Up Blood

sis), one of the blood vessels within the bronchi may break open. This can also happen with tracheitis, or inflammation of the windpipe. Within the lung itself, congestion can put enough pressure on blood vessels to cause them to rupture. Congestion can be due to a narrowing of the valve between the upper and lower chambers of the heart (mitral stenosis), or blockage of a lung artery by a clot (pulmonary embolism). Lung cancer can also weaken and eventually rupture a blood vessel, causing hemoptysis.

Diagnosis. The appearance of the blood coughed up can give clues to the underlying disorder. Only rarely is the blood bright red and unmixed with other secretions. It may have a pink, foamy, or streaked appearance, or take the form of clots.

A cough that persists for months, worsens dramatically, and produces blood may be an indication of lung cancer. A high fever and shortness of breath may suggest pneumonia. A chest x-ray can be done to detect abnormalities in the lungs and respiratory tract. In some cases, visual examination of the respiratory tract with a bronchoscope may be performed.

Treatment. Treatment may include antibiotic drugs for bacterial infections, diuretics to reduce fluid retention, and anticoagulant drugs to prevent abnormal blood clotting. *See also* CONGESTIVE HEART FAILURE *and* HEART FAILURE.

Cramp

A sudden, painful contracting of the muscles.

Painful muscle spasms or cramps are common in healthy people and usually last only a few minutes. Cramps may result from vigorous activity or remaining in the same position for an extended period.

Causes. Cramps that occur during or just after strenuous exercise are caused by a buildup of lactic acid in the muscles. A muscle cramp may also indicate a minor injury to muscle fiber. Prolonged exercise accompanied by excessive sweating can lead to a loss of electrolytes and cause cramps in resting muscles. Some individuals experience leg cramps at night while sleeping; this may be caused by poor blood circulation to the leg muscles.

Symptoms. Attempting to move a cramped muscle causes the muscle to vigorously contract. If pressure is placed on the cramped muscle,

Crohn's Disease

the pain is temporarily eased.

Treatment. A cramp usually lasts only a few minutes and will improve by itself. Gently massaging and stretching the muscle can help to ease the cramp. To prevent cramping, it is important to drink plenty of water and stretch properly before exercising. Adding calcium to the diet and raising the legs may relieve leg cramps.

Writers' Cramp. Writers' cramp is a series of muscle spasms that makes writing painful. Half of people with writers' cramp develop a tremor in the arms. It may be a form of dystonia (an involuntary muscle spasm), or it may be psychological in origin, as often writing is the only affected movement. However, the cramp does not generally respond to psychotherapy. The main treatment is rest; muscle relaxants are usually ineffective.

Crohn's Disease

Also known as ileitis or regional enteritis

A disease of unknown origin, characterized by chronic inflammation and ulceration of the intestines.

Crohn's disease is a chronic and progressive inflammation of the intestine, involving the lower part of the small intestine (ileum) and, in some cases, the colon. However, Crohn's disease may also affect any portion of the digestive tract from mouth to anus.

Incidence and Cause. Crohn's disease occurs in one in every 50,000 people. In recent years, the disease has become more prevalent in the United States and other Western countries. The typical patient suffering from Crohn's disease is Caucasian and between the ages of 15 and 35. The disease may be inherited, and it is suspected that it may result from an abnormal reaction of the immune system to a substance in the digestive tract.

Symptoms. Symptoms of Crohn's disease include periodic pain and cramping on the right side of the abdomen or around the navel, abdominal swelling or tenderness, chronic diarrhea, nausea, a low-grade fever, fatigue, malaise (a generalized feeling of illness), weight loss, and lesions, especially in the intestine and around the mouth. Crohn's disease is thought to be hereditary; if an individual has a family history of symptoms, there is a greater chance of that individual developing the disease.

Diagnosis. Crohn's disease is diagnosed with barium x-rays, which reveal abnormal areas of the intestine. Parts of the intestine may ap-

Crohn's Disease

pear narrower and more rigid than normal. Colonoscopy, also used, may reveal a cobblestone-like texture of ulcerations in the lining of the intestines.

Complications. The diarrhea that characterizes Crohn's disease can be quite debilitating and can result in severe malnutrition, as nutrients are not properly absorbed by the intestines. Abdominal pain helps suppress the appetite, resulting in further weight loss. Other complications include progressive obstruction of the small intestine, development of abnormal connections (fistulas) and fissures in the rectal and anal areas, bleeding, and development of abscesses.

Treatment. There is no single cure for Crohn's disease. Supplements of certain vitamins and minerals, such as vitamin B_{12}, are often needed to counter reduced absorption of nutrients. A special diet may be required. Generally, foods that are difficult to digest, such as high-fat or high-fiber foods, as well as irritants, such as caffeine and spicy foods, should be avoided. Some physicians recommend liquid diets or intravenous feeding during severe attacks, to give the intestine a chance to rest.

No specific treatment is required if the patient does not exhibit symptoms. Mild symptoms can be helped by antidiarrheal medications and adequate intake of fluid.

ALERT   ALERT   ALERT

WHEN CROHN'S DISEASE RESULTS IN DEHYDRATION

Dehydration may not seem very threatening to overall health, but it can cause serious damage. Young children can dehydrate rapidly, causing serious damage to the digestive tract and even death. Adults, too, should pay attention to frequent spells of diarrhea. Oral rehydration therapy is simple and effective: replace what diarrhea takes out of the body by drinking glasses of water mixed with a half-teaspoon of salt or baking soda. Dementia in the elderly may be a sign of dehydration.

More severe cases can be helped by anti-inflammatory medications such as s-amino-salicylate drugs and corticosteroids. If only the rectum is affected, corticosteroid enemas may suppress inflammation. Immunosuppressive therapy may also be effective, including a recently introduced drug called infliximab. All of these treatments can provide relief from symptoms of Crohn's disease, but they cannot cure the disease itself.

Surgery is performed for complications such as obstruction, abscesses, and perforation. The large intestine may be removed if the disease is limited to one area and medications have proven ineffective.

Crush Syndrome

When the disease is found only in the small intestine, the diseased segment is removed and the healthy portions joined together.

Approximately 70 percent of patients with Crohn's disease require surgery at some point. Surgery is not a permanent cure; recurrence of the disease in other areas of the intestinal tract is common.

Prevention. Since Crohn's disease is most likely caused by genetic factors, there is no way to prevent this condition. Individuals with the disease should get plenty of rest.

Crush Syndrome

Also known as compression syndrome

Failure of the kidneys, resulting from violent compression of muscle tissue.

Victims of collapsed buildings or auto accidents often suffer crush syndrome. The damaged muscle tissue releases large amounts of protein into the bloodstream. This sudden deluge interferes with the ability of the kidneys and liver to remove toxins from the blood. Crush syndrome is a life-threatening condition, since toxic substances build up to high levels in the blood instead of being excreted in the urine.

Crush syndrome is almost always complicated by shock. Hospitalization with artificial cleansing of the blood (kidney dialysis) removes high levels of toxins in the blood, while allowing the kidneys to recover. *See also* ACCIDENTS *and* SHOCK.

Dacryocystitis

Also called tear sac infection

An inflammation of the tear sac that occurs when the nasolacrimal duct is obstructed.

The nasolacrimal duct runs between the nose and the tear sac. When it is obstructed, it may result in an infection that is called dacryocystitis.

Dacryocystitis is marked by the discharge of mucus or pus from the eyelid whenever light pressure is applied. It may also cause redness, some pain, and swelling on the inside corner of the infected eye.

Dacryocystitis will regularly cause tearing to occur. In severe cases, there may be an abscess in the tear sac, where tears are stored before exiting the body when the eyes water or when an individual is crying.

Causes. Dacryocystitis can be caused by an infection, nasal polyps, or trauma. Dacryocystitis often appears after serious facial traumas, particularly those involving the nose; this may explain the increased incidence in children.

Treatment. A warm compress applied to the affected region of the face may help treat some of the pain and redness. A health care professional should be consulted as soon as possible in order to ensure that the infection is not serious.

Antibiotics may be prescribed to combat any infection related to the dacryocystitis. Although medication usually heals dacryocystitis, the most severe cases may require surgery.

Deafness

A complete or partial inability to hear.

Impaired hearing is the single most common physical disability in the United States. It can vary in severity, cause and prognosis and can be the result of disease, injury, or old age.

Types. Deafness can be classified as either conductive, sensorineural, or a combination.

Conductive hearing loss refers to a mechanical problem that blocks the transmission of sound through the outer- or middle-ear. It is frequently a result of damage to the eardrum or the middle-ear bones. In a healthy ear, sound enters the outer-ear and passes down the ear canal to the eardrum (tympanum). The sound causes the eardrum to vibrate, activating the middle-ear bones, which then carry the vibrations to the inner-ear.

Deafness

Conductive hearing loss has a number of possible causes. Earwax blocking the outer ear canal is the most common cause in adults, while middle-ear infection (otitis media) is the most common cause in children. The eardrum may become perforated due to middle-ear infection or ear surgery, or the eardrum or middle-ear may be damaged by abrupt pressure changes (barotrauma).

Sensorineural Hearing Loss. This is the result of damage to the inner-ear, auditory nerve, or nerve pathways. Vibrations reach the inner-ear but are not transmitted to the brain. Common causes include: genetics; injury to a developing fetus because of exposure to German measles (rubella); repeated exposure to loud noise; and fluid in the labyrinth of the ear.

Diagnosis. Several hearing tests are used to determine the type and severity of hearing loss. A person's responses to different sounds in each ear, both heard through the ear and transmitted through the bone at the back of the ear, can help a physician determine the location of the impairment and the underlying cause.

Treatment. Proper diagnosis is crucial for the treatment of hearing loss. An accumulation of fluid or wax can be drained or removed, and hearing will be restored. Children that suffer from continuous otitis media can be treated with antibiotics and, if necessary, surgery can drain accumulated fluid (myringotomy). A perforated eardrum that fails to heal naturally can be surgically rebuilt (tympanoplasty).

In cases in which there is no cure for deafness, a hearing aid is recommended. Basically, hearing aids consist of a microphone, an amplifier that makes sounds louder and clearer, and a speaker. Different hearing aids meet different individuals' needs; there are many types that vary in clarity, ease of adjustment, and visibility. Presently, hearing aids have been developed that are controlled by computer to adjust for different environment, such as a crowded restaurants or a quiet room. Those with hearing impairments can also purchase amplifiers that attach to telephones and doorbells.

Cochlear Implant. If a hearing aid is not effective, a cochlear implant may be surgically embedded in the ear. The implant consists of internal and external coils, electrodes, a speech processor, and a microphone. The microphone accumulates sound waves that the processor then transforms into electrical impulses. These impulses are transmitted from the external coil through the skin to the internal coil and then to the electrodes, which activate the auditory nerve. After the surgery, the patient must work with a speech therapist to learn how to interpret the sounds produced by the implant.

Decompression Sickness

Also known as the bends

Physical problems caused by an overly rapid ascent from deep under water.

When decompression sickness was an occupational disease of workers in high-pressure conditions, such as underwater construction and marine bioengineering, it was called caisson disease. Now it is largely a hazard for scuba divers.

In high-pressure environments, such as deep water, gases build up in the tissues of the body. If pressure drops suddenly when a diver rises to the surface too quickly, those gases will expand and form bubbles that block blood vessels.

Symptoms can occur within 24 hours after the event. They include severe pains of the larger joints, itching, chest tightening, and mottling of the skin. Decompression sickness can cause neurological problems such as visual disturbances or difficulty with balance. If the blood vessels blocked by the bubbles are in the heart or lungs, the condition can be fatal.

Decompression sickness is treated by putting the person in a decompression chamber, where high pressure dissolves the bubbles; the pressure is then reduced gradually so that excess gas can be breathed out. A carefully timed, slow ascent from a deep dive is necessary to prevent decompression sickness.

Defibrillation

The technique of giving the heart a brief electric shock to terminate a rapid, irregular, and ineffective heartbeat and restore normal heart rhythm.

In an emergency situation where an abnormal heartbeat such as ventricular fibrillation or ventricular tachycardia is life-threatening, paddles are placed over the heart and a shock is given to restore normal electrical activity.

Defibrillation is also used routinely to restart the heart after open-heart surgery. Defibrillators are standard equipment in ambulances and are carried by emergency medical teams. Persons with conditions that place them at high risk of life-threatening arrhythmias now often have implanted defibrillators that are programmed to detect an arrhythmia and administer a shock automatically.

Dehydration

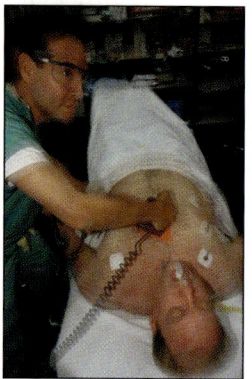

Defibrillation. Left, a physician is using a defibrillator to restart a man's heart. All physicians and emergency medical technicians, as well as others, are trained in defibrillator use. Early defibrillation is essential to effective emergency heart treatment.

EXPERIENCE NOT MANDATORY
Automatic defibrillators are available in many public places, such as airports and stadiums, so that persons with even minimal training can use them in the short period, only a few minutes long, when restarting the heart can save a life. Defibrillation using advanced devices does not require extensive training.

Dehydration

A loss of water through vomiting, diarrhea, inadequate fluid intake, or perspiration.

If not restored by fluid intake, dehydration can have many serious consequences, including low blood pressure, loss of consciousness, heart failure, and, in the most extreme cases, death. Water enters the body through the ingestion of food and liquids. Water leaves the body in the form of urine, perspiration, vomiting, in the stool, and as air that is exhaled. Most of the water retained in the body is in the cells themselves or in the spaces surrounding the cells.

Only about eight pounds, or four to five quarts, of water is needed in the bloodstream, so there is always a large reserve available in the rest of the body when the water in the blood is depleted. The water in the bloodstream acts as the vehicle for the various types of blood cells, and it also carries dissolved mineral salts necessary for bodily functions. The percentages of sodium and potassium in the bloodstream are carefully monitored by the body. If the percentage rises, the body attempts to reduce loss of water through the kidneys. Thirst increases causing greater water intake and retention. When the body's sodium percentage lowers, the body excretes more water through the kidneys. This mechanism is controlled in part by the pituitary gland in the lower part of the brain, which senses the need to retain water and secretes an antidiuretic hormone.

When this hormone is present in the bloodstream, the kidneys drain less water from the blood, and other cells of the body give up their retained water. When blood volume and pressure is at healthy levels, the pituitary gland ceases to release the antidiuretic hormone,

Dehydration

and the kidneys resume their normal draining function.

Causes. Dehydration occurs when there is an imbalance between intake and outflow of bodily fluids—when the body loses more water than it takes in. This can happen during strenuous exercise with heavy perspiration or when the person is in hot, dry environments. Fluid loss can be the result of diarrhea and vomiting. Inadequate ingestion of water or foods with high water content can result in dehydration, particularly among the elderly, whose thirst- and hunger-signaling mechanisms may be impaired. Dehydration is also a consequence of many diseases, such as diabetes or virus infections. In children too young to feed themselves, dehydration may be caused by parental neglect.

> **OVER 60 AND UNDER 6**
> *Dehydration is particularly dangerous to small children and the elderly. Over two million infants die of dehydration every year, often because of diarrhea.*
> *An elderly person does not respond as quickly to the signals of low water content and may be slow to replenish the depleted water supply. In addition, older people have underlying conditions that predispose them to dehydration. They are more likely to suffer from diarrhea due to diseases that are more common among the elderly (such as diabetes) and from medications, including some antibiotics. The elderly are also at risk of kidney failure caused by the reduced bloodflow to the kidneys when dehydrated.*

Symptoms. In the early stages, a person with dehydration becomes very thirsty. An infant may cry without tears. Symptoms include dry mouth and nasal passages; a flushed face; dry, warm skin; dizziness and weakness; cramped limbs; confusion; headaches of varying degrees of intensity; and decreased urinary output. Severe dehydration can produce low blood pressure leading to a loss of consciousness; this is a medical emergency.

Treatment. Mild dehydration is easily treated by drinking water. There are a number of commercial drinks specially fortified with potassium and sodium that can be used to treat dehydration. Before, during, and after exercise, a person should drink plenty of fluids and increase salt intake. People with heart or kidney problems should consult a physician before starting heavy exercise; they should also be cautious in utilizing any supplemental salt or potassium preparations.

In emergencies involving blood loss, severe dehydration, or shock, medical personnel will apply intravenous solutions of salt water.

If the kidneys excrete too much water (leading to dehydration), a doctor may prescribe medication. If the dehydration is caused by diarrhea, the cause of diarrhea must be addressed by whatever means necessary, or the rehydration process will be ineffective.

Dehydration in Infants

Dehydration in Infants

Water and salt (electrolyte) loss as it pertains to infants.

Dehydration in infants is most commonly caused by vomiting, diarrhea, or inadequate fluid intake. Parental neglect often plays a part in allowing this to occur. The viral or bacterial forms of gastroenteritis, an infection of the digestive tract, also often causes the condition.

Other possible causes of acute diarrhea include: contaminated foods; consuming poisons, such as iron, arsenic, or pesticides; ingestion of too many laxatives; food intolerance; emotional stress; and constipation with fecal soiling. Diarrhea can also be caused by a reaction to antibiotics, acquired sugar intolerance, Hirschsprung's disease (a condition in which the large intestine is obstructed due to inadequate muscular motion), milk protein allergy, upper respiratory infection, and urinary tract infection.

ALERT ALERT ALERT

WHEN TO CALL A DOCTOR

Infants and children dehydrate more rapidly than adults. Parents need to know the warning signs of dehydration and be aware of certain other factors and situations that may exacerbate or increase a child's susceptibility to dehydration. A child's chronic medical condition, especially if he or she is less than two months old, may contribute to a dehydration. Parents should call a doctor if they observe any of these conditions:

- *the soft top of the infant's head has shrunken;*
- *the infant has gone eight to twelve hours without wetting a diaper;*
- *bloody, particularly pungent, or increased frequency or amount of bowel movements;*
- *crying brings no tears;*
- *increased heart rate;*
- *a weak, raspy cry or decreased activity;*
- *mouth, eyes, or skin are dry;*
- *the child shows signs of malnutrition; or*
- *frequent vomiting.*

Symptoms. In addition to diarrhea, fever, abdominal pain, or an upper respiratory infection may be present when an infant is dehydrated. There is also the possibility of parasitic infection. Vomiting, which will often cause dehydration in an infant, is usually due to upper respiratory infection, flu-like infection, or gastroenteritis.

Delirium

Infants who are five percent dehydrated will probably show signs of a poor appetite, fever, dry mucous membranes, concentrated urine output (that is, very dark urination), dry and sunken eyes, drowsiness, and a slightly increased heart rate.

An infant or child who is 10 percent dehydrated will usually have a depressed fontanel, or soft spot, as well as the symptoms listed above.

The most severely dehydrated infants—those who are more than 15 percent dehydrated—experience decreased blood pressure (hypotension) or shock. *See also* HYPOTENSION *and* SHOCK.

> **ROTAVIRUS AND DIARRHEA**
> *Rotavirus, which kills about 600,000 children a year worldwide, causes an acute form of diarrhea that leads to life-threatening dehydration. In the past, how the disease worked was a mystery. It now appears that the rotavirus attacks nerves in the wall of the gut, stimulating the secretion of water and salt. This discovery has led to new treatments for viral gastroenteritis in children.*

Treatment and Prevention. The best way to prevent dehydration in an infant is to maintain sufficient electrolyte balance and to replace fluids lost through diarrhea or vomiting. Since dehydration can be serious in an infant, it is important for a doctor to examine a sick child and evaluate severity on a case-by-case basis.

Treatment regularly includes intravenous fluids and electrolytes. For treatment of slight dehydration, a nonprescription drink, such as Pedialyte, may be used to balance the infant's electrolytes, unless the child's pediatrician recommends otherwise.

Delirium

Acute and sudden onset of abnormal mental symptoms resulting from physical illness.

Delirium is characterized by extreme confusion, often accompanied by agitation. The individual often appears disoriented, frightened, and confused. Symptoms may also include disorganized speech, screaming, threatening, visual and auditory hallucinations, and mood swings. The person's mood, memory, and awareness fluctuate significantly, so he or she may be calm and lucid at times and extremely agitated and incoherent at others. Delirium usually disappears as abruptly as it arrives, often after a few days. It may, however, be an early sign of chronic dementia and it may even be life-threatening.

Dementia

There are many physical causes for delirium, including brain injury or disease, metabolic disorders, low blood sugar, vitamin deficiency, infection, and anesthesia. Diagnosis is urgent so that the underlying illness may be treated. *See also* DEMENTIA.

Dementia

The loss of mental agility.

Dementia is the term used to describe the mind in old age. Usually caused by brain disease, such as Alzheimer's or cerebrovascular disease, dementia can affect a person's memory, intellect, emotional stability, sense of direction, and attention to personal health and hygiene. The onset of symptoms may go unnoticed at first. People may get lost in their own neighborhood or become confused in what should be familiar situations—many people try to cover up what they cannot do. *See also* DELIRIUM.

Dengue

Also known as breakbone fever or dandy fever

An illness caused by any of the numerous dengue viruses.

There are many viruses that cause dengue fever and dengue hemorrhagic fever. This class of viruses includes West Nile and O'nyong-nyong fever. Dengue hemorrhagic fever sets in when multiple viruses infect the victim at the same time or when another dengue virus infects an individual who previously suffered from dengue fever.

Symptoms. Victims of dengue will experience the sudden onset of a very high fever, often above 104° Fahrenheit. That usually coincides with the onset of a severe headache; muscle and joint pains will come later in dengue hemorrhagic fever than in dengue fever. Appetite virtually disappears and vomiting may also occur.

After a few days, in the later phase of dengue hemorrhagic fever (the most severe form of dengue), the victim will experience shock-like symptoms, including perspiration, clammy skin, and restlessness. This will be accompanied by a rash all over the body and petechiae, which looks like a bruise bleeding under the skin.

Diagnosis. An examination will find the pulse has quickened and blood pressure is below normal levels; an external examination of the liver will find it enlarged—a condition known as hepatomegaly—so

Dental Emergencies

that it can be felt with the fingertips below the edge of the ribcage on the right side. A "tourniquet" test will reveal petechiae just below where it is applied and chest x-rays will show that the lungs are filled with fluid, a condition known as pleural effusion. Blood tests will show antibodies to dengue viruses.

Prevention. The virus is transmitted by mosquitoes (*Aedes aegypti*), so repellent and wearing long sleeves in areas where it is known to occur may help. At night, beds and mattresses should be covered by mosquito netting. It may also be beneficial to research the "mosquito season" if a destination is known to harbor infected insects.

> **DENGUE WARNINGS FOR TRAVELERS**
> Dengue is a particular concern among many people going overseas. Dengue is particularly virulent in the Caribbean islands, however, it also shows up in places such as the tropical regions of Asia, Africa Central, and South America. Infected mosquitoes have also been found in the Northeastern United States.

Treatment. The only course of action involves treating the symptoms that result from the virus. An intravenous unit is used to rehydrate the patent and normalize electrolyte levels. The fever should be treated with acetaminophen.

Transfusions and injections of platelets to treat bleeding problems are common as is oxygen therapy. If dengue is treated before shock sets in, the prognosis is good; if shock sets in, there is about a 50 percent mortality rate. There is not yet a vaccination for dengue; preventative measures are the best steps to take. *See also* DEHYDRATION; FEVER; *and* INSECT BITES AND STINGS.

Dental Emergencies

Injury to, or severe pain in, the teeth.

Dental emergencies require immediate medical attention either because the pain is debilitating or because a slow response might result in infection, deformity, or other complications.

Tooth Avulsion. A tooth that has been knocked out or badly loosened (avulsed) in an accident is treatable. The more immediately it is tended to, the better the chances are that the tooth or teeth will be reimplanted. The procedure involves attaching the tooth or teeth to surrounding teeth, or dental splinting; this is a process similar to placing a cast on a broken bone.

Depression

Fractured Tooth. Another dental emergency is a fractured tooth. Treatment varies, depending on the size and location of the break. A fracture in the lower portion of a tooth (root) is often repaired by dental splinting, but sometimes this is unsuccessful and the tooth is removed. Fractures in the upper part of the tooth (crown) receive fillings that prevent pain and infection. A fracture of this sort, which affects the inner nerve and blood vessels of the tooth, requires a root canal.

Broken Jaw. If the jaw breaks, the parts are wired together, immobilizing them in order to heal.

Swelling, inflammation, and general pain in the mouth can be caused by toothache, dental abscesses, or gingivitis. Sometimes pain can be relieved simply by brushing and flossing. If these measures are insufficient, a visit to the dentist is usually necessary.

Depression

> A disorder characterized by pervasive depressed mood, pessimism, and thoughts and feelings of despair and hopelessness, accompanied by a loss of interest in otherwise pleasurable activities and changes in eating and sleeping habits.

Depression is the most common of all mental disorders and is seen twice as often in women than in men. It is also one of the most treatable mental illnesses. Depression often goes untreated because it tends to be tolerated or denied by those suffering with it.

Situational Depression (Grief). Feelings of sadness and depression are normal reaction to certain situations, such as losing a loved one due to a breakup, divorce, or death; relinquishing an important goal; retirement; or experiencing a long-term frustration. Anyone may suffer from transient feelings of hopelessness or despair.

Often, this sort of depression will eventually fade without intervention. When dark thoughts and depressed mood persist longer than several weeks, making it difficult to perform everyday activities, get up in the morning, experience happiness, or function normally, it may be useful to seek treatment, particularly if there are prominent feelings of guilt or thoughts about suicide.

Major Depressive Disorder. Major depression overwhelms a person with feelings of sadness and hopelessness that do not seem to have a specific cause or are out of proportion to a troubling situation. Depressed patients lose the zest for life and may become suicidal. These

Depression

feelings are accompanied by physical symptoms, including exhaustion, decreased concentration, sleep disturbances, and appetite problems.

Major depressive disorder is often (although not always) a recurring disorder. Once a person has experienced this problem, the likelihood of a relapse is higher and increases with each occurrence. For this illness to be diagnosed, at least five criteria must be continuously present for at least two continuous weeks.

Dysthymic disorder is a chronic form of depression with similar but less severe symptoms than major depressive disorder.

It usually starts at an early age and continues throughout life. A general feeling of melancholy envelops a person with this disorder; those affected suffer from low self-esteem and tend to view life with a sense of regret and dissatisfaction.

SIGNS OF MAJOR DEPRESSIVE DISORDERS

Sufferers of major depressive disorders feel sad all the time; they are down, often tearful, guilt-ridden, and hopeless. They no longer enjoy doing things that previously gave them pleasure.
- There are significant changes in appetite: either the sufferer loses all interest in food or else or he or she feels the need to overeat.
- Sleeping habits are also altered so that an individual with major depressive disorders sleeps significantly more or less than usual. He or she may experience major sleep disturbances, often in the middle of the night.
- Sufferers have a diminished ability to concentrate, to think clearly, and to make decisions. Anxiety and agitation are common in individuals with major depressive disorder.
- Thoughts of suicide—or the wish no longer to be alive—are common in a depressed person, who may express these feelings to others.

If these signs should appear in an individual, persuade him or her to seek the care of a trained professional—clergy, counselor, or psychiatrist.

While those with this disorder function on a higher level in common social situations—such as at work and in day-to-day interactions with others—than those with major depressive disorder, their symptoms limit their enjoyment of life. People with dysthymic disorder may be difficult to be around and may have a limited social circle, which exacerbates their sense of isolation. Consequently sources of emotional support in times of need are limited.

CAUSES

The tendency to be depressed may be inherited or may be associated with childhood trauma. Some medications, including antihyperten-

Depression

sives and sleeping pills, may trigger depressive episodes. Certain diseases, such as stroke or hypothyroidism, are also associated with depression. The risk of depression increases after surgery, particularly heart surgery, or childbirth (postpartum depression). People who suffer from seasonal affective disorder experience bouts of depression in the winter that are related to lack of daylight.

TREATMENT

Depression is a highly treatable disorder. A number of therapies address the physiological, biochemical, emotional, and cognitive aspects of depression.

Antidepressant Medication. Antidepressants have become safer and more tolerable recently because the number of side effects has been dramatically reduced. These new medications may require three or four weeks to take effect and can take up to two months to reach full potency. The likelihood that these medications will work is high, although one may need to try several different drugs to find one that is effective in a particular case.

If an antidepressant medication is effective, it can be taken safely for a long period of time; these drugs are not addictive. The most widely prescribed antidepressant medications are fluoxetine (Prozac), sertraline (Zoloft), and paroxetine (Paxil). Although side effects are usually minimal, some people may experience nausea, upset stomach, headaches, or sexual side effects.

Electroconvulsive Therapy. ECT is a safe and effective treatment for individuals with depression that does not respond well to medication. The electrical current that passes through the brain improves chemical imbalances associated with depression. Negative attitudes towards ECT are fostered by fictional depictions of inappropriate use.

Cognitive Therapy. Because many depressed people feel hopeless, helpless, and worthless, cognitive therapy can be helpful in addressing the negative thinking patterns that perpetuate a depressed individual's downward spiral in mood.

Other Treatments. Insight psychotherapy helps a patient define the unconscious psychological conflicts that may have contributed to depression. Behavior therapy attempts to affect mood by changing behavior first. For example, a lethargic person will take part in physical activities, in the hope that alleviating the symptoms of depression will also alleviate the depression. In light therapy, which is appropriate for those affected by seasonal affective disorder, a patient is exposed to a source of bright light during the winter months.

Diarrhea

Detergent Poisoning

Poisoning brought about by the intake of any product containing cleaning agents.

The chemical ingredients of many household products, including shampoos, laundry detergents, and cleaning fluids, are very dangerous when ingested. In some cases the pH is very high and creates a caustic hazard to the gastrointestinal (GI) tract. Accidental detergent poisoning is particularly common in small children, who are drawn to these products because of their pleasant scent or attractive color. Symptoms of detergent poisoning may include nausea, difficulty in swallowing or breathing, and unconsciousness. If a child ingests detergents, first contact the poison control center. Then the label of the household product should be checked for emergency instructions. The victim should drink lots of water to dilute the poison.

Diarrhea

An increase in the volume, wateriness, or frequency of bowel movements.

As waste products pass through the intestines, water is removed and wastes are compacted into a solid form that is eliminated. If too much water is removed, stools will become hard and dry; if insufficient water is removed, the result is diarrhea.

Causes. The most common causes of diarrhea include:
- bacterial, viral, fungal, and parasitic infection;
- inflammation of the intestinal lining;
- altered intestinal transit; and
- antibiotics.

The most common cause of diarrhea is infection. Viral infections that affect children are quite common; a minor epidemic of "stomach flu," which is usually a viral infection causing both diarrhea and vomiting, will occur in a school from time to time. Most infectious causes of diarrhea are self-limiting or easily treated. Common infectious causes of diarrhea include:

Rotavirus affects mostly children under two, but is also implicated in epidemics in nursing homes.

Norwalk virus is similar to rotavirus and it is often contracted through

Diarrhea

exposure to contaminated water or eating contaminated shellfish.

Cytomegalovirus occurs in people with compromised immune systems.

Campylobacter is the most common bacterial cause of infectious diarrhea in young adults; it is caused by the consumption of contaminated foods such as raw milk and poultry.

Salmonella causes a third of all cases of diarrhea. It comes from contaminated food.

Parasitic infestations include *Giardia lamblia*, *Entamoeba histolytica* and *Cryptosporidium*. All of these parasites cause diarrhea.

ALERT   ALERT   ALERT

COMPLICATIONS ARISING FROM DIARRHEA

Diarrhea may lead to serious complications or indicate a serious underlying disorder if it is accompanied by high fever, severe abdominal pain, painful passing of stools, or bloody or black diarrhea. In these cases, or if diarrhea persists for more than a few days, a physician should be consulted.

The most common complication of diarrhea is dehydration. Symptoms of dehydration include weakness, rapid heartbeat, confusion, and a loss of skin elasticity. In infants, the soft spots (fontanelles) may appear sunken. If any of these symptoms occur, seek medical treatment immediately.

Malabsorption can be caused by a malabsorption syndrome, in which the body is unable to digest certain foods, or by laxative drugs, which contain soluble substances (such as magnesium) that are poorly absorbed by the intestines. Poorly absorbed soluble substances cause the intestines to retain extra water. Malabsorption of fats, which do not dissolve in water, results in water retention, but may cause the intestines to excrete more salts and water than they are able to reabsorb (secretory diarrhea).

Malabsorption syndromes include an inability to process milk sugar, (general malabsorption disorders) and an inability to process gluten. Other related to malabsorption include problems of the pancreas, surgical removal of part of the intestine, lack of sufficient enzymes in the small intestines, and liver disease.

Inflammation can also cause diarrhea. When the lining of large intestine is inflamed, ulcerated, or engorged, proteins, blood, and mucus are excreted. The colon or rectum may also be more sensitive to distention, leading to increased urgency and frequency of bowel movements. The intestinal lining can become inflamed as a result of diseases such as ulcerative colitis, Crohn's disease, tuberculosis, lymphoma, and cancer.

Altered intestinal transit occurs when feces are moved too quickly

Diarrhea

through the large intestine. As a result, the intestine does not have time to absorb enough water. This may be caused by hyperthyroidism, surgical removal of part of the small or large intestine or stomach, damage to the vagus nerve, antacids, caffeine, and laxatives that contain magnesium.

Bacterial overgrowth refers to the abnormal growth of bacteria that are normally found in the intestinal tract.

Antibiotics such as clindamycin, ampicillin, and cephalosporins can alter the normal intestinal environment, killing necessary intestinal bacteria and allowing harmful bacteria to flourish—most commonly *Clostridium difficile*.

COMPLICATIONS

Severe diarrhea carries the risk of dehydration as well as malnutrition. Dehydration can result in a precipitous fall in blood pressure, leading to shock. Electrolyte levels can be disrupted, leading to abnormal blood acidity (metabolic acidosis).

DIAGNOSIS AND TREATMENT

Diagnosis of the cause of diarrhea often requires an examination of a stool sample as well as a description of the symptoms and when the condition began.

Treatment ultimately depends on the cause. For minor cases of diarrhea, this simply involves making sure fluids are replaced; if the diarrhea is accompanied by vomiting, small amounts of fluid should be taken frequently. High fiber foods and bulking agents such as psyllium, found in commercial fiber supplements, may absorb water and add some solidity to the stools. Over the counter medications such as attapulgite and loperamide hydrochloride also add bulk and reduce the frequency of bowel movements.

In cases of more severe diarrhea, prescription drugs including diphenoxylate, codeine, and loperamide can be administered to bring bowel movements to a halt. These should be used only after consulting a physician. Antiemetic drugs may be prescribed to control vomiting.

PREVENTION

The easiest way to prevent infectious diarrhea is to practice proper hygiene. Wash your hands before and after using the bathroom and before handling or eating food. It is important to make sure all utensils and plates are clean. Children should be taught not to put objects in their mouths.

Discharge

D Discharge

Secretion or excretion of pus, feces, urine or other material from the body. Also the material itself.

Abnormal discharges from the body usually indicate an underlying disorder that needs treatment. Often, the the discharge may be used diagnostically in order to identify the nature of a disease or ailment.

Discharge from the Eye. There are several types of irregular discharge that issue from the eyes because of illness or inflammation. Conjunctivitis results from an inflammation of the tissues protecting the eye surface and inner eyelid, producing a clear or yellowish crusting discharge that may be viral or bacterial in nature. Both are highly contagious and may be transmitted through the discharge. Other eye disorders producing discharge include corneal ulcer and dacryocystitis.

Pus. A variety of bacterial and viral wound infections are accompanied by the discharge of pus, a by-product of inflammation composed of white blood cells, albuminous substances, and thin fluid. The color, texture, and occasionally the smell of this pus can indicate the particular form of infection. Pus is generally yellow. Blue or green pus indicates the presence of *Pseudomonas aeruginosa*, a species of bacteria. Discharges of pus may also occur in the urine, and may indicate any of the following: cystitis, pyelitis, urethritis, tuberculosis of the kidney, infection of the genitourinary tract, or trauma.

Blood. Abnormal discharges of blood from any of the bodily orifices are of particular concern. Such discharges, particularly vaginal, are not uncommon and may indicate a range of disorders. Any atypical discharges should be reported to a health care professional for diagnostic analysis and, when needed, treatment.

Dislocation, Joint

The displacement of two bones in a joint, so that they no longer touch each other.

Joint dislocation often occurs with an injury, usually a car accident, sports injury, or a fall. Tearing of ligaments and additional injury to the joint capsule may occur; one of the bones involved may fracture as well.

Symptoms of joint dislocation include severe pain, lack of mobility, and swelling. Dislocation of one of the vertebrae can lead to paralysis. A shoulder or hip dislocation that injures surrounding nerves can also

Dizziness

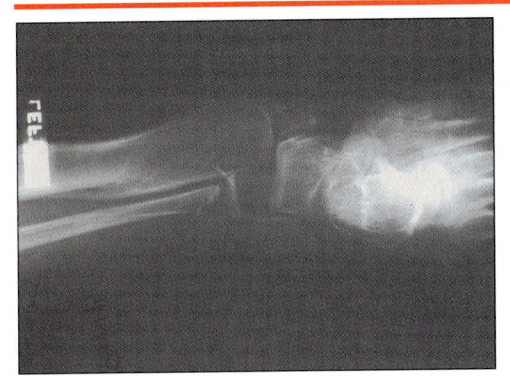

Joint Dislocation X-Ray Imagery. Dislocations can be seen most clearly under the scrutiny that x-ray images offer. Due to the nature of dislocations, any more complex imaging techniques, such as MRIs or CAT scans, are usually excessive. Dislocations can be seen with or without contrast agents (radiopaque dyes that cause disorders to show up more clearly).

result in paralysis of the limb. *See also* EMERGENCY, FIRST STEPS; FALLS IN THE ELDERLY; FIRST AID; FRACTURE; HEAD, NECK, AND BACK INJURIES; HIP, FRACTURED; *and* SWELLING.

> **ALERT ALERT ALERT**
>
> **NOT FOR BEGINNERS**
>
> *Nonprofessionals should not try to pop dislocated joints back into place. Unqualified people may not know how to avoid additional nerve damage and may not be able to tell if fractures are present. A splint or sling may be worn to restrict movement until a doctor is available to correctly reset the bones. In most cases, a physician will test to see if there are any additional fractures, then may simply manipulate the bones back into place. In extreme cases, surgery may be necessary to reposition the bones. Afterwards, a splint or cast may be fitted to restrict movement as the affected area heals.*

Dizziness

A condition in which an individual feels a general sense of lightheadedness or that the surroundings are spinning around.

Dizziness is a symptom of a malfunction in the ear, along the nerve pathways, or in the brain itself. Dizziness can refer to either fainting or vertigo. Fainting is a classification of dizziness characterized by a sensation of grogginess, lightheadedness, queasiness, and nausea. Vertigo is a form of dizziness in which a person may feel as though the room is whirling about or that he or she is falling down. Vertigo may last for a few minutes or continue for a period of days. The condition may be improved by lying down flat.

Causes. Most episodes of dizziness are innocuous. They can be caused by either a temporary reduction of the blood pressure to the

Double Vision

D brain or a change in the pressure of the fluid in the inner ear. This can be manifested when abruptly leaping out of bed or bending to pick up an item from the floor. Dizziness is also a side effect of anemia, epilepsy, heart trouble, blockage in the arteries that supply the brain, and inner-ear disorder. It may also be caused by malfunctioning balance-controlling organs located in the inner-ear or along the nerve impulses traveling to the brain. Common causes for vertigo include:

- bacterial infections;
- viral infections;
- brain tumors;
- abnormal pressure;
- nerve inflammation;
- labyrinthitis (infection in the labyrinth, which controls balance in the ear);
- Ménière's disease (fluid in the labyrinth, increasing pressure);
- motion sickness;
- drugs, such as alcohol or tranquilizers; and
- multiple sclerosis.

> **WHEN IS DIZZINESS AN EMERGENCY?**
> Dizziness can be a symptom of several severe disorders, including brain tumor, hematoma, myocardial infarction (heart attack), and subdural hemorrhage. If dizziness is accompanied by weakness in the arms or legs, numbness or tingling in any part of the body, blurred vision, speech difficulties, or nausea, it is essential that a physician be consulted immediately.

Treatment. Episodes of dizziness usually pass by themselves; lying down may make a person less disoriented. Prolonged and repeated attacks of dizziness should be brought to the attention of a physician. Treatment then depends on diagnosing and treating the underlying cause. Drugs that may be effective in treating vertigo include meclizine, dimenhydrinate, and scopolamine.

Double Vision

Also known as diplopia

The sensation of seeing two images of everything in the visual field.

When the eyes are working properly, an individual sees a single three-dimensional image of the world; this is called stereovision. The brain filters and interprets information about the visual field from

Dressing

both eyes to make one image. This also allows an individual to perceive depth. However, when there is a disorder in either eye, in the pathways that transport information about the visual field from the eyes to the brain, or in the image processing function of the brain, double vision may be the result.

> ### When is Double Vision an Emergency?
> Double vision is often cause for concern, as it may be a symptom of a brain tumor, aneurysm, head trauma, or neurological disorder. These conditions all require immediate attention. Because prompt treatment increases the chances of survival, it is essential that any prolonged or frequent bout with double vision be reported to a physician so that further testing may be performed.

Types. There are two principal types of double vision: monocular and binocular. Monocular double vision is often caused by a disorder in one eye. If one eye is covered and the visual field is double, then the disorder is probably located within the eye itself. The person could be suffering symptoms associated with astigmatism from an abnormality in the lens, retina, cornea, or a cataract.

Binocular double vision usually has a neurological basis or is associated with defects related to a misalignment of the eyes—this is similar to symptoms associated with crossed eyes. If one eye is covered and the double vision is relieved, then the particular case of double vision is binocular.

Treatment. Usually, double vision is not a disorder in itself, so it can be alleviated by treating underlying ailments. Trauma to the head, myasthenia gravis, multiple sclerosis, nerve palsy, or a brain tumor may need to be treated before double vision disappears. Glasses with the proper prescription may treat some cases, while surgery on the muscles that control the eyes may correct vision in others.

Dressing

Protective covering placed on wounds.

Dressings are used to control bleeding and aid the healing process by absorbing secretions and preventing contamination by bacteria. Sterile, absorbent dressings are placed directly over wounds to promote dryness and thereby discourage growth of microorganisms. The dressing should be left undisturbed unless the wound needs to be cleaned.

Dressing

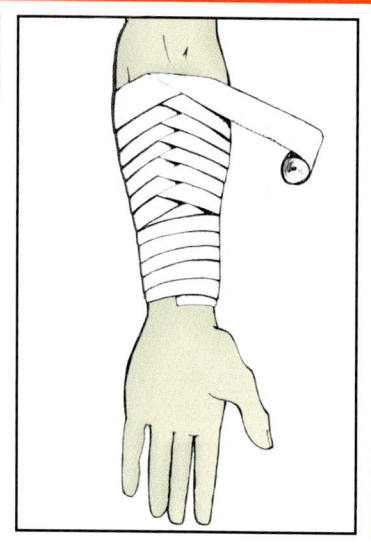

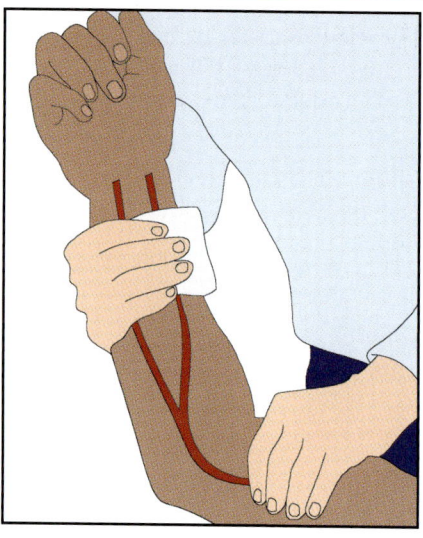

Dressings. Dressings are used to protect wounds from infection and to stop bleeding. Types of dressings include cloth bandages (above left), elastic bandages, and gauze (above right). Above left, an injured arm is wrapped in a bandage. Above right, gauze is applied to a postoperative wound.

Types. Dressings come in several forms, including adhesive and elastic bandages, gauze, butterfly bandages, roller gauze bandages, and circular bandages. In emergency situations, clean, absorbent materials such as clean handkerchiefs and sheets can be used as substitute dressings.

Gauze can be placed directly on a wound and is made either of cotton (woven or nonwoven) or a synthetic material. It is held in place by a bandage, by adhesive strips or by first-aid tape. The commonly used Band-Aid® is a smaller, name-brand variation of this gauze-and-adhesive strip configuration. Gauze is usually applied dry, but sometimes contains a substance to promote healing and regrowth of tissue in a deep wound.

Alginate dressings, derived from brown seaweed, are a relatively new form of dressing used mostly for moderate to high exuding wounds. They form a gel capable of absorbing up to 20 times its weight in fluid. An innovative blood-clotting fibrin bandage, made of natural proteins, is currently being tested by the American Red Cross and the U.S. Army. *See also* BANDAGE; BLEEDING, TREATMENT OF; EMERGENCY, FIRST STEPS; *and* FIRST AID.

Drowning

Death by suffocation in water or some other fluid.

When a person is subjected to prolonged immersion in water, death can be caused by suffocation and a lack of oxygen (hypoxia). Drowning can occur in two ways. In one instance, a person inhales liquid into the lungs. In the other, no liquid enters the lungs, as the water is instead diverted into the stomach. In these cases, the drowning death is completely caused by oxygen deprivation; this is called dry drowning. Near-drowning describes an event in which a drowning victim is resuscitated back to life. Drowning is the third leading cause of accidental death in the United States, following auto accidents and falls.

More than a third of all drowning accidents involve alcohol consumption. There are many physiological reactions to alcohol consumption that may be problematic in drowning incidents. The major problem, however, is that alcohol impairs both judgment and physical coordination, thereby greatly increasing the likelihood of a drowning death.

> **SPINAL CORD DAMAGE**
> Divers rescued from drowning in shallow water or surf might also be victims of spinal cord damage if they slipped and hit their head on a hard surface, or if the strength of the surf tossed them onto the floor of the ocean, resulting in head or neck injury. If a spinal cord injury is suspected, the swimmer should be moved as little as necessary to restore breathing and should be kept still until medical assistance arrives.

Process. In the first moments of drowning, an automatic protective reflex is triggered and a muscle at the entrance of the windpipe tightens to direct water to the stomach, rather than the lungs. But this esophageal reflex also interferes with normal breathing, which can lead to a lack of oxygen in the blood that causes loss of consciousness. Dry drowning occurs when a person has a particularly strong esophageal reflex that cuts off their oxygen supply. In this instance, the person drowns from lack of oxygen, even if only little or no water has entered the lungs.

Rescue. The best help for a drowning person comes from a trained lifeguard, since a panicking swimmer can pull an untrained rescuer down. The person in danger should be given something—a rope, a large floating object, or the end of an oar—to hold onto while the rescuer gets him or her ashore or into a boat.

Drowning

Drowning Assistance. There are several methods one can use when trying to rescue a drowning victim. If available, toss a floating object (a) to the drowning victim to keep him or her afloat until help arrives. Otherwise, try to offer an object such as a board (b), pole, or stick to the victim and attempt to pull him or her out of the water. One should not place him or herself at risk when rescuing a drowning victim, but as a last resort the human chain method (c) may be attempted.

Once the victim is on a firm surface, the rescuer should immediately check for the presence of breathing and a pulse. It is important to remember that even a swimmer who has suffered cardiac arrest can sometimes be revived. Artificial ventilation or cardiopulmonary resuscitation (CPR) should be provided as needed. If a phone is available, 911 should be called and emergency services contacted.

Drug Overdose

The accidental or deliberate ingestion of an excessive amount of a drug.

Deliberate and unintentional drug overdoses are leading causes of poisoning and death in the United States. The Food and Drug Administration decides which drugs are safe to be sold over the counter, which require a doctor's prescription, and which are illegal. Considerations for a given drug's safety include whether the drug can be harmful when taken by itself and whether it is habit-forming.

Legal drugs are usually safe when a recommended dosage is taken, but they can be dangerous if too much is consumed at once or if they are combined with other drugs. Some accidental medication overdoses occur because a patient believes that increasing the dosage will speed up or enhance the drug's effect. For patients prone to forgetfulness, the dosage should be written and highlighted on the label. Sometimes overdose occurs as a complication of kidney or liver mal-

Drug Overdose

function, in which case the medication is not effectively processed and builds up in the bloodstream.

Illegal Drugs. The effects of illegal drugs vary; an overdose can often cause unpredictable reactions. Because such drugs do not have to pass any regulations before they are sold, users may expose themselves to illegal drugs that have been mixed together or diluted with potentially harmful substances.

Accidents. Children are at high risk for accidental drug overdose, because they may not realize what they are consuming. It is important to keep drugs out of childrens' reach and in childproof containers, as well as to educate older children about drug safety.

> **DRUGS AND AGE**
> *The elderly are particularly sensitive to drugs like barbiturates and benzodiazepines. Psychoactives and alcohol can lower the body temperature, and nonsteroidal anti-inflammatory drugs can cause gastrointestinal bleeding and kidney malfunction.*

Signs of an Overdose. Indications of a drug overdose vary depending on the drug and the dosage. Symptoms include: abnormal breathing; slurred speech; lack of coordination; abnormal pulse rate; abnormal body temperature; enlarged or constricted pupils; sweating; drowsiness; convulsions; and hallucinations.

In Case of Emergency. If the victim is a child, his or her mouth should be checked for pills or other medication, which must be removed at once. If the victim is an adult and unconscious, make sure he or she is breathing. Act immediately if there is any sign of bluish coloring. The air passages should be checked for obstructions. Opening the air passageways to allow the person to breathe is essential. This is done by pushing on the forehead while pulling the jaw upward. This is also good preparation in case the victim is still not breathing and needs mouth-to-mouth resuscitation (artificial respiration). In addition to the air passages, it is important to check breathing, temperature, and pulse. Cardiopulmonary resuscitation (CPR) should be administered if necessary.

A poison control center should be called immediately. Information about the specific drug ingested is vital to determining proper treatment. Vomiting should not be induced unless it is specifically advised by the poison control center or a qualified health professional.

If a victim is conscious and hallucinating, convulsing, or breathing slowly and shallowly, emergency medical help should be called. Do not administer anything by mouth.

Drug Poisoning

D Drug Poisoning

The accidental or intentional overdose of over-the-counter, prescription, or illegal drugs.

Drug poisoning can occur in a variety of ways. Many medications can be deadly if taken in amounts greater than prescribed, or if combined with alcohol or other medications. Patients should inform a doctor of all chronic and short-term conditions and all prescription and over-the-counter medications being taken, including vitamins and supplements, herbs, laxatives, antibiotics, pain-relievers, cold and allergy medicines, oral contraceptives, and antibiotics. Filling prescriptions at the same pharmacy reduces the possibility of dangerous medicinal reactions, as the pharmacist can identify negative drug interactions.

If drug poisoning is suspected, a poison control center should be called, even if no symptoms have appeared yet. The drug container should be on hand in order to read the ingredients to the poison control center operator. It is thus recommended that medications be kept in their original packaging.

The operator will ask for a description of what was taken, the quantity, and how recently, and will also want to know the person's age and whether he or she is conscious, drowsy, vomiting, convulsing, or experiencing changes in body temperature or skin color.

ALERT   ALERT   ALERT

PRECAUTION FOR CHILDREN

Children are extremely curious. All drugs should be kept out of their reach, as they are potential sources for poisoning. Vitamins and other supplements behave as drugs and can be dangerous, especially to children. Medications and vitamins should be kept in their original packaging and also put out of reach. The strengths of most medicines are calibrated for adults, and even a small amount can be toxic to a child. All medicine containers need to be childproof. Also, taking medication in front of children is not advised, as they like to mimic adult behavior.

Vomiting should not be induced unless directed by medical personnel. For such situations, it is wise to keep a bottle of ipecac syrup in the medicine cabinet, as well as activated charcoal, which is indicated for certain cases of poisoning, and which may be purchased at most pharmacies. Activated charcoal should be used only when advised by a physician.

If the victim loses consciousness, stops breathing, or is having convulsions, an ambulance should be called immediately.

Dysentery

A disease characterized by inflammation of the intestines.

Dysentery refers to painful, often bloody bouts of diarrhea accompanied by abdominal pain. The two major types are amoebic dysentery, caused by a shapeless microscopic organism called *Entamoeba histolytica*, and Sonne dysentery, which is caused by the *Shigella* bacteria.

In amoebic dysentery, the parasite infects the large intestine. Direct transmission occurs through contact with infected feces, usually because of poor sanitation or through sexual contact. Even when the individual does not have an active case of diarrhea, the parasite may form cysts through which it can be spread. Dysentery caused by the *Shigella* bacteria is acquired by the ingestion of contaminated food or water. Most often, this occurs in unsanitary environments where food is handled.

Symptoms include constant diarrhea, increased gas, and abdominal cramps. Extreme weight-loss (emaciation) as well as low oxygen level in the blood (anemia) frequently occur. Dehydration can also occur. The dysentery-causing organism may spread through the bloodstream and infect the lungs and brain, as well as the skin and any sustained wounds.

Treatment. Replenishing fluids lost from diarrhea is advised for the treatment of the resulting dehydration. A stool sample is required for accurate diagnosis, after which several different amoebicide drugs, such as iodoquinol, paromomycin, and diloxanide, can be administered to kill the parasite. Metronidazole is usually prescribed in severe cases or when the infection has moved beyond the intestines. Stool samples must be examined at one, three, and six month intervals to ensure that the patient is cured.

Dysmenorrhea

Severely painful menstrual periods that cannot be tolerated without medication.

Severe cramping occurs in only about 10 percent of women. If the pain is not a sign of another gynecological problem, the condition is called primary dysmenorrhea. This is relatively common during adolescence or until a woman gives birth to her first child. Primary dysmenorrhea is caused by excessive levels of prostaglandins, chemicals that are found in menstrual fluids and semen and that trigger uterine contractions. Se-

Ear, Discharge from

vere cramps may also be due to internal "gridlock"—a lot of fluid and tissue attempting to exit all at once through a relatively small opening. Pain therefore persists until enough material has been expelled.

Secondary dysmenorrhea is suspected when cramps and pain extend past the first three days of a period, occur between periods, or precede a period by a few days, accompanied by vaginal bleeding. Secondary dysmenorrhea is caused by an underlying condition such as noncancerous growths (fibroids, endometriosis, or adenomyosis), a sexually transmitted disease, a pelvic inflammatory disease, or an ovarian cyst.

Diagnosis of dysmenorrhea may involve investigation through a fiberoptic viewing tube, a pelvic exam, or an ultrasound.

Treatment involves routine medication to alleviate pain in cases of primary dysmenorrhea. Secondary dysmenorrhea is treated by determining and correcting the underlying condition.

Ear, Discharge from

Fluid passing out of the ear.

Ear infections, whether viral or bacterial, usually cause inflammation in the tissues within the ear that prevents fluids from draining. The result is a buildup of fluid that will begin to leak out via the ear canal.

Middle-ear infections (otitis media) allow fluid to gather in the middle-ear cavity, behind the eardrum. The pressure from the fluid may cause the eardrum to rupture, allowing the fluid to drain out of the ear.

Outer-ear infections (otitis externa) form in the ear canal, outside the eardrum, and may extend to the exterior cartilage that shapes the ear (the pinna); in this case, there may be a discharge directly from the ear canal, or there may be pus from a boil. Occasionally, head injuries may cause a leak of cerebrospinal fluid or blood from the ear.

Discharge from an ear should be investigated by a physician. A sample may be taken and analyzed to determine what bacteria or virus is present.

Ear, Foreign Body in

Matter in the ear that causes an obstruction.

Occasionally, objects may become lodged in the outer-ear canal, either accidentally or by intent. Flies or other insects may enter and then become trapped in the ear canal. During accidents, an object may be forced into the ear canal. Children frequently insert objects into their

Earache

ears, such as small toys, beads, buttons, or stones. Small children also often force certain foods, such as peas, into their ears.

Treatment. If an insect has flown or crawled into the ear, a physician may have to remove it. A person should not attempt to remove any type of matter from the ear canal. In these cases, the object should be left alone until a physician can attend to it. Do not attempt to remove foreign objects by flushing the ear with water, as that may cause some objects to swell. A trained physician can safely remove the object with a syringe, tiny forceps, or other specialized suction devices. Occasionally, anesthetic may be required for this procedure.

Earache

Pain or pressure in or around the ear.

Earaches, one of the most common pains experienced in childhood, usually take place in the outer-ear or middle-ear, often caused by infections and, on occasion, by earwax or jaw problems. An earache may result in throbbing, tenderness, pressure, or splitting pain that occurs inside the ear or in the surrounding areas. Infants and children commonly suffer from infections that cause earaches.

TYPES

Outer-ear infections (otitis externa) are the result of a blockage or build-up of pressure in the outer-ear. Often called swimmer's ear, the most common cause of this type of pain is water build-up in the ear, a recurring problem for frequent swimmers. While the water sits in the ear, bacteria may grow. The ear may itch and the contact with the skin, plus any dirt or residue on it, will cause the bacteria to multiply, resulting in an infection. In addition to pain, symptoms of this type of earache may include itching, a small discharge, and minor hearing loss.

Middle-ear infections (otitis media). The most common type of earache, otitis media is an accumulation of fluid in the middle-ear, causing pressure on the eardrum. The fluid build-up is the result of an obstruction in the Eustachian tube, the small tube that carries air from the middle ear to the nasal passages. Infections from bacteria or viruses, as well as allergies, may cause the tube to become inflamed or blocked. Fluid from the mucous membranes in the tube build up, causing the pressure that results in an earache.

Otitis media is characterized by a sharp, stabbing pain. There may also be a rise in temperature and a slight loss of hearing. Children may

Eardrum, Perforated

pull on their ears, or cry and become irritable. If the eardrum ruptures, a discharge of fluid will follow.

Tooth infections, sinus infections, or injuries to the jaw can all cause earaches—as can foreign objects lodged in the ear.

Treatment. Care at home for minor outer-ear infections consists of over-the-counter pain-relievers, antihistamines, and nose drops. A vaporizer can help to thin the mucus in cases of inner-ear infections. If symptoms persist for more than a few days, a visit to a doctor is recommended. Doctors usually prescribe antibiotics for middle-ear infections, as well as stronger forms of antihistamines or decongestants that will help open the Eustachian tube. For severe cases, an ear tube may be inserted to drain fluid.

Eardrum, Perforated

A break in the eardrum.

The eardrum is a thin, round fibrous membrane, covered by skin, that separates the middle-ear from the inner-ear. There are several ways this membrane may break: a puncture from a sharp blow or object; a loud noise or explosion; or a change in air pressure, as may happen during flying or diving. The common cause, however, is a middle-ear infection, or otitis media. This is characterized by a buildup of fluid in the middle-ear cavity when inflamed airways prevent the proper drainage of fluid. The pressure may build up to such a level that it ruptures the eardrum, allowing the fluid to burst through and flow out of the ear.

Treatment. A suspected eardrum rupture should be kept clean and dry to avoid infection. A physician will prescribe antibiotics to further reduce the possibility of infection. In most cases, a rupture will heal on its own. If this does not happen within six months, a physician may perform a myringoplasty, a procedure that repairs the break with tissue from another part of the body.

Electrical Injury

Also known as electrical shock

Injury to the skin or internal organs resulting from exposure to an electrical current.

The human body is a good conductor of electricity. Because of this, direct contact with an electric current is potentially fatal. While some re-

Electrical Injury

sulting burns look minor, the shock is still capable of inflicting serious damage to internal organs.

An electric current can injure the body in three main ways. Cardiac arrest can result from the effect of an electric current on the heart. Massive muscle destruction can be caused from the current passing through the body. Finally, contact with the electrical source can cause thermal burns.

Incidence. In the United States, about 1,000 people die annually of electric shock. Statistically, children under two have a slightly higher risk of electrical injury.

Cause. Electrical injury occurs through exposure to an electric current. Accidental contact with the exposed part of an electrical appliance or wiring, lightning, and contact with high-voltage electric lines are the common sources of electrical injury.

ALERT   ALERT   ALERT

PREVENTING ELECTRICAL INJURY IN CHILDREN

Young children are especially prone to accidental exposure to electricity. They may bite or chew an electric cord or poke a sharp object into an electrical outlet. For that reason, it is important to keep child-safety plugs on all outlets. Children should be taught the dangers of electricity, and parents should take whatever steps possible to minimize electrical hazards in the home. Electrical devices and cords should be kept out of the reach of children, and electrical appliances should be kept out of the bathroom and away from sinks.

Symptoms. Electrical injury causes a diverse range of symptoms. Fatigue, headache, dizziness, fracture, heart attack, muscle spasms, muscular pain, skin burns, unconsciousness, and loss of vision are some of the signs that exposure to an electric current may have resulted in bodily injury.

Treatment. The first step in treatment is to ensure that you are not at risk for electric shock. Having done so, if possible, try to remove the source of the electric current. Often, turning off an appliance will not stop the flow of electric current. The appliance must be unplugged, or the fuse removed from the fuse box. The immediate source of the current should not be touched. If the current cannot be turned off, a nonconducting object, such as a broom or rubber doormat, can be used to push the victim away from the source of the current. Call for medical help. Once the source of the electricity has been stopped, check for signs of breathing and a pulse. If either has stopped, CPR is necessary.

Embolism

Clothing should be removed from burned areas. The victim's head and neck should remain immobile in case internal or spinal injuries have been sustained.

Prevention. Simple measures can help to prevent exposure to electric current. Electrical appliances should not be used while showering or while wet. Never touch an electrical appliance while touching a faucet or water. Frayed or exposed wires should also never be touched and should be replaced to prevent fires.

Embolism

> A partial or complete blockage of an artery by something travelling in the bloodstream.

A substance that causes a blockage in an artery resulting in an embolism is called an embolus. An embolus can be a piece of tissue, a clump of bacteria, a bit of bone marrow or cholesterol, or a number of other substances (a pregnant woman can suffer an amniotic fluid embolism, in which amniotic fluid escapes from the uterus), but most often it is a blood clot that has broken away from an artery wall and has traveled to a spot where it causes blockage. A moving clot is referred to as a thrombus.

LOCATION

An embolism can occur almost anywhere in the body. The damage that an embolism inflicts is directly related to the site where it occurs.

Leg. An embolism in an artery of a leg or an arm causes pain, numbness, and inflammation in the area that loses its blood supply, sometimes accompanied by cramps and a sensation of cold and pain. If the blood supply is not restored quickly, gangrene can set in, and the tissue of the affected area will die from a lack of oxygen.

Lung. An embolism in an artery supplying the lung can cause chest pain, breathlessness, loss of consciousness, and sudden death if not treated quickly.

Brain. An embolism affecting an artery supplying the brain causes a stroke (cerebral embolism), which occurs when a thrombus (a small clot that forms in an intact blood vessel) breaks off from a blood vessel and travels toward the brain. It is distinguished from a stroke caused by cerebral thrombosis, in which the clot in an artery grows large enough to block the entire diameter of the blood vessel. People at highest risk of cerebral embolism include those with coronary artery disease or a condition affecting the heart valves.

Embolism

SYMPTOMS

The symptoms of stroke may be mimicked by a transient ischemic attack, TIA, which differs from a stroke in that it does not last long—sometimes only a few minutes, sometimes a few hours. TIAs of longer duration are more likely to be caused by an embolism, while briefer ones are usually due to the narrowing of an artery. A TIA is an important warning for stroke. Persons with cardiac conditions, such as atrial fibrillation, a disease of a heart valve, congestive heart failure, or endocarditis are at risk for TIAs. An individual with an artificial heart valve or who has suffered a heart attack is also at increased risk, as these increase the chance that an embolus will form.

ALERT   ALERT   ALERT

THE NEED FOR A SPEEDY DIAGNOSIS

Quick and accurate diagnosis of an embolism is vital, because arrested blood flow can result in serious, life-threatening death of tissue. If a patient has the symptoms of an embolism, the tests that can be used to make the diagnosis include angiography—an x-ray procedure in which dye is injected to help locate the site of the blockage; an ultrasound examination using computer analysis to detect abnormalities in the flow of blood; and a CT (computerized tomography) scan, which also uses computer processing to produce an image of the blood vessels.

TREATMENT

An embolism can be treated either by surgery or by medication. Drug treatment consists of a clot-dissolving (thrombolytic) agent that is injected into the affected artery. Sometimes, the drug is administered through a catheter, a thin tube that is inserted in the artery. The process by which the clot dissolves, which can last as long as 48 hours, can be monitored by angiography. Brain damage from a stroke caused by embolism can usually be prevented if treatment is administered within three hours after the onset of symptoms.

Angioplasty. If surgery is required because of an immediate threat of death or major damage, the most common procedure is balloon angioplasty. Alternatively, laser angioplasty may be performed in facilities equipped for this advanced technique, in which the tip of a catheter inserted into the artery carries a metal probe or a fiberoptic probe that focuses intense laser light on the embolus to dissolve the clot. Laser angioplasty is still being perfected. Angioplasty has replaced embolectomy, the surgical procedure once used for embolism, in which an incision was made in the artery at the site of the blockage, so that the embolus could be sucked out.

Emergency, First Steps

E Emergency, First Steps

Critical situation that requires immediate medical attention.

In the United States, a complete network of emergency services exists, including medical, fire, police, and psychological departments. Emergency vehicles range from helicopters to ambulances to boats. Dialing 911 anywhere in the United States activates a connection between a caller and the nearest emergency service dispatcher. However, in an emergency situation, a bystander must often take the first critical steps before emergency medical assistance is available. In such instances, important considerations include:

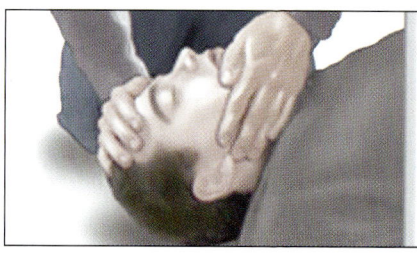

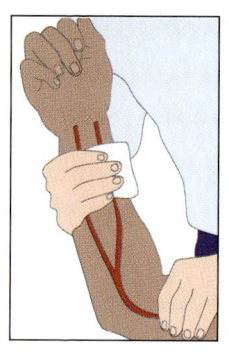

First Steps in Handling an Emergency. If a victim has lost consciousness, it is important to find out if he or she is breathing by checking for a pulse. If it appears that the victim is not breathing, open the airways (above) and perform mouth to mouth resuscitation or CPR. At right, if the victim is bleeding, it is important to bandage the wound and put pressure on the blood vessel until help arrives.

Breathing. Are the victim's air passages clear, and is he or she breathing? If there is a foreign object lodged in the throat, use the Heimlich maneuver. If the passages are clear but the victim is not breathing, use artificial ventilation.

Bleeding. Use some form of pressure to control bleeding. If an artery has been injured, a tourniquet may be required as a last resort, but the use of pressure is far more preferable. A cut artery will spurt or pulse; it

Recovery Position. An unconscious victim who is still breathing should be placed in the recovery position until help arrives. The casualty should lie on the stomach with the near arm and top knee bent forward (as pictured).

118 • Cornell Illustrated Emergency Medicine & First Aid Guide

Emergency Hospitalization

is far more serious than a cut vein. In contrast, the blood from the latter will have a tendency to ooze. If a ruptured artery is suspected, treat the wound immediately, as a victim can die in minutes.

Heartbeat. Is there a detectable pulse? If not, the patient will require cardiopulmonary resuscitation (CPR) or artificial ventilation.

Protect Yourself. Avoid exposure to the blood or bodily fluids of a victim, as they may be a major source of infection.

Emergency Hospitalization

The treatment and care that an individual receives during a medical emergency.

Emergency departments are designed to deal with unexpected, life-threatening situations that require immediate medical attention, although people often go to the emergency room to treat relatively minor problems.

Triage. Once in the emergency department, patients who are the most severely ill or injured will be treated first. As a result of this need-based system of seeing patients (known as triage), someone with a minor problem may have to wait several hours to be examined. In addition to the wait, the cost of treatment in an emergency department can be as much as three times higher than that of a doctor's office. It can also be difficult to convince some HMOs to reimburse a patient for the costs of a visit to an emergency ward.

What to Expect. Upon arrival at the emergency room, unless you are severely ill or injured and require immediate attention, you will be interviewed by a staff member who will obtain personal and medical insurance information and have you sign treatment consent forms. After you are triaged, you will either be promptly treated and released or admitted into the hospital for extensive care, depending on the nature of your injury.

Even if your life is not in immediate danger, there are still a number of symptoms that may require hospitalization. These include: severe bleeding (especially from an artery); loss of consciousness; pain; high fever; convulsions; difficulty breathing; severe headache; shock; weakness; and numbness in the extremities. All of these symptoms require emergency care, especially if the victim's physician is unavailable. *See also* ACCIDENTS; BLEEDING, TREATMENT OF; EMERGENCY, FIRST STEPS; *and* HOSPITALS, TYPES OF.

Epileptic Seizure

> A chronic nervous system disorder characterized by recurring seizures.

Seizures are characterized by a partial or complete loss of consciousness, generally accompanied by convulsions or uncontrolled movements. Seizures result from a breakdown in orderly communication between nerve cells (neurons). Neurons in the brain communicate by sending electrical signals back and forth in an orderly manner. During a seizure, electrical signals from one group of neurons become excessively strong and overwhelm neighboring neurons, resulting in a chaotic pattern.

In epilepsy, seizures are recurrent and are not caused by a non-neurological disorder, such as a fever. About one million people in the United States have epilepsy.

Symptoms. There are two different classifications of seizures: generalized and partial. Generalized seizures affect most or all of the brain, influence the entire body, and produce a loss of consciousness. In contrast, partial seizures are caused by a misfiring of a smaller area of the brain and do not necessarily result in loss of consciousness. Many epileptics do not exhibit any symptoms between seizures. Some recognize when a seizure is imminent because of an aura, an often unpleasant feeling or hallucination that precedes an attack.

GENERALIZED SEIZURES

Generalized seizures consist of grand mal and petit mal seizures:

Grand mal seizures affect the entire body. The person may cry out and then fall to the ground. The muscles will first be rigid for a few moments and will then proceed to spasm. Breathing may be irregular or absent; if the seizure lasts for more than one or two minutes, there is danger of brain damage.

Status epilepticus is a type of grand mal seizure in which the convulsions do not cease, producing a medical emergency. It is accompanied by strong muscle contractions, rapid electrical discharge throughout the brain, and difficulty breathing. The patient must get medical help immediately to prevent brain damage or death.

Petit mal seizures are characterized by a temporary loss of consciousness without any abnormal behavior. They generally occur in children, usually before age five, and disappear after adolescence. A child may appear to be daydreaming but in reality loses awareness for a few seconds. Afterwards, the child continues as if nothing has hap-

Epileptic Seizure

pened. Petit mal seizures can occur countless times during a day and can impede a child's scholastic performance.

PARTIAL SEIZURES
Partial seizures can be subdivided into simple seizures, in which the victim maintains consciousness, and complex seizures, in which the person loses consciousness.

Simple seizures occur when a chaotic electrical flow in an area of the brain remains confined. The accompanying symptoms are spasm-like movements, tingling of the skin, and hallucinatory sensations. The sufferer remains conscious. In a Jacksonian seizure, movements begin in a hand or foot and slowly travel up the body but remain on one side of the body. The seizure ends after a few minutes.

Complex seizures are characterized by a lack of awareness of surroundings for an interval of a minute or two. The sufferer may perform repeated movements, such as picking at clothes, wandering aimlessly, or babbling without conscious intent (automatism).

ALERT   ALERT   ALERT

FIRST AID FOR AN EPILEPTIC SEIZURE
- *Do not restrain the person or attempt to put anything in his or her mouth.*
- *Do not move the person unless he or she is in danger of injuring himself/herself.*
- *Loosen the clothing around the neck and, if possible, move the head to one side so saliva can drain out of the mouth.*
- *When the attack has subsided, place the person in the recovery position.*
- *Remain with the person until he or she regains consciousness, and help reorient him or her.*
- *If the seizure lasts more than a couple of minutes or if the person does not regain consciousness, seek emergency medical help.*

TREATMENT
Treatment begins with addressing abnormal conditions that are easily correctable, such as high or low blood sugar or sodium levels. At times, this is sufficient to eliminate or reduce seizures. If epileptic attacks persist, anticonvulsant drugs are prescribed to control these attacks; however, these drugs can cause marked drowsiness. A combination of more than one drug may be needed. Fifty percent of patients who successfully respond to anticonvulsant drug therapy can eventually suspend the treatment without relapse. Brain surgery is considered if drug therapy has failed and brain damage in the temporal lobe is the cause of the seizures.

Extradural Hemorrhage

Extradural Hemorrhage

Also known as epidural hemorrhage

Uncontrolled bleeding into the space between the inner surface of the skull and the dura mater, the outer layer of the tissue that covers the brain.

Extradural hemorrhage can be caused by a blow to the head that fractures the skull and ruptures blood vessels on the upper side of the dura mater. These vessels bleed profusely, and a pool of blood (hematoma) can rapidly develop, pressing against the brain and causing severe damage.

> **ALERT   ALERT   ALERT**
>
> **WHEN TO SEE A DOCTOR**
>
> A headache that occurs after a head injury, accompanied by symptoms such as drowsiness, vomiting, and seizures, may indicate an extradural hemorrhage. Any head injury that causes loss of consciousness calls for an examination by a doctor.

The injured person may lose consciousness briefly and then appear normal. Symptoms may not appear for hours or even days. An extradural hemorrhage can be diagnosed by a physical examination and CT scanning of the head. It is treated by craniotomy, surgery in which an opening is made in the skull so that the blood can be drained and injured blood vessels repaired. *See also* HEAD INJURY *and* HEMATOMA.

Eye Injuries

Trauma to the eye, including foreign objects in the eye, chemical damage, and burns.

Injuries to the eye are almost always accompanied by pain or intense itching; some may impair vision. Bleeding, redness, or fluid discharge may occur. The person may become extremely sensitive to light and develop a headache. The pupils of the eye may appear to be different sizes.

Trauma. All trauma to the eye should receive treatment from trained medical personnel. Both eyes should be lightly covered until medical treatment occurs. Pressure should never be applied to the eye, and the victim should not rub the injured area. An object that has penetrated the eye should not be removed. Contact lenses should not be removed unless medical assistance is delayed.

Chemical Burns. If the eye has come into contact with chemicals, it should be flushed as quickly as possible with large amounts (at least three to five quarts) of saline solution or clean water. If a household

Eye, Foreign Body in

chemical is involved, the label should contain emergency instructions. If no instructions are available, water should be used. Contact lenses should be removed after rinsing.

Burns. Eye burns may result from fireworks, gas explosions, or even sunlight or sunlamps. If the skin around the face has peeled or blistered, and sunglasses designed to filter out ultraviolet radiation have not been used, the eyes have probably been damaged. A cool compress gently placed over both eyes may reduce pain. Emergency medical help should be contacted.

Abrasions. A scratch on the cornea may come from a foreign object in the eye or from rubbing the eye with a finger or fingernail. Contact lenses that trap an object under them or lenses that fit poorly and have been worn for too long may also damage the eye. The eye should be kept closed and should not be rubbed. Because all corneal abrasions carry the risk of deeper injury and infection, they should be examined by a medical professional.

Black Eye. With a black eye, purple bruising appears around the eye and on the eyelid from burst blood vessels. There may be swelling of the eyelid. Over time, the color changes to yellow and green. This is essentially an external injury, though frequently the eye is also injured. Cool compresses applied gently but immediately will reduce pain and swelling. Normally, a black eye will not require a doctor's attention unless there is continued pain, double vision, or light sensitivity, or if the discoloration does not subside in a few days.

Eye, Foreign Body in

An object that is touching or has entered the eye.

Any foreign object that has entered the eye can cause tearing, blurred vision, light sensitivity, or swelling of the eyelid. The white of the eye can become red and irritated. The object may scratch the eyeball's transparent tissue (cornea). Scratched eyes may become infected by bacteria.

Washing the Eye. Sometimes the eye's own tears are enough to wash away the object. If they do not, the eye should be flushed with clear water or saline solution for fifteen minutes. Contact lenses should be left in place. The head should be held to one side, and the eyelids held open, although the eye itself must not be touched. If both eyes are involved, the person may wish to use a shower, holding the face up to the shower head and allowing a gentle flow of water into the eyes. Alterna-

Eye, Foreign Body in

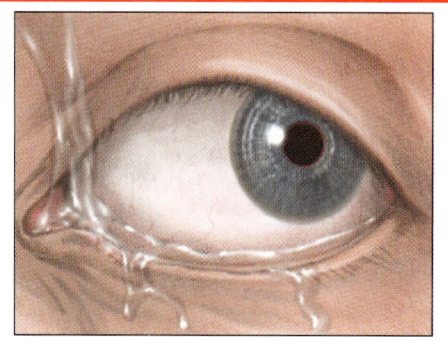

Eye, Foreign Body in. When a foreign body irritates the eye, above, it generally causes pain, redness, tearing, and blepharospasm (uncontrollable eyelid contractions).

tively, the person may immerse his or her head in a large bowl of water until the eyes are covered. The eyes should remain open—blinking repeatedly may scratch the cornea.

Removing Objects. Sometimes a foreign body can be removed. If the object is visible, it may be possible to remove it with a cotton swab or the corner of a clean cloth. However, too much pressure may cause the object to become more deeply embedded. **Removal of a foreign body should not be attempted if it is on the cornea. Never attempt to remove an object that is embedded in the eye.**

If the object cannot be removed easily, the entire eye should be covered with a light bandage, and medical attention should be sought. The doctor will examine the eye with a microscope and remove the object with a tweezer, needle, or other instrument. An antibiotic ointment will be applied to fight infection, and drops will be put into the eye to relax the muscle. An eye patch may be put in place to protect the eye from further injury and to keep the eyelid closed while it heals. If an object has penetrated the eye, it must be removed by an ophthalmologist.

Occasionally a small irritation, known as a stye, may swell into a bump on the inner surface of the eyelid; this may feel like a foreign object. The doctor will roll the eyelid over a thin stick to examine the inner surface of the eyelid to see if a stye is responsible. An antibiotic ointment and rest, with an eye patch in place, usually eliminates this irritation. *See also* ACCIDENTS; EMERGENCY, FIRST STEPS; *and* EYE INJURIES.

Facial Pain

A feeling of discomfort in part or all of the face.

Facial pain may be a result of actual injury to the face, teething in a baby, wisdom tooth eruption in an adult, or partial dislocation of the jaw. Less commonly, facial pain may originate from another point in the body (referred pain) or may arise for no apparent reason.

Infection. Commonly, inflammation of the nasal passages (sinusitis) can cause acute pain near the eye sockets and in the cheekbones. An infected toothache or abscess can cause pain that spreads to the face, as can a boil or other inflammation in the nose or ear.

Nerve Damage. Damage to the nerves of the face can cause pain, which sometimes occurs on one side of the face (trigeminal neuralgia) and may also involve facial tics (tic douloureux). Facial palsy, or Bell's palsy, is a disorder in which the main facial nerve becomes damaged, causing weakness of the face. Shingles (herpes zoster) may also damage the main facial nerve, causing pain and blistering.

Cardiac Causes. If face pain occurs with chest, shoulder, neck, or arm pain, it may indicate a heart attack. Emergency medical help should be sought immediately.

Treatment. Analgesics can be prescribed for temporary pain relief. In general, the underlying cause should be diagnosed and treated.

Fainting

Temporary loss of consciousness due to a lack of oxygen in the brain.

Weakness, nausea, or dizziness may precede fainting. The vagus nerve regulates breathing and circulation; in a vasovagal attack, fear, stress, or pain may overstimulate the vasovagal nerve and cause loss of consciousness. Sitting for long periods and suddenly standing causes blood to collect in leg veins, depriving the heart of blood to send to the brain and possibly resulting in fainting. When bloodflow through the neck and brain is obstructed, this may cause fainting, preceded by difficulty speaking or weakness in the limbs. Stokes-Adams syndrome, in which the heartbeat is irregular, may also be a cause.

After fainting, a person should lie down for up to fifteen minutes. If a person feels lightheaded, sitting can prevent fainting. Recurrent fainting or a delay in regaining consciousness demands immediate medical attention. *See* LOSS OF CONSCIOUSNESS.

Falls, Preventing

Accidents are the sixth leading cause of death in the United States; among those over 65, falls are the leading cause of injury-related deaths. Half of all people over 65 fall each year. Five percent of those falls result in broken hips or other fractures; bruises and head injuries are also common. Of the more than 200,000 older adults who fracture a hip, nearly a third die, and fewer than half regain full mobility, with many requiring long-term care.

Causes. Many conditions can lead to an increased incidence of falls, particularly in the elderly. Vision often degenerates with age, resulting in a lessened ability to judge distances or see small objects that may cause an individual to trip. A number of prescription drugs, including tranquilizers and antidepressants, may cause dizziness or drowsiness. Some medical conditions, such as heart disorders, lung disorders, and arthritis, may also lead to a greater likelihood of falling.

Many causes of falls are less directly age-related. Alcohol consumption can impair balance and coordination. Diseases such as influenza, pneumonia, epilepsy, and anemia also increase the chances of falling.

Prevention. Quick reflexes and strong muscles are the best defense against falling. Regular exercise can help maintain muscle tone, and frequent social interactions and mental activities can sustain alertness. Reducing activity due to fear of falling is not an effective preventive measure; less activity leads to decreased fitness and thus can actually increase the chances of falling. A balanced diet, especially one that includes adequate calcium and vitamin D to enhance bone strength, may also help prevent accidents.

Feces, Abnormal

Feces whose content, color, consistency, or odor are out of the ordinary.

Causes. Bleeding in the gastrointestinal tract can result in blackened or bloody feces; darkened feces may also result from a large intake of iron. Bloody or darkened feces could be a sign of cancer or diseases such as ulcerative colitis and should be brought to the attention of a doctor. Unusually light-colored feces can be the result of a disease such as celiac sprue, which reduces the absorption of fats in the intestinal tract. Ulcerative colitis and other intestinal disorders, as well as an infection such as gastroenteritis, may change the consistency of feces, causing them to be very loose and liquefied. Diarrhea is an obvious cause of loose, liquid feces and can also cause them to be abnormally light in color. Constipation can result in unusually hard feces and fewer than normal bowel movements.

Diagnosis. A number of tests can be done to identify the cause of abnormal feces. Samples can be tested for the presence of specific bacteria and other infectious agents. If there is blood in the stool, a physical examination can help determine if the blood originates from hemorrhoids, intestinal growths, or another disease.

Fever

> Elevated body temperature, usually in response to an illness or infection.

Body temperature is controlled by the hypothalamus, which acts as a natural thermostat, keeping temperature within a normal range. Normal body temperature ranges from 97° to 99°F, with an average of 98.6°F. Body temperature follows a 24 hour cycle, reaching its peak at around 4 P.M. and its lowest level in the early morning. During a fever, the hypothalamus works to maintain body temperature a few degrees above normal; after a fever breaks, the range returns to normal.

Causes. Fever is one of the body's generalized responses to infection. Substances that trigger a fever are known as pyrogens; they include bacteria and other microorganisms, as well as the toxins they produce. Body temperature becomes elevated during an illness, because microorganisms do not survive well in an environment that is too hot. Therefore, it may not be necessary or even wise to bring a fever down quickly, unless body temperature rises to a dangerous level.

In addition to infection, fevers may be caused by dehydration, heat stroke, reactions to medication, autoimmune reactions, hormonal disorders, and cancer. They may also have no known cause.

Symptoms. A fever can often be felt as a warmth and flushing of the skin, as blood vessels near the surface of skin dilate to eliminate excess heat. A person with a fever may also experience chills.

A fever may regularly fluctuate, with temperature rising and falling in a regular pattern. This is accompanied by the alternating chills and flushing experienced in many illnesses. A spike occurs when temperature elevates sharply within a very short period of time. In small children, it is not uncommon for a fever to spike suddenly at the beginning of an illness.

Fever

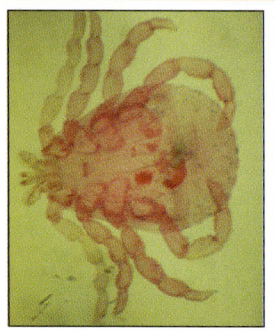

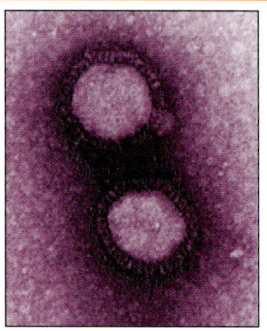

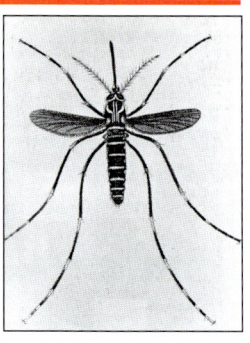

Fever. Above, are magnifications of bacteria and insects that cause fever. A fever can be caused by bacterial or viral infections such as influenza, or tonsillitis. In such cases, proteins called pyrogens are released when the body's white blood cells fight the microorganisms responsible for the illness. The proteins raise body temperature to try to destroy the invading microorganisms.

When a fever breaks, the patient often sweats profusely, which helps to lower the temperature.

Treatment. Over-the-counter drugs such as aspirin, ibuprofen, and acetaminophen are effective at lowering a fever. Aspirin should not be given to children, because Reye's syndrome, a potentially life-threatening condition, may develop in children with viral infections who have taken aspirin.

Cold compresses and sponging with lukewarm or cool (never cold) water can lower fever and make the patient feel more comfortable. A person with a fever should rest and drink plenty of fluids.

Febrile Seizures. A febrile seizure is a seizure caused by a fever.

ALERT   ALERT   ALERT

EMERGENCY SITUATIONS

A fever is considered an emergency if it is accompanied by a severe headache, a stiff neck, severe swelling in the throat, or mental confusion.

A very high fever can also be an emergency. The temperature at which a fever becomes dangerous varies according to age:

- *In infants from newborn to six months of age, a fever over 100.5°F is cause for concern, and above 101°F is serious.*
- *In children and adults, a fever of 103°F is serious, and a fever of 105°F or more is considered dangerous and potentially fatal.*

If a fever is 101°F and persists for three days or more, or if a low-grade fever persists for several weeks, a doctor should be consulted.

Food Allergy

There is a brief period of unconsciousness and the seizure may be accompanied by convulsions.

Febrile seizures occur in approximately two to five percent of all children under the age of five. The tendency for febrile seizures runs in families. In most cases, a child prone to febrile seizures usually outgrows them.

Febrile seizures usually occur when the temperature is either falling or rising rapidly. If a serious disease such as meningitis or encephalitis has been ruled out and the period of unconsciousness lasts only a few minutes, the seizure should not be a major cause for concern.

Anticonvulsant medication may be prescribed to reduce the likelihood of future occurrences.

TAKING A TEMPERATURE

Body temperature can be measured with a thermometer. Thermometers come in many varieties, and measure temperature in degrees Fahrenheit and Centigrade. Some have a digital readout.

The most common type of thermometer is the oral thermometer. It is placed under the tongue for three minutes, and then removed and read.

For an infant or young child, who may not be able to hold a thermometer in the mouth for three minutes, rectal thermometers are the preferred choice. The bulb end of the thermometer is lubricated and inserted gently into the anus. It should not be forced, and the parent should not let go of the other end while it is inside. If the child protests or is otherwise uncomfortable, the thermometer can be removed after only one minute, as the majority of the temperature registers by that time. Temperatures obtained rectally are usually 1° warmer than those obtained orally. For this reason, it is important to tell the child's physician how the temperature was obtained.

A thermometer can also be placed in the child's armpit. This temperature reading usually produces results that are 1° cooler than those obtained orally.

Newer models of thermometers can be placed in the ear; the temperature registers in less than a minute. There is some evidence, however, that suggests that the ear thermometers are not very accurate.

Food Allergy

An allergic reaction caused by a component in food.

As in any other type of allergic reaction, the immune system of a person with a food allergy will treat relatively innocuous molecules as foreign invaders and will mount a response, complete with the release of histamines and antibodies designed to specifically combine with and neutralize the invader. A food allergy is not the same thing,

Food Poisoning

chemically speaking, as a food intolerance, although they may share some of the same symptoms.

Causes. The foods most likely to provoke an allergic response are cow's milk, egg whites, peanuts and other legumes, nuts, and wheat. The tendency to have food allergies, though not the specific allergy itself, runs in families.

Symptoms of food allergy include nausea and vomiting; diarrhea; hives; swelling of the lips, eyes, face, and tongue; nasal congestion; breathing difficulties; convulsions; and even anaphylactic shock, a severe and life-threatening allergic reaction involving a sudden drop in blood pressure.

The seriousness of a food allergy varies greatly according to the individual. Some people find them a source of mild distress; others have increasingly severe symptoms. In the most severe cases, an individual may go into anaphylactic shock and death may result without immediate medical intervention. As with any allergy, more than one exposure to the allergy-causing agent (allergen) is required for a reaction. In most instances, digestive symptoms from dairy products are caused by a lactose intolerance, not an allergy.

Diagnosis. Determining the cause of the allergic reaction often takes time, as it is necessary to isolate each suspected food and eliminate it from the diet.

Treatment. Antihistamines can be administered to alleviate the majority of the symptoms, including hives. However, if a person is having a severe allergic reaction, medical attention should be sought.

Prevention. Once a food allergy has been established, that particular food should be avoided.

Food Poisoning

> **Result of contamination by a variety of bacteria that have entered the food supply.**

Food poisoning is generally caused by endotoxins, that is, toxic substances produced by bacteria such as *Salmonella, Campylobacter, Staphylococcus aureus, Listeria,* or *Escherichia coli.* These bacteria contaminate the food before or during preparation, and survive the cooking process. Sometimes food poisoning occurs because foods are left unrefrigerated for prolonged periods of time. If live bacteria inhabit food that is consumed, they may continue to multiply in the intestines and make the sufferer very sick. *Salmonella, Campylobacter, E. coli,* and *Listeria* are all present in uncooked food and thrive in the gastrointestinal (GI) tract. *Staphylococcus aureus* and *Clostridium botulinum* bacteria, for example, produce toxins that can cause anaphylactic shock and, in rare cases, death.

Food may be tainted after cooking by cooks who do not wash their hands after touching raw meat and handle the finished dish.

Symptoms of food poisoning generally pass so quickly that the organism responsible is rarely identified. Symptoms are usually abrupt in onset and generally include stomach cramps and abdominal pain, diarrhea, vomiting, and general weakness. Fever usually does not occur in cases of food poisoning—if fever is present, another diagnosis is more probable.

Food poisoning usually lasts only between 24 and 36 hours and concludes without treatment. It can, however, be life-threatening in the very young, the very old, and those with compromised immune systems. Infection by *E. coli* is particularly dangerous for these individuals.

If you suspect severe food poisoning in a high-risk individual, immediately contact your doctor or go to the emergency room. If you or someone you know has food poisoning and is unable to stop the diarrhea or vomiting, is feeling dizzy or faint, or is having difficulty breathing, call a doctor.

Drinking water (hydration) is essential in situations of prolonged vomiting or diarrhea. In severe cases, it may be necessary to inject fluids into the veins (intravenously) or to have prescription medicine inserted (suppository) in the rectum—such as promethazine (Phenergan) or prochlorperazine (Compazine).

Foreign Body

An object or particle in the human body that does not belong in the location in which it is found.

A foreign object in the body may obstruct function and could jeopardize a person's health or life. Generally, foreign objects are introduced into the body accidentally, but they are sometimes introduced deliberately by certain individuals. Children and people under the influence of alcohol and other drugs are most likely to deliberately inhale, swallow, or otherwise introduce a foreign object into their systems.

Airway Obstruction. A foreign object may become lodged in the airways and cause choking, which may require application of the Heimlich maneuver. If the object becomes lodged in the lungs, it may

Fracture

cause pneumonia or collapse of the lung. Foreign objects in the airway require emergency medical intervention.

Foreign Objects in the Gastrointestinal Tract. An estimated 80 to 90 percent of foreign bodies in the gastrointestinal tract pass through the digestive system spontaneously and without complications. Another 10 to 20 percent of foreign bodies require medical assistance and less than one percent require surgical intervention. Sharp objects require surgical removal from the stomach to prevent serious problems, such as perforation of the intestines.

Foreign Objects in the Ear. A foreign object in the ear should be removed by a physician, as attempting to remove it without proper instruments could have the opposite effect, pushing the object further into the ear canal.

Other Common Foreign Object Obstructions. Foreign bodies also commonly become lodged in the urethra, rectum, and vagina. Splinters in the skin are also considered foreign bodies. *See also* FIRST AID *and* HEIMLICH MANEUVER.

Fracture

An injury that causes a break in a bone.

A fracture occurs when more force or pressure is applied to a bone than it can bear. The force may come from a direct blow or torsion applied to the bone. The weight of a person's own body can cause a fracture if the person steps or falls at an angle at which bone must suddenly bear the weight of the whole body.

TYPES

The speed, angle, and weight of the responsible object determines just how the bone will break. Bones usually break at an angle, but they may also split lengthwise from torsion. Fractures are organized into two categories, closed and open. Within these two main categories are many different types of fracture.

Closed (or simple) fractures are those in which the broken bone remains below the skin. Because the surface is not breached, there is little chance of infection.

Open (or compound) fractures occur when the ends of the bones break through the surface of the skin and are exposed. In these cases, there is a great risk of infection, as the bones and tissues are exposed to the typically nonsterile environment.

Fracture

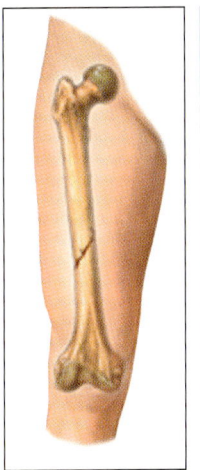

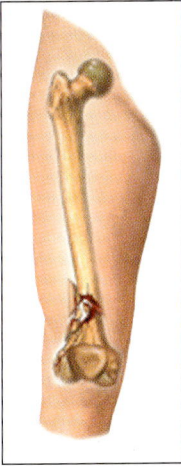

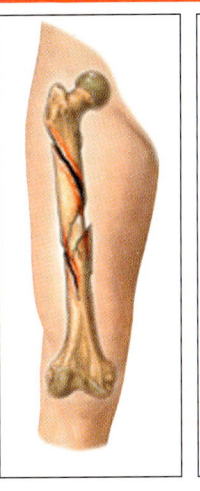

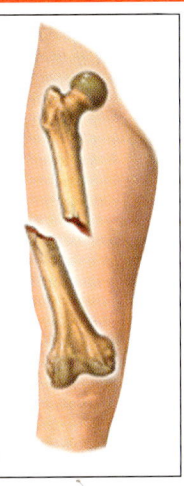

Fracture. Breaks in bones that occur in fractures can be of varying types, as shown in the diagrams above. A bone is usually broken across its width, but it can also be broken lengthwise, obliquely, or spirally.

Spiral fractures are caused by twisting of the bones, such as those that may occur in skiing accidents.

Transverse fractures are horizontal breaks directly across the bone. Stress fractures, which are caused by a repetitive, damaging motion, such as running or jumping, are usually transverse.

Greenstick fractures, usually the result of sudden force, are characterized by a splintering of the top layer of the bone; they resemble a piece of bark peeled from a tree. They are most common in children.

Comminuted fractures are those in which the bone shatters into fragments. Comminuted fractures are caused by severe force, such as that experienced in a car accident.

SYMPTOMS

The following signs suggest a fracture:
- A limb that is visibly deformed or out of place—an open fracture is obvious as the ends of the bone can be seen;
- Limited movement, or movement that intensifies the pain;
- Swelling;
- Tenderness;
- Bruising;
- Inability to bear weight.

Even if a fracture is not immediately obvious, a doctor should be

Fracture

consulted. A break that is not noticeable or easily detectable can still heal incorrectly and cause serious problems in the future if it is left to heal on its own.

TREATMENT

Bones begin to heal very rapidly, so it is important that a fracture be treated by a physician in order to ensure that the bones heal in the correct position. Until a physician can be reached, however, the following temporary measures may be taken:
- The injured person should be moved as little as possible;
- If the person must be moved, the affected area should be splinted in order to immobilize it;
- The injured person should not be given food or water; this can impede the function of anesthesia if surgery is deemed necessary.

The first thing a doctor will do to treat a fracture (usually after x-rays) is to move the bone ends back together; this process is called a closed reduction. A splint or cast may be applied after the closed reduction. If an operation is necessary, then it is called an open reduction. After an open reduction, the injured area must be immobilized so that the bones will stay in place as they heal. This may be done with a plaster cast. In more serious cases, pins or screws may have to be inserted to stabilize the bone.

When a bone heals, a blood clot is first formed to seal the ends of the blood vessels. Thus, for a period of time, painkillers that inhibit the clotting of blood should not be given to patients with bone fractures. After the ends of the blood vessels are sealed, the body begins to dispose of any debris from the break that is left in the injured area, and a mesh-like layer forms between the bone ends to provide a base for the new bone. A callus of new bone then fills into the fracture and bone ends, and over a period of weeks denser and stronger bone with calcium builds on top.

Bone grafts may be necessary if the bone ends cannot meet adequately. If a bone heals incorrectly, surgery may be needed to rebreak and reset the bone so it can heal properly.

REHABILITATION

A fracture takes a number of weeks to heal. During the healing period, the injured area must remain immobilized. Depending on the severity and location of the break, physical therapy may be necessary to restore strength and movement in the injured area.

Frostbite

Damage to the skin and underlying tissue caused by exposure to extreme cold.

Symptoms. Frostbite is distinguished by the cold, hard, pale appearance of skin that has been exposed to cold for an extended period of time. The area may feel numb, but there is also usually a sharp, aching pain. Any part of the body may get frostbite, but the hands, feet, nose, and ears are the most commonly affected areas.

The first symptom of frostbite is usually a "pins and needles" sensation, followed by numbness. The skin is hard and has no feeling. As the affected area thaws, the skin will become red and painful. While the area is warming, it is common to feel pain and tingling, a sensation called chilblains or pernio. In severe cases of frostbite, blisters may appear. Frostbite is often found in conjunction with hypothermia, a lowering of the body's core temperature. Symptoms of hypothermia include slurred speech, shivering, and memory loss.

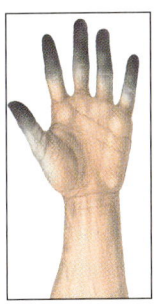

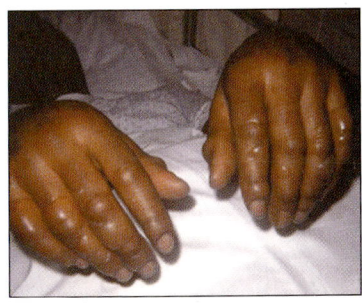

Frostbite.
Frostbite can be extremely damaging to the hands and extremities. The diagram and photo at left show frostbite's effects on the hands after exposure to severely cold temperatures—below 32°F (0°C).

Treatment. Rapid warming of the affected area is recommended, such as in water of 104° to 105°F. The affected area should not be rubbed with snow, as this may cause further damage to the area. Following immediate treatment, it is important that affected areas be rested and protected from any trauma.

Risk Factors. People who take beta-blockers, which decrease blood flow to the skin, are particularly susceptible to frostbite. People with atherosclerosis—thickening and hardening of the arteries—are also at high risk. Other factors that increase the chances of frostbite include smoking, exposure to windy weather, diabetes mellitus, and peripheral neuropathy or Raynaud's phenomenon. *See also* FIRST AID; GANGRENE; HYPOTHERMIA; *and* NUMBNESS.

Gallstones

> Accumulations of crystallized minerals that form in the gallbladder or in its ducts.

Normally, gallstone formation is inhibited by bile acids. However, if cholesterol levels are high, the cholesterol crystallizes and forms stones. Stones in the gallbladder itself may not cause any problems, but stones that lodge in the cystic duct (which leads from the gallbladder to the bile-duct) or bile-duct can cause pain and inflammation.

Gallstones may be smooth or rough, and can range in size from small grains to stones the size of golf balls. Most gallstones are composed of cholesterol; up to 20 percent of gallstones, however, are made up of calcium salts from bile.

Incidence. Approximately one in ten people develop gallstones. Women have a higher incidence of gallstones than men.

Symptoms. A gallbladder attack is known as biliary colic. The symptoms of biliary colic are a sudden sharp pain on the upper right side of the abdomen (occasionally migrating to the shoulder blade), nausea, vomiting, fever, and jaundice. Jaundice is usually an indication that the stone has become lodged in the common bile duct. Fever is attributed to inflammation of the gallbladder or infection of the bile duct, in addition to the obstruction.

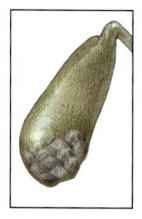

Gallstones. Left, gallstones accumulate in the gallbladder or its ducts and are made up of crystallized cholesterol. Stones located in the gallbladder are not as serious as stones in the ducts, which may result in a blockage of bile.

Treatment. Surgical removal of the gallbladder, called a cholecystectomy, can be performed after an acute episode of biliary colic has been resolved. This is the preferred method for treating gallbladder disease, and is usually performed by laparoscopy rather than open surgery. Stone dissolution, in which stones consisting of cholesterol are broken down chemically, is a newer alternative. Biliary lithotripsy is the use of high-frequency sound waves to shatter the stones, but the procedure is seldom used any longer.

Noninvasive treatments for gallstones include the administration of a medication called urodeoxycholic acid, which can dissolve cholesterol gallstones. However, this drug works best for small stones that have not formed obstructions. It takes several months for the drug to dissolve the stone, and the chance of recurrence is high.

Gastritis

Gangrene

Damage or death of body tissue due to poor blood supply.

Any injury, surgical wound, or disease that restricts or stops the flow of blood to tissue can cause the tissue to die. This process is called gangrene. Injuries that occur on the surface of the body, such as bedsores, chemical and deep burns, and frostbite, can result in gangrene. Decreased bloodflow within the body can also result in gangrene.

Types. "Dry" gangrene is usually associated with diabetes or arteriosclerosis. Gangrene complicated by bacterial infection is considered "moist" or "wet," and is not as common.

Symptoms. One of the earliest signs of either type of gangrene is a reddening of the dying tissue. Initially, dry gangrene is painful, but the area becomes increasingly numb. The skin turns purple and then black. Moist gangrene may begin with blisters and swelling. The infection spreads quickly, causing bruise-like discolorations as the tissue dies. The infection may also release a foul smell, and immediate hospitalization is necessary to treat the condition.

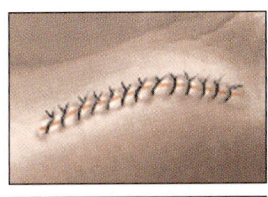

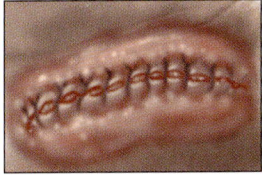

Gangrene. Gangrene is the death of body tissue, caused by poor blood supply to the area. Top, a normal wound can be contrasted with a gangrenous wound, bottom. The first sign of gangrene is generally a reddening of the dying tissue.

Treatment. Antibiotics are administered as soon as gangrene is suspected. Damaged tissue must be removed surgically. Individuals suffering from moist gangrene may be put into a hyperbaric chamber, in which oxygen under pressure helps to kill the bacteria.

Gastritis

Inflammation of the stomach lining.

Gastritis may be acute, in which the patient suffers from sudden attacks, or it may be chronic, in which the condition develops over a long period of time.

Types. There are several types of gastritis, each of which has distinct

Gastrointestinal Bleeding

G symptoms:

Atrophic gastritis, in which the stomach lining becomes atrophied, is seen in the elderly and patients whose stomachs do not produce enough acid. It may be an endproduct of *Helicobacter pylori* infection.

Chronic erosive gastritis can be caused by medicines, especially aspirin and other nonsteroidal anti-inflammatory drugs (NSAIDs). It can also be caused by other conditions, such as Crohn's disease or bacterial and viral infections. This form of gastritis develops slowly. Gastric (peptic) ulcers may result from this condition.

Causes. Causes of gastritis include infection by *Helicobacter pylori* or other bacteria; viral infections; NSAIDs; stress, burns, or other severe injuries; Crohn's disease; and vitamin B_1 deficiency.

Symptoms. Common symptoms of gastritis include nausea, vomiting, upper abdominal discomfort, and loss of appetite.

Diagnosis. Gastritis is diagnosed by a barium x-ray of the stomach or a gastroscopy, in which a tube is passed into the stomach so that the doctor can view the stomach lining.

Treatment. Antacids and other medications that limit acid production in the stomach are used to treat mild cases of gastritis. If the problem is caused by other underlying conditions, those conditions should be treated first.

Gastrointestinal Bleeding

Bleeding in the gastrointestinal tract, which includes the mouth, the esophagus, the stomach, and the intestines.

The appearance of blood or hemoglobin in the feces is the sign of a disease or abnormality within the gastrointestinal tract. Upper gastrointestinal bleeding involves a source near the lower outlet from the stomach (pyloric valve). Lower gastrointestinal bleeding involves a source farther down in the intestines.

Causes. Gastrointestinal bleeding can occur at any age, and for a number of different possible reasons. In children, the appearance of blood in the feces is most commonly due to swallowed blood from a nosebleed, milk allergies, or disorders such as intussusception or Meckel's diverticulum. Adolescents and young adults may suffer from gastrointestinal bleeding as the result of bleeding ulcers, Crohn's disease, and colitis. Middle-aged and older adults are susceptible to disorders like colon cancer and diverticulitis, which may cause gastrointestinal bleeding.

Symptoms. The symptoms of gastrointestinal bleeding include blood in the stools and vomiting blood or material that looks like coffee grounds. Gastrointestinal bleeding can range from occult or microscopic bleeding (where the amount of blood is so small that it can only be detected by laboratory testing) to massive hemorrhaging. Prolonged occult bleeding can lead to severe iron loss and subsequent anemia. Acute massive bleeding can lead to shock and death.

Treatment. Gastrointestinal bleeding may be indicative of an underlying cause requiring immediate medical intervention. If blood is noticed in the feces or in vomit, medical help should be sought as soon as possible. Intravenous fluids and medications, blood transfusions, drainage of the stomach through a nasogastric tube, and other medical measures may be required. Once the condition is stable, the doctor will attempt to ascertain the cause by means of various diagnostic tests, and treat the underlying condition.

Glands, Swollen

An enlargement of the lymph nodes or glands, generally a clear sign of infection.

Background. The lymph system parallels the blood circulatory system. Just as blood flows through the blood vessels, lymphatic fluid moves through the tissues of the body and the spaces between cells. Lymphatic fluid is a clear, watery fluid that acts as an intermediary between the blood and the cells. The fluid moves through a network of vessels the thickness of a single hair. Dead or damaged white and red blood cells are allowed through the porous walls of the vessels. These substances then accumulate in the glands.

The glands are grouped in various areas throughout the body. Areas where the glands can be felt include the armpits, the groin, under the jaw, the neck, and behind the ears.

Causes. The most common cause of swollen glands is infection. Glands play a crucial role in the body's response to infection by bacterial, fungal, and viral pathogens (disease-causing agents). The glands can become swollen even if the infection is so small as to go undetected by the infected individual. If a person is infected by a pathogen,

Head Injury

G the gland will swell and become painful to the touch.

A less common cause of swollen glands is cancer. Leukemia and Hodgkin's disease are two types of cancer that can cause swelling of the glands. If the glands enlarge slowly and painlessly, it is possible that a cancerous tumor may be the cause.

Treatment. Swelling of the glands caused by infection generally disappears spontaneously if the underlying infection is treated. It may take up to a couple of weeks for the glands to return to normal size after an infection. If the cause of the swelling is cancer, the cancer must be treated with radiation therapy or chemotherapy.

Physical Examination

In a physical examination, one of the first things a physician will examine is the area under the patient's jaw and neck. If there is an infection in the body, the lymph glands in this area will be swollen. The physician will also check other areas of the body in which glands are present to determine if those glands are swollen as well. The location of the swollen glands points to the part of the body that is infected, though it does not indicate the specific underlying cause of the infection.

Head Injury

Damage to the scalp, skull, or brain as a result of a blow to the head.

Head injuries may occur as a result of any blow to the head. In minor head injuries, the skull protects the brain from damage. A significant blow to the head may fracture the skull or cause brain damage. In addition, injured blood vessels in the brain can bleed (hemorrhage), and significant brain damage can result.

CONCUSSION

A concussion is a form of injury to the brain that is sometimes associated with a brief loss of consciousness. Symptoms of a concussion may include loss of memory, dizziness, nausea, and headache. Progressively worsening symptoms may indicate a more serious head injury, and medical attention should be sought.

SKULL FRACTURES

Skull fractures may damage arteries and veins, causing bleeding around the tissue of the brain. The fractures may allow foreign material into the brain, leading to bacterial infection.

Head, Neck, and Back Injuries

SERIOUS INJURIES
More serious injuries result in damage to the brain itself. Bruising or tearing of brain tissue can result in permanent loss of brain function. Pools or clots of blood between the brain and the skull can put pressure on the brain, causing swelling and destruction of brain tissue. Symptoms such as severe headache, dizziness, repeated vomiting, visual changes, pupils of different sizes, and diminished consciousness may indicate serious head injury; anyone who exhibits such symptoms requires immediate medical treatment.

Brain damage may be indicated by an extended loss of consciousness, followed by memory loss (amnesia) of the period before or after the injury. The longer the period of unconsciousness or memory loss, the more severe the damage may be. Damage to the brain may result in symptoms such as muscular weakness (paralysis), speech impairment (aphasia), or changes in mental capabilities or personality.

TREATMENT
Patients who become dizzy or unconscious should be placed under medical supervision. Blood clots and severe skull fractures, which can be life-threatening, require surgical repair. Serious, progressive brain damage along with loss of consciousness always requires emergency intervention, often involving life support and surgery.

PROGNOSIS
The survival rate of patients who have had major head injury has improved. However, some head injuries cause permanent physical or mental incapacity or personality changes. There is also an increase in the chance of seizures after a head injury. Recovery can be slow; improvement can take years after injury.

Head, Neck, and Back Injuries

Injuries in areas vital to human function.

The head, neck, and back contain the central nervous system—the brain and spinal cord. Falls, sports injuries, and other traumas can cause damage to these areas.

A severe blow to the head can fracture the skull, causing brain damage and amnesia. Prolonged unconsciousness can cause paralysis and brain damage. The survival rate after major head injury has improved, but recovery is slow.

Heart Attack

An injury at birth or skin contracture—shrinkage of scar tissue owing to burns or injuries—can cause wryneck, or torticollis, a condition in which the head is permanently twisted to one side. Paralysis or death may result from dislocations, fractures, or whiplash of neck vertebrae. Strangulation can cut off breathing and blood flow, while lacerations to the jugular vein or carotid artery can cause serious blood loss or death.

Severe injury to the spine may cause paralysis. Heavy lifting and carrying, prolonged sitting in the workplace, and obesity can cause muscle pulls and tears, ligament strains, and spinal or nerve damage, making life a daily struggle.

Heart Attack

Also known as a myocardial infarction

The death of heart tissue caused by interruption of the supply of oxygen-rich blood to the heart.

The immediate cause of a heart attack is the blockage of a narrowed coronary artery. The section of heart muscle that loses its blood supply can die in minutes. The risk to a person's life depends largely on which part of the heart is affected. Death of tissue that controls the electric impulse system (heartbeat) can precipitate lethal heart rhythm irregularities. If a less vital part of the heart muscle is affected, survival is possible, even if 30 percent or more of the heart muscle dies.

Symptoms. Chest pain is perhaps the most noticeable symptom of a heart attack, but chest pain can occur in different ways: as a severe, crushing feeling in the center of the chest; as a persistent but dull ache; or as pain that spreads from the chest to the shoulders and sometimes to the arms, neck, and jaw. Chest pain is occasionally ignored by patients because it is similar to the symptoms of indigestion. In some cases, a heart attack can occur without pain.

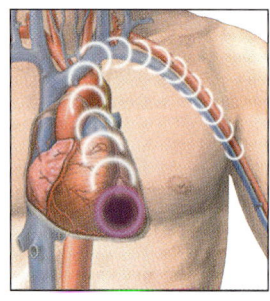

Heart Attack. Left, pain in the chest or radiating from the chest down the left arm may be a warning sign of a heart attack.

Other symptoms of a heart attack include cold sweats, dizziness, or weakness (sometimes enough to cause fainting); nausea and vomiting; shortness of breath; and a shallow, irregular pulse. When these symptoms occur, medical help should be sought at once by call-

Heart Attack

ing 911. Prompt treatment can be life-saving and can limit the damage to the heart. While quick treatment of any kind is vital for survival and recovery, the best source of medical help is a hospital emergency department that is associated with an intensive care unit specializing in cardiovascular crises.

Diagnosis and Treatment. The diagnosis of a heart attack may require an electrocardiogram that shows abnormal electrical activity of the heart, as well as blood tests that can detect the molecules secreted by dying heart cells.

In the most severe cases, if the heart is fibrillating, normal rhythm can be restored by transmitting an electrical impulse from a defibrillator to the heart muscle through electrodes held to the chest. If the heart has stopped, emergency department personnel will try to maintain the pumping action by performing cardiopulmonary resuscitation (CPR) and administering various medications. Because most heart attacks are caused by blood clots, patients will often be treated with reperfusion therapy, which may involve the injection of thrombolytic (clot-dissolving) drugs into a vein, or a direct intervention, such as balloon angioplasty performed via cardiac catheterization. Experience has shown that thrombolytic therapy can dissolve clots and salvage heart tissue if it is given in the first few minutes or even hours after a heart attack occurs. In addition to thrombolytic agents, the patient will also be given aspirin and heparin, both of which are drugs that reduce clotting in the body.

ALERT   ALERT   ALERT

HEART ATTACK RISK FACTORS

Each year, 1.5 million Americans suffer heart attacks, and more than 500,000 of these people die. Smoking, an unhealthy diet, obesity, and lack of exercise place people at serious risk for a heart attack. The most important fact about heart attack symptoms is that 60 percent of deaths occur before a patient reaches a hospital. Sometimes this happens because death is sudden, but often treatment is not sought in time because the symptoms of a heart attack are not recognized or are ignored.

Prognosis. After emergency department treatment, patients usually go to a coronary care unit (CCU), an area of the hospital staffed by specially trained doctors, nurses, and technicians. A CCU will have sophisticated electrocardiogram equipment and a variety of devices that allow minute-by-minute monitoring of the patient's condition. This equipment will recognize any heart irregularities and sound an alarm. The CCU will also be equipped with defibrillators and other life-saving

Heat Exhaustion

equipment on hand for immediate use.

Patients typically stay in a CCU for several days, until the heart and other vital organs are functioning regularly. At that point, the patient may be moved to a regular hospital room. The duration of the hospital stay for a heart attack victim depends on the degree of damage detected by electrocardiograms, blood tests, cardiac stress tests, and other diagnostic procedures.

A second heart attack can occur in up to 25 percent of first heart attack patients. If the risk is high, bypass surgery or balloon angioplasty may be performed to maintain blood flow to the heart.

Full recovery from a heart attack usually takes several months. A rehabilitation program to enable restoration of normal or near-normal activity, accompanied by drug treatment that can include aspirin, heparin, and beta-blockers, is successful in a large percentage of cases. See also ARRHYTHMIA, CARDIAC; ATRIAL FIBRILLATION; CARDIAC ARREST; CARDIOVASCULAR DISORDERS; CHEST PAIN; CORONARY HEART DISEASE; DEFIBRILLATION; EMERGENCY, FIRST STEPS; FIRST AID; INDIGESTION; NUMBNESS; and WEAKNESS.

Heat Exhaustion

An upset in the balance of nutrients in the blood and an increase in blood pressure as a result of exposure to high heat over a period of time.

Heat exhaustion usually follows a period of strenuous exercise in hot weather when fluids in the body are not replaced. Salt lost through sweating is also a factor, upsetting the balance of sodium and potassium in the bloodstream. The elderly are particularly vulnerable to heat exhaustion, as are chronic alcoholics, the obese, and those taking medications such as antihistamines and antipsychotic drugs.

Symptoms of heat exhaustion include: fatigue; weakness; hot, moist, and flushed skin; nausea; dizziness; and headache. The pulse is rapid and weak. Breathing may be fast and shallow. The victim may be confused and may faint.

Treatment is aimed at cooling the affected person off and replacing lost fluids. Shade, air conditioning, a cool wet towel, and immersion in cool water are all means of treatment. The victim should be given sport drinks, electrolyte beverages, or water. Emergency medical personnel may provide fluids with salt directly into the bloodstream (intravenously). Recovery is usually rapid. See also FAINTING; FIRST AID; HEADACHE; HEAT STROKE; and NAUSEA.

Heat Stroke

Body temperature high enough to incapacitate the body's cooling mechanisms.

Heat stroke is the most severe of the heat-related syndromes. It results from excessive exposure to very high temperatures and is accelerated by heavy exertion and direct sunlight. Especially on very humid days, the victim cannot sweat enough to reduce body temperature. Diabetes, alcoholism, vomiting, and diarrhea add to the risk of heat stroke in hot weather.

Symptoms of heat stroke include a body temperature of above 105°F, headache, vertigo, and fatigue. The affected individual does not sweat. The skin is red, hot, and dry. The pulse is weak and rapid, breathing becomes fast and shallow, and the pupils are often dilated. The victim is likely to be confused and may experience convulsions and lose consciousness. Heat stroke can be fatal if left untreated.

Treatment and Recovery. If the temperature of a victim of heat stroke is not reduced quickly, permanent brain damage may result. The victim should be wrapped in cool wet sheets or immersed in cool water. Emergency medical assistance (911) should be called immediately. The body temperature should be monitored constantly to make sure it is not lowered too far. Drugs may be administered to control convulsions. The body temperature of the victim may vary erratically for days or even weeks afterward.

PREVENTING HEAT STROKE

Heat stroke is a potentially dangerous medical situation. The following simple measures can help to prevent heat stroke:
- *Do not leave a child or elderly person in a closed, parked car during hot weather.*
- *Do not leave an elderly person in a closed room or apartment without air conditioning during summer heat waves.*
- *At the first signs of heat exhaustion, move to a shady area and drink cool liquids.*
- *Do not exercise during the hottest times of the day (between 12 and 3 PM).*
- *Wear light, loose-fitting clothing and a hat.*
- *Drink lots of liquids and monitor urine color. Urine should be clear or light yellow. Sip often; do not drink large quantities at once.*
- *Limit time in a hot tub or sauna to fifteen minutes during summer months.*
- *Limit consumption of alcoholic beverages or caffinated beverages in hot weather.*
- *Do not wrap an infant in blankets or heavy clothing in hot weather, as the cooling system of infants is not fully developed.*

Heimlich Maneuver

Heimlich Maneuver

Method for clearing an obstruction from the air passages.

The Heimlich maneuver is only applied to a conscious adult or child older than one year of age with complete airway obstruction. Patients with complete airway obstructions will be unable to speak and may use the universal sign of choking, placing their hands around their throats. If these signs are present, the victim should be approached from behind and "hugged" below the ribs, just above the navel. With one fist grasped by the other hand, five thrusts are delivered in quick succession, pulling inward and slightly upward. The thrusts should be firm and sharp. If the obstruction is not removed, the process is repeated. If the airway is cleared and the victim is not breathing, emergency help must be called and artificial respiration started immediately.

A child victim requires gentler thrusts to prevent injury. If the victim is an infant, he or she should be held face down with one hand supporting the chest, and the head held slightly lower than the body. With the heel of the other hand, the child should be struck between the shoulder blades five times in quick succession. If this does not clear the obstruction, the baby should be turned on his or her back. Using the forefinger and second finger, five thrusts should be made to the breastbone. If the object can be seen, it should be removed. If not, careful attention should be paid not to push the object further down the throat. Emergency help should always be summoned. *See also* CHOKING.

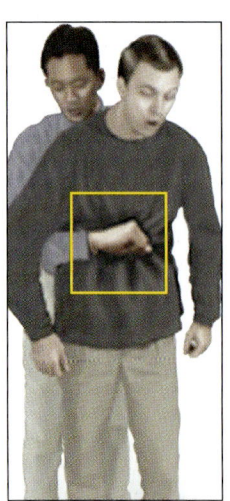

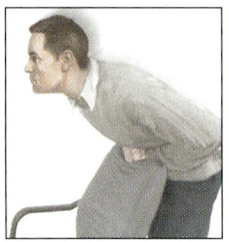

Heimlich Maneuver. Left, a choking adult should be firmly grasped around the abdomen from behind. A fist should be placed just under the breast bone, and pulled up and in quickly to dislodge the blockage (top right). If choking when alone, a person should thrust his or her body weight on the back of a chair (bottom right).

Hiccup

Spasm of the lungs and vocal cords, producing a sound resembling a chirp.

A hiccup is the sudden, involuntary movement of the breathing muscles (diaphragm), followed by the sudden, involuntary closure of the vocal cords. Hiccups usually occur in clusters and can be caused by sudden excitement, a surge of emotion, cigarette smoking, excess alcohol intake, or sudden stress.

Chronic hiccuping is much more serious; it can be due to a number of conditions, including pregnancy, gout, asthma, injury, pneumonia, and gastric ulcer. Some drugs, including steroids, barbiturates and benzodiazepines can also cause chronic hiccups. Severe chronic hiccuping can result in exhaustion, insomnia, inability to eat, and cardiac abnormalities. Medications such as baclofen, chlorpromazine or phenytoin can help in some cases. Acupuncture or hypnosis have been reported to be effective for some patients. If all else fails, the nerve controlling the diaphragm can be blocked by surgery.

Hip Fracture

A fracture involving the hip joint.

What is commonly referred to as a hip fracture is actually a fracture of the thigh bone, or femur, which meets the pelvis to form the hip joint. Elderly people are the most common sufferers, usually owing to a fall. Surgery is required if the upper end, or neck, of the femur is displaced. If it is impacted, the person must be kept bedridden for a few weeks and undertake daily exercises in bed to facilitate natural healing.

Hives

Also known as urticaria

Raised red welts on the surface of the skin that are usually associated with allergies.

Hives usually occur in batches. Histamine and other factors in the skin cause itching and swelling of hives. They are more common among individuals who suffer from fever or asthma. There are many substances that can trigger hives outbreaks through allergic reactions. These include: medications, certain foods (such as some kinds of fruit, berries,

Hospitals, Types of

shellfish, nuts, eggs, and milk), pollen, animal dander, and insect bites. Exposure to water or sunlight, as well as stress may also cause hives in some individuals. There are also many infections or illnesses that may trigger outbreaks of hives. These include: dermographism, cold urticaria, lupus erythematosus, dog tapeworm, hereditary angioedema, Henoch-Schönlein purpura, mononucleosis, hepatitis, and mastocytosis. Symptoms of hives may include itching and swelling of the skin into welts, which may enlarge and join together to form large, raised areas.

Hives may be treated with antihistamines, epinephrine, terbutaline, cimetidine, corticosteroids, sedatives, and tranquilizers to reduce itching and swelling. When hives occur in the throat, they may obstruct the airway and must be treated. Although hives are uncomfortable, they are usually not serious and may disappear on their own.

Hospitals, Types of

Different categories of institutions designed to diagnose and treat sick individuals.

A hospital is an institution equipped to treat the sick and injured and house patients while they are treated. The most well-known type of hospital is a general hospital. These institutions offer a variety of services to the community by means of departments equipped with specially trained staff and a variety of sophisticated equipment. General hospitals are only one type of hospital, however. There are many other types, and two main ways to classify them; most hospitals differ either by ownership or by the type of service offered.

Ownership. Some hospitals are owned by local or national governments, while others are owned by private institutions. Government-owned hospitals are supported by tax revenue. Nongovernmental hospitals further divide into two categories. Proprietary hospitals are operated on a for-profit basis for private gain. Other nongovernmental hospitals are operated on a nonprofit basis for the communal good. Hospitals in the latter category are often operated by churches, fraternal orders, universities, or independent associates. Hospitals run by these non-profit organizations are referred to as voluntary hospitals.

Outside the United States, most hospitals are government-owned. In most countries, however, a few small proprietary institutions exist, often with a capacity of fewer than 50 beds. Nongovernmental hospitals account for less than five percent of the hospitals in the world.

Services. Hospitals may be classified as general or special. A general

Hot Flashes

hospital, as described above, treats most types of medical and surgical cases. General hospitals also provide maternity service and treatment for children. Special hospitals, however, provide services for only one or two classes of patients, or types of illness. Some hospitals treat only mental illnesses, contagious diseases, or cancer. Special hospitals account for nearly 1,000 of the 6,500 hospitals in the United States.

There are also a number of other ways to classify hospitals. Hospitals are civilian or military institutions. Military hospitals treat sick or wounded soldiers. Military physicians and their assistants provide treatment. Some military hospitals are known as mobile field hospitals. Staff and equipment for these hospitals follow the movement of troops to provide emergency treatment to the wounded.

Some hospitals affiliated with universities are teaching hospitals. Doctors train at these hospitals by providing treatment as part of their medical schooling or post-medical school training. Teaching hospitals are more likely to have cutting-edge technologies and experimental treatments than most other types of hospitals. *See also* EMERGENCY HOSPITALIZATION *and* OPERATING ROOM.

Hot Flashes

Brief sensations of heat, a common symptom of menopause.

Changes in hormonal levels can often cause unpleasant side effects while the body tries to adjust. The loss of estrogen caused by menopause, ovary removal, or in men the removal the testes, can lead to the symptom known as hot flashes. This usually consist of a feeling of heightened body temperature, accompanied by reddening of the face, neck, and upper body, along with excessive sweating. The flashes usually last about two or three minutes. They are most likely to occur at the end of the day, overnight, or during times of stress. Hot weather, food, or beverages may exacerbate them.

Hot flashes may continue to occur for as long as it takes the body to adjust to its new level of hormones. Until then, some measures may be taken to reduce their effects. Avoiding substances such as alcohol and caffeine can help, as can exercise and other methods of stress reduction. If the hot flashes are severe and disruptive, estrogen replacement therapy may be recommended for women and testosterone is suggested for men if there is no medical reason to withhold the therapy. Estrogen or testosterone may be taken orally or released through a transcutaneous patch.

Hyperemesis

Hyperemesis

Excessive vomiting during pregnancy.

Hyperemesis usually occurs in the first trimester of pregnancy, and it is different from the more common "morning sickness." This condition is related to hormone production and may be aggravated by stress. Other symptoms include an inability to eat, nausea, and persistent retching.

This will cause dehydration, fevers, and (in some cases) jaundice; the blood may contain bile, and acute cases of starvation may result. Since the dehydration and nutrient deficiencies can be severe, intravenous nutrient administration is not uncommon. Sedatives may also be administered.

Hyperglycemia

When the blood sugar is abnormally high, often a consequence of diabetes.

In a normal digestive system, carbohydrates and sugars are converted into glucose. The pancreas releases the hormone insulin to regulate blood glucose. When the blood glucose level goes up, the pancreas secretes insulin that moves the glucose into the body's cells and tissues.

Cause. People with diabetes produce too little insulin (if they produce any at all) or they produce insulin at inappropriate times. Without the control that insulin provides, glucose levels gets too high. Without the necessary insulin in the blood, the body breaks down fat

ALERT ALERT ALERT

DIABETIC EMERGENCIES

High blood sugar (hyperglycemia) can lead to coma, and low blood sugar (hypoglycemia) can lead to shock. Either can render a person unconscious. These are potentially fatal emergencies and must be dealt with immediately. A person who is known to be diabetic and has fruity breath is suffering from diabetic ketoacidosis caused by hyperglycemia. The person may seem to be inebriated, or may be unconscious; he or she may be feeling extremely thirsty; urinating frequently; or breathing heavily. If a person is sweaty, he or she may be suffering from hypoglycemia. People suffering from hypoglycemia may sweat heavily and act paranoid or belligerent. Consuming sugary food should lead to recovery—if a person is unconscious, emergency assistance must be contacted immediately.

Hypotension

in order to supply energy to the cells. Too much fat breakdown can raise blood acid levels, leading to an emergency situation.
Treatment and Prevention. Medications and home therapy devices are available to regulate glucose. Insulin can be taken by injection; drugs that enhance insulin production or action may be taken orally. An individual with diabetes must learn to regulate his or her treatment to avoid hyper- or hypoglycemia.

Hyperventilation

Abnormally rapid or deep breathing.

The immediate symptoms of hyperventilation include a sense of not being able to catch one's breath and feelings of panic or anxiety. Rapid, deep breaths may result in a high level of oxygen and low level of carbon dioxide in the blood. This causes increased blood alkalinity, which can causes numbness in the fingers and toes, as well as faintness and painful spasms of muscles in the hands and feet. These physical effects can add to the psychological effects, resulting in the mental distress called hyperventilation syndrome. Hyperventilation can be stopped by increasing the level of carbon dioxide in the blood. A person experiencing hyperventilation should breathe into a paper bag; a plastic bag should not be used because of the danger of suffocation. If someone faints from hyperventilation, breathing returns to normal almost immediately.

Hypotension

Dangerously low blood pressure.

While hypertension (high blood pressure) is a major cardiovascular risk factor if it is uncontrolled, hypotension generally is not a cause for concern, although its symptoms can be rather bothersome. Those symptoms occur only when blood pressure is so low that the brain does not get an adequate supply of blood. Hypotension can occur naturally in some younger persons whose heart and blood vessels are normal but who have below normal blood pressure. In older people, it may be a side effect of medications taken for high blood pressure.
Diagnosis. A resting blood pressure reading of less than 90 over 50, or a drop in blood pressure of more than 20 mm Hg when getting up

Hypotension

from sitting or lying down is sufficient to diagnose hypotension.

Causes. If blood pressure falls enough to reduce blood flow to the brain, dizziness or fainting will occur. Hypotension is classified by the occasions when it occurs. Orthostatic hypotension, the most common type, occurs when someone stands up after being in a stooped or reclined position. Normally, blood vessels in the legs contract to keep the supply of blood to the heart and brain constant. In orthostatic hypotension, this reaction does not occur, and the result is a temporary

ALERT   ALERT   ALERT

SUDDEN HYPOTENSION

Sometimes hypotension can be a sign of a serious, even life-threatening, condition. A sudden onset of unusually low blood pressure can be due to an injury that has caused severe loss of blood, or by burns that cause a major reduction in blood volume. A heart attack or failure of the adrenal glands are among the major crises that can bring on a sudden reduction in blood pressure. Any unexpected, severe and sudden attack of hypotension is a clear signal that immediate medical help should be sought, either by going to a hospital emergency room or by calling the emergency medical service.

period of dizziness or near-fainting. This can also occur when someone gets up very quickly after sitting or lying down for a long period. Orthostatic hypotension is also a side effect of some antidepressant drugs.

Postural hypotension occurs while standing. It is common among older people who are taking medications, such as beta-blockers, to treat hypertension. Sometimes the medication works too effectively, widening the arteries and slowing the heartbeat so much that the brain does not get enough blood even during moderate activity. Hypotension sometimes affects teenagers and young women because of an imbalance in the blood's saline content. Sweating during exercise can lead to a temporary condition of low pressure.

Treatment. Medical help should be sought if the symptoms of low blood pressure become troublesome. Often, low blood pressure can be treated with common sense. If it occurs during exercise or physical activity, care should be taken to be sure the body gets enough water and salt to replace what is lost through perspiration. There are a number of sport drinks designed to meet those particular needs.

Someone who consistently experiences the symptoms of orthostatic hypotension can follow a routine of getting up slowly after lying down, sitting for a short period with the legs dangling before standing up. A chair, table, or other support should be close at hand to provide support if dizziness does occur.

Hypothermia

Dangerously low body temperature.

Hypothermia is the condition in which the body is incapable of maintaining a temperature greater than 95°F. Individuals with poor circulation, such as those with diabetes, congenital heart failure, and alcoholics, are especially susceptible. Prolonged exposure to icy water, or exposure to environments with cool temperatures and high humidity (especially when coupled with drinking alcoholic beverages in such environments), can cause hypothermia.

Symptoms. The onset of hypothermia is slow and subtle. A person's reaction time slows; the or she may become confused, loose coordination, and may even begin to have hallucinations. The affected person often becomes sleepy and unmotivated. For example, if hypothermia sets in while a person is in icy water, he or she may cease trying to swim or struggle and simply drown. In the most extreme cases, the muscles can become rigid, heartbeat can become irregular, and the person with hypothermia becomes drowsy and has difficulty speaking. If help is not provided, the person soon becomes unconscious, lapses into a coma, and may die.

ALERT ALERT ALERT

HYPOTHERMIA MORTALITY IN THE ELDERLY

The risk of mortality by hypothermia is five times greater for a person over 75 than it is for middle-aged and young people. The metabolism of the elderly is slower and less capable of keeping the body temperature stable. There is less fat and muscle tissue, and the blood vessels near the surface of the skin are less able to constrict and thereby preserve heat. Moreover, the shivering response and an awareness of the cold are reduced in the elderly. In addition, many conditions of the elderly can themselves lower the body temperature or leave people vulnerable to hypothermia. These include malnutrition, thyroid disease, stroke, Parkinson's disease, diabetes, and congestive heart failure.

Treatment. Whenever possible, move the victim to a warm environment; all wet clothing should be removed and replaced with warm, dry clotting. The victim should be wrapped in a blanket. If he or she is awake and alert, warm beverages, without caffeine or alcohol, may be given. If the or she is not breathing and has no pulse, cardiopulmonary resuscitation (CPR) should be administered, and emergency help should be summoned immediately *See also* CARDIOPULMONARY RESUSCITATION; COLD INJURY; FIRST AID; *and* FROSTBITE.

Hypovolemia

Hypovolemia

The loss of 20 percent or more of the body's total blood volume.

The cause of hypovolemia is often a traumatic accident in which a person sustains an injury that bleeds copiously. It can be caused by internal bleeding from the stomach, or intestines, or even by diarrhea and vomiting, if fluid loss is extreme enough and liquids not replenished fast enough. Burns can produce hypovolemia when they result in an excessive loss of body fluids from the brined skin surface.

Symptoms. A person suffering from hypovolemia exhibits classic symptoms of shock. He or she is initially tired, light headed or confused. Blood pressure is low, the pulse is weak and fast, and the respiration rate is high. The skin becomes cool, pale, and clammy.

Treatment is first aimed at finding and treating the cause of the fluid loss. The person should be kept warm and placed in a horizontal position with her or his legs elevated. As soon as possible, emergency medical technicians should be summoned.

Ice Packs

Use of ice to reduce pain or swelling, and aid in healing.

Cold can help treat injuries in a number of ways. It lessens pain or inflammation, and stops bleeding by causing the blood vessels to contract, which decreases the flow of blood. Ice packs are best used for bruises, sprains, injuries that swell, arthritic joints, and reducing pain after surgery or during physical therapy. Ice packs should not be used on areas of skin that lack sensation due to diseases, such as diabetes or paraplegia, or areas where injury or surgery have caused an inadequate blood supply. After intense exercise, ice baths may be used to minimize muscle soreness.

MAKING AN ICE PACK

Ice should not be applied directly to the skin, but should be placed in some kind of container, such as a bag or cup, or wrapped in a cloth. Do not leave on for more than 15 or 20 minutes, and apply every two hours, more or less, depending on the severity of the injury. Do not apply directly on the nerve at the elbow or heel as this may lead to temporary nerve palsy.

To make an ice pack, mix 1/3 cup of rubbing alcohol with 2/3 cup water. Put into a recloseable plastic bag and leave in the freezer until frozen to a slush. This pack may be refrozen and reused.

Injury

Indigestion

Upper abdominal discomfort often due to difficulty digesting food.

Indigestion is a general term used to describe a number of symptoms referring to upper abdominal discomfort. Also called dyspepsia, this condition occurs most often after eating.

Causes. Specific causes can rarely be found, but certain foods—particularly those that are unfamiliar or highly spiced—can provoke an attack of indigestion. Habits, such as eating too fast or too much, may also cause indigestion. Excessive amounts of alcohol can also be a factor. Some individuals experience indigestion on a regular basis; others, only occasionally.

It is important to note that indigestion, while not a serious condition, can be a symptom of another disorder, such as cholecystitis, gallbladder disorders, gastritis, an ulcer, stomach cancer, or a ruptured appendix.

Injury

A trauma to any part of the body.

The term injury covers a wide variety of circumstances that can result in harm to the body. They generally are considered problems that are due to some kind of external attack, rather than diseases. Injuries may include: fractures, sprains, strains, joint dislocations, cuts, burns, cold-related trauma, bites, stings, and sickness from poison.

All injuries need to be treated according to the specifics of their condition. Some general rules include:

Fractures and Sprains. Immediate care for suspected fractures or sprains is commonly called RICE: Rest the injured part; Ice the area; Compress with a bandage; Elevate the injured part to help the blood flow away from the area.

Animal Bites and Scratches. Apply pressure with a clean bandage or towel to stop bleeding. Clean the area, and call a physician to find out if antibiotics or shots, such as tetanus, may be needed; try to note as many details as possible about the animal that caused the wound.

Poison. Find out what the victim has swallowed or how the poisoning occurred. Call an ambulance, or the local poison control center.

Burns. For minor burns, run the injured part under cold water or apply an ice pack until pain subsides. Clean and bandage the burned area to avoid the possibility of infection.

Insect Bites and Stings

Insect Bites and Stings

Any bites, caused by insects, that may produce swelling, irritation, itching, or disease.

Most insect bites do not require medical attention, though a few can lead to serious, even fatal, results. Many common insects can produce anaphylactic shock in persons with heightened allergic sensitivity to insect saliva or venom. A number of insects are carriers for viral and bacterial infections, some of a grave nature. Identifying symptoms and, whenever possible, the insect responsible for the bite or sting will help in recommending treatment.

TYPES OF INSECT BITES

- Mosquito bites are among the most common insect bites. Generally, the small, itching bumps subside quickly, posing no threat to health. Some species of mosquito do, however, transmit serious diseases, including malaria, dengue fever, encephalitis, and yellow fever;
- Common flea bites acquired through contact with dogs or cats produce irritation and itching. Some species of fleas, however, may carry diseases such as plague and murine typhus;
- Bedbugs are likewise often benign, irritating pests, but may carry Chagas' disease;
- Spiders, though not truly insects, sometimes inflict painful bites on humans. While generally nonthreatening, some species, including the black widow and brown recluse, inject a highly toxic venom;
- Various species of louse may infest the head, body, or pubic area, producing an itching, excoriated skin rash; in some cases they transmit diseases such as trench fever, epidemic typhus, or relapsing fever.

Treatment. Insects should be removed from the skin and the area cleaned. Where itching, pain, or irritation are severe, an ointment containing antihistamine and corticosteroid will reduce swelling and offer pain relief. In cases of bedbug or flea infestation, an entire residence may need to be treated with insecticides. For lice, insecticidal lotions effectively treat infestation.

While stings of wasps, ants, bees, yellow jackets, and other insects are often painful, they are by and large not a serious risk to health. It's not the piercing of the skin, but the insect's injection of a swelling and irritation–inducing liquid (venom) that causes pain. This discomfort is usually minor and lasts one to two days. However, some people exhibit severe allergic reactions in addition to the characteristic swelling, redness, and discomfort normally associated with such stings. In cases of

Insect Bites and Stings

Insect Bites. Insects such as the Lyme tick, top left, and mosquito, bottom left, can pose some serious health risks to humans. Lyme disease is a bacterial infection transmitted to humans by lyme ticks that live on deer. Symptoms of the disease include headache, fever, lethargy, and muscle aches. Mosquito bites can be life-threatening to humans because they transmit diseases such as dengue fever, malaria, and encephalitis. **Insect Stings.** Wasps, above, are not known to carry human diseases, but allergic reactions to their venom and to the venom of insects such as yellow jackets and bees, can cause reactions in humans ranging from mild to fatal.

allergy, these individuals may experience anaphylactic shock, a potentially life-threatening condition.

Bees and Wasps. In the United States, bee and wasp stings are common. In general, a person may withstand ten such stings per pound of body weight without risk of serious complication. Attacks involving multiple stings can cause circulatory collapse or cardiac arrest. Certain aggressive species of bee, such as the Africanized honeybee, or killer bee, pose another threat due to their tendency to attack in swarms with little provocation.

Fire ants produce painful, occasionally fatal stings and are common to the American South. Such stings produce immediate pain, followed by swelling and blistering. When the blister ruptures after 30 to 70 hours, a secondary infection may develop and in some cases the entire limb may swell. Fire-ant stings are likewise capable of inducing anaphylactic shock, which acts to constrict the air passages and lower blood pressure, although this reaction occurs in fewer than one percent of those stung.

Treatment. Bees, fire ants, and wasps may leave a stinger embedded in the skin following attack. Care must be taken to gently remove the stinger without squeezing it, which will inject more venom into the skin. Scraping with a dull table knife or credit card against the skin next to the embedded stinger will help to remove it. Tweezers should be avoided. Ice may be applied to reduce the pain. Antihistamine or corticosteroid cream is helpful in reducing swelling and for pain relief. It is critical that the area be repeatedly washed during the healing process to avoid infection. Consult a physician if an infection develops.

Alert. Individuals known to have allergies to stinging insects should

Internal Bleeding

I

carry allergy kits including antihistamines and syringes for injecting epinephrine to improve breathing and circulation. Symptoms of a whole-body reaction to insect stings include nausea; hives; facial swelling; shortness of breath; difficulty swallowing; light-headedness and fainting; chest and throat tightness; and swelling or redness over most of the body. The onset of symptoms can occur anywhere from within minutes to several hours later. Emergency services must be contacted immediately after symptoms of an allergic reaction appear.

Internal Bleeding

Bleeding that occurs inside the body or from any of the internal organs.

Internal bleeding is a potentially hidden danger. Injury, illness, or a disorder can cause bleeding within the body—from blood vessels, tissues, and organs into cavities, other tissues, or organs—that is not immediately or visibly apparent. It must be suspected after a vehicular accident, fall, or major blow to the head or body.

Symptoms. Pain in the chest, abdomen, or pelvic region; abdominal muscle spasms; a weak, rapid pulse; clammy skin; spitting, vomiting, or coughing up blood or extremely dark sputum; bleeding from orifices; or blood in the stool or urine can all be signs of internal bleeding. However, there may also be no symptoms whatsoever. Days or even weeks may pass before any signs appear, thus the need for immediate medical examination following cases of impact—even those that seem mild—to the body. A failure to seek prompt attention may be life-threatening. Until help arrives, if there is no risk of spinal injury, lay the person down and elevate the feet. Monitor breathing and pulse.

Ipecac

A substance used to induce vomiting in cases of poisoning.

Syrup of ipecac is an emetic—that is, a substance that induces vomiting. It is used to bring about vomiting in the case of accidental poisoning. It should be an essential component of the medicine cabinet, especially if there is a child under the age of 12 in the house. Syrup of ipecac should be used only on the advice of a doctor, pharmacist, or poison control center, since certain poisons can cause further damage if they are vomited. Never use ipecac if the person has swallowed lye, as it may cause severe esophageal erosions.

Jellyfish Stings

Painful, itching stings caused by marine jellyfish.

Jellyfish are a type of coelenterate equipped with specialized stinging cells capable of penetrating human skin. Such cells are concentrated in the jellyfish's tentacles. Contact with the jellyfish or its tentacles typically produces a painful, raised rash appearing in a linear pattern. Jellyfish stings may be quite painful and are usually accompanied by itching. The rash may yield to raised, pus-filled blisters, which eventually rupture. Additional symptoms include nausea, muscle spasms, headache, breathing difficulty, and heart irregularities. The sting of one type of jellyfish, the Portuguese man-of-war, is potentially lethal.

Jellyfish stings may be treated with vinegar for 30 minutes to neutralize the toxin. Embedded spines or tentacles should be removed with sterile tweezers. Baking soda may be used after the wound is cleaned, to relieve pain. Ointments containing antihistamine and corticosteroid may be applied to reduce swelling and alleviate discomfort. Antivenom treatments exist for some but not all coelenterates. Seek medical help if there are signs of an allergic reaction (i.e., difficulty breathing or loss of consciousness); CPR may be necessary.

Kidney Failure

Partial or total loss of kidney function.

The body's two kidneys filter waste products from the blood, control the levels of water and salt in the body, and help regulate blood pressure. The kidneys also play a vital role in the production of a hormone called erythropoietin and in the production of the active form of vitamin D. Erythropoietin is critical for the production of near normal numbers of blood cells, thereby preventing anemia (a low red blood cell count). Vitamin D is responsible for the absorption of calcium from food, and for the maintenance of healthy bones. When the kidneys fail to do their job, the result is a buildup of waste products, accompanied by other abnormalities that can cause a variety of symptoms.

Causes. Acute (sudden) renal failure can be caused by a number of medical problems. These include conditions that block the flow of urine, such as bladder tumors, bladder stones, or an enlarged prostate gland in men. Major bleeding or burns can reduce blood flow to the

Kidney Stones

kidneys enough to cause acute renal failure; a heart attack can have the same effect. Chronic (over time) renal failure can result from untreated high blood pressure (hypertension), diabetes, polycystic kidney disease or amyloidosis. Overuse of painkillers for a number of years can also result in chronic kidney failure.

Symptoms. If renal failure is acute, symptoms can include a severe decrease in urine production, drowsiness, nausea, vomiting, muscle cramps, headache, and breathlessness. Chronic renal failure, brings about all the symptoms of acute failure, as well as a growing sense of weakness, lethargy, anemia, and paleness of the skin. If progressive renal failure cannot be reversed, it can be fatal.

The complications caused by acute kidney failure include an increased risk of infection and internal bleeding. Chronic renal failure can cause anemia, nerve damage, and degeneration of muscle tissue.

Treatment. The treatment of acute kidney failure is aimed at diagnosing the underlying condition and correcting it, for example, removing a stone that is blocking urine flow. Diuretic drugs may be given to increase the production of urine. In severe cases, artificial kidney treatment (dialysis) may be given until a crisis is over. Treatment of chronic kidney failure can start with dietary changes and include drugs to remove excess fluid from the body and reduce high blood pressure. When these measures cannot prevent end-stage renal failure, continuing dialysis or a kidney transplant can prolong life.

Kidney Stones

A calculus, which is a crystalline mass formed from precipitating fluids (such as those found in urine or bile), in the kidney.

There are various kinds of kidney stones (urinary tract calculi). In most cases, the calculi are formed from crystals that separate from concentrated urine; these crystals, which are often composed of calcium oxalate or phosphate, build up in the kidney. Kidney stones can also be caused by urinary tract infections (struvite or infection stones). Uric acid or cystine stones occur in less than five percent of cases.

The pain that kidney stones cause is usually an intense cramping sensation in the lower abdomen; this may spread to the groin. The pain is usually caused by the movement of the calculi into the urinary tract, leading to blockage and sometimes, to infection. If a fever is also present, call a physician immediately, as it is a sure sign of infection.

Loss of Consciousness

Fortunately, very few stones require surgery. After the presence of a stone has been identified, often during a routine x-ray examination, a person will be directed to drink lots of water, and take pain-relief medications (aspirin or ibuprofen) as necessary. Only the largest stones and stones that cause infection, will require surgery. Non-invasive techniques have improved over the last few years, so the hospital stay tends to be quite short. Still, prevention methods, as recommended by a primary care physician, are a much preferred option in nearly all situations. *See also* OPERATING ROOM.

Life Support

Process in which a person is kept alive artificially with a ventilator, to maintain breathing, and/or a pacemaker, to sustain the heart beat.

Life support devices are used for a short period to keep a victim alive in times of emergency, or for a lengthier time in the event of serious illness. Life support is designed to supply oxygen, food, and water to the patient. It is also used to maintain body temperature, blood pressure control, carbon dioxide disposition, and the proper removal of waste. *See also* EMERGENCY HOSPITALIZATION.

Loss of Consciousness

A state of being unable to respond to external stimuli resulting from reduced brain activity.

Someone who has lost consciousness may be suffering from something as minor as fainting, or as serious as a stroke. Unconsciousness can result from injuries to the head, shock, stroke, a loss of blood to the brain, hypotemia which is too little oxygen in the blood, hypoglycemia which is too little sugar in the blood or other chemical changes, drug overdoses, or exposure to toxins. *See also* DRUG OVERDOSE *and* FIRST AID.

The first step in dealing with an unconscious victim is to check the victim's airways to make sure he or she is breathing. If the victim is not breathing, remove any obstruction from the airways and begin artificial respiration or CPR if necessary. Call for medical help, but try not to leave the unconscious person unattended. Do not give food or drinks to anyone who is unconscious. *See also* COMA.

Menstruation, Disorders of

Menstruation, Disorders of

AMENORRHEA

Amenorrhea is the absence of any menstrual periods in premenopausal women who are not pregnant.

Primary amenorrhea is diagnosed in young girls who have not begun menstruating by age 16. Menarche can be delayed in athletic or very thin girls whose body fat level is below a certain percentage.

Secondary amenorrhea is defined as the absence of menstruation for six months or longer in adult women who are not pregnant. Secondary amenorrhea has a variety of causes, including sudden weight loss and prolonged bouts of exercise. Stress and either too few or too many fat cells in the body can prevent the ovaries from producing estrogen in a normal cycle. Taking oral contraceptives can often affect a woman's monthly cycle, even for a few months after discontinuing use. Nursing mothers often fail to menstruate for several months. As a woman approaches the age of menopause, it is normal to begin skipping periods.

It is important to note that even if a woman isn't menstruating, she may still be ovulating and may still get pregnant.

Treatment. If amenorrhea is caused by an underlying disorder, that should be treated. Estrogen therapy may be recommended. A sufficient level of estrogen is needed for the prevention of bone weakness (osteoporosis) later in life.

DYSMENORRHEA

Dysmenorrhea refers to painful menstrual periods. More than half of all women experience mild cramps during the first few days of a period. Dysmenorrhea, which occurs in about ten percent of women, involves severe pain that cannot be tolerated without medication.

Primary Dysmenorrhea. If the pain is not a sign of another gynecological problem, the condition is called primary dysmenorrhea. It is caused by excessive levels of prostaglandins, chemicals that are found in menstrual fluids and semen which trigger uterine contractions. Severe cramps may also be due to internal "gridlock"; a lot of fluid and tissue attempting to exit all at once through a relatively small opening. Pain therefore persists until enough material has been expelled. After a woman has given birth, the opening has been somewhat stretched, and this problem may cease.

Secondary dysmenorrhea is caused by an underlying condition such as

Mercury Poisoning

abnormal growths in the uterus (fibroids, adenomyosis, endometriosis) or a sexually transmitted disease.

OLIGOMENORRHEA

Oligomenorrhea is diagnosed when a woman experiences fewer menstrual periods than the usual 11 to 13 per year. Some women never have regular periods; others may suddenly begin to experience irregular cycles for no apparent reason. This irregularity is not related to approaching menopause but may be caused by an insufficient amount of estrogen. If erratic menstrual cycles are accompanied by acne and an increase of body and facial hair, the cause may be an excess of male hormones known as androgens.

Treatment. In most cases, oligomenorrhea presents no health threat unless a woman is trying to become pregnant. If the condition is due to insufficient estrogen production by the ovaries, hormone supplements should restore normal menstruation. Oligomenorrhea caused by an excess of androgens is treated depending on the underlying cause.

MENORRHAGIA

Menorrhagia refers to abnormal menstrual periods that last longer than seven days or involve unusually heavy bleeding. Heavy periods may be caused by hormonal disturbances in a woman's cycle, fibroids, pelvic infection, endometriosis, or the presence of an IUD. A one time heavy period which arrives late may be due to a miscarriage.

Menorrhagia may result in anemia, due to heavy blood loss, but is otherwise not considered a serious condition.

Treatment. A combination of estrogen and progesterone, usually in the form of oral contraceptives, are prescribed to reduce bleeding. A physician may also wish to perform a D&C (dilation and cutterage) to determine if there are any other causes. Bleeding due to fibroids or endometriosis is treated by those conditions. An IUD that causes bleeding must be removed. *See also* INTERNAL BLEEDING.

Mercury Poisoning

Complex of symptoms caused by exposure to mercury or compounds containing mercury.

Mercury has long played a significant role in industrial production and craft, and mercury poisoning has accompanied such work. The phrase "mad as a hatter" refers to the psychosis that hatmakers in

Migraine

the nineteenth century exhibited due to exposure to toxic levels of mercury.

Exposure to mercury generally occurs from environmental pollution, including atmospheric fumes from refining, smelting, mining, or from the burning of fossil fuels. Marine environments are often contaminated by industrial runoff and the dumping of mercury-containing materials. Organic mercury compounds are found in fish, shellfish, and in grains treated with the fungicide methylmercury.

Mercury and its compounds may be ingested, absorbed through the skin, or inhaled. Ingestion or inhalation of mercury can be fatal. If mercury exposure is suspected, call a poison control center and seek immediate medical attention.

Symptoms of acute mercury poisoning include a metallic taste, stomach pain, coughing, chest tightness, and breathing trouble. Pneumonia may develop, which can be fatal. Exposure to inorganic mercury compounds can cause nausea and vomiting, diarrhea (possibly bloody), and kidney damage.

Symptoms of chronic mercury poisoning include loose teeth, excessive salivation, painful or numb limbs, and emotional and mental changes, possibly including mood swings, irritability, loss of motivation, inability to concentrate, hallucinations, and memory loss.

The prognosis for mercury poisoning depends on the amount of mercury involved, length of exposure, and speed of treatment. Acute exposure may result in complete recovery, but it may be fatal. Fetuses and young children are particularly at risk for permanent developmental impairments. *See also* POISONING.

Migraine

Severe form of headache, usually recurrent and affecting only one side of the body.

Migraines can affect anyone at any age. Most migraine sufferers begin to get migraines between the ages of ten and 30 and continue until the age of 50. Twenty-five percent of women and eight percent of men complain of migraine headaches. The majority of migraine sufferers have close relatives who also suffer from migraines, indicating that there may be a genetic predisposition for these headaches.

Cause. The reason for migraines is not understood. Two theories exist for the physical process of migraines. One is that the arteries to

Migraine

the brain narrow (constrict) and then widen (dilate), triggering pain receptors that produce the migraine. The second, and latest, theory surmises that proteins are released in the brain, inflaming blood vessels and nerves, resulting in pain.

Symptoms. There are two forms of migraines: migraines without an aura (a set of symptoms preceding the migraine) and migraines with an aura. An aura may consist of an alteration in vision, numbness in the face, arms, and hands, muscle weakness, or difficulty speaking. Aura symptoms last no longer than one hour and affect only one side of the body.

Whether a migraine is preceded by an aura (classic migraine) or is not (common migraine), symptoms may include:
- pulsing pain centralized on one side of the head that can curtail the ability to function;
- at least five attacks per year that last four to 72 hours;
- pain upon physical exertion;
- nausea or vomiting; and
- light sensitivity or sound sensitivity.

Before a physician can diagnose a migraine, he or she must ascertain that the patient has no other diseases that could produce the same symptoms.

Treatment. If migraine attacks occur more than once a month, a person should determine what triggers his or her attacks and avoid the triggers, thus limiting the number of attacks.

Aspirin or acetaminophen, along with an anti-nausea drug, can treat a mild migraine. An acute migraine may need to be treated with ergotamine—a vasoconstrictor that narrows blood vessels, preventing the dilation that causes pain. Medications for high blood pressure and heart disease, such as beta blockers and calcium-channel blockers, have also been found to provide relief in some sufferers of migraine.

TRIGGERS

Although the underlying cause of migraines is unknown, the attacks are often triggered by specific conditions. A variety of situations can produce a migraine attack in a vulnerable individual, including:
- Anxiety;
- Climactic changes;
- Ingestion of chocolate, aged cheese, red wine, nuts, and fried food;
- Loud noises, intense smells, and strong lights;
- Menstrual cycle and birth control pills; and
- Smoking and fatigue.

Morning After Pill

Also known as ECP, emergency contraceptive pill or post-coital contraception

Colloquialism for high doses of oral contraceptives taken to prevent pregnancy after a single act of unprotected sex.

An emergency contraceptive pill (ECP) must be taken within 72 hours of intercourse to be effective. Most physicians prefer not to use the term "morning after pill," as it implies that the pill can be used often and should only be taken in the morning, neither of which are particularly advisable. While the failure rate of post-coitial contraceptives is rather low, it is still higher than that of oral contraceptives (one of the most effective contraceptive options), making them ineffective and unreliable as conventional contraceptive alternatives.

ECP's are not to be confused with so called abortion pills such as mifepristone (RU-486); which induce miscarriage. ECP's prevent conception by thickening the cervical mucus, making it difficult for sperm to pass through, and by thinning the endometrial lining, thereby decreasing the chances that an egg will implant. Side effects include nausea, breast tenderness, and an irregular menstrual cycle. *See also* VAGINAL BLEEDING.

Mushroom Poisoning

Adverse effects from eating toxic species of fungi.

Mushroom poisoning occurs frequently when novice mushroom hunters mistake a toxic species for an edible one. Children are also at risk for eating wild mushrooms. A wild mushroom should never be eaten unless there is complete certainty that it is edible—some species that are toxic enough to kill immediately if ingested closely resemble non-poisonous varieties.

Mushroom. Wild mushrooms (shown left), which are toxic can easily be mistaken for those that are edible. The toxicity in some wild mushrooms can even cause death.

Nausea

The effects of mushroom toxicity vary greatly according to species, and may even have diverse effects on different people who have eaten them.

> **ALERT   ALERT   ALERT**
>
> **POISON MUSHROOMS**
> If it is suspected that someone has eaten an unidentified wild mushroom and is experiencing toxic effects, immediately contact the closest poison control center. If possible, bring a sample of the mushroom to the emergency room.

There are four types of mushroom toxins (mycotoxins): gastrointestinal irritants that cause abdominal cramping, diarrhea, nausea, and vomiting; neurotoxins, whose symptoms include hallucinations, spastic colon, depression, and agitation; protoplasmic poisons, which result in the destruction of cells, followed by organ failure; and disulfiram-like toxins, which are usually nontoxic unless alcohol is drunk within 72 hours of eating the fungi, causing a temporary toxic syndrome. *See also* POISONING.

Nausea

Abdominal sensation that leads to vomiting.

Nausea may be accompanied by retching, dizziness, abdominal pain, considerable salivation, clamminess, and lowered blood pressure. Nausea is a common symptom in many different diseases or conditions affecting the gastrointestinal system or the kidneys.

Causes. Any of the following may bring on nausea, which in turn is usually followed by vomiting: strong or unpleasant odors; medications; viral infections; sea-sickness or motion sickness; migraine headaches; morning sickness during pregnancy; food poisoning; food allergies; chemotherapy in cancer patients; emptiness of the stomach; heat exhaustion; or intestinal obstruction.

A person who is not pregnant and has experienced nausea for a prolonged period of time should consult a healthcare professional.

Treatment. When the cause of nausea and vomiting is known, the underlying disorder can be treated. If vomiting occurs, the patient should take in as much fluid as possible without upsetting the stomach further. Antiemetic drugs may be prescribed to suppress nausea.

Neck Rigidity

N | Neck Rigidity

Immobility of the neck.

When muscles in the neck and spine clench in a spasm, they cause the neck to become rigid. Occasionally, the spasm may cause the neck to arch back.

Muscle spasms and rigidity of the neck can occur as a result of stress, injury, arthritis, or even from sleeping in an odd position. In many cases, pain can be relieved with anti-inflammatory drugs. Neck spasms and rigidity can be reduced by strengthening the muscles in the neck and upper back and adopting correct positions for sleeping and carrying heavy objects.

A patient with neck rigidity accompanied by numbness, tingling, or weakness should be attended to by a physician, as this may indicate a more serious injury.

Nerve Injury

Damage or laceration to a nerve that severs all or a portion of its conducting fibers.

Nerve damage is often caused by accidents. Nerve injury can result from lacerations (open wounds), fractures, or crush injuries. In each case, nerve injury can result in a loss of feeling and muscular control in the affected area.

In a nerve injury, the individual nerve fibers within the peripheral nerve may be disconnected while the nerve trunk generally remains intact. The severed fibers at the point of injury may degenerate. If the ends of the nerve fibers remain intact, they can regenerate themselves.

Complete severance of a nerve is often caused by a power tool accident or a knife wound. If the nerves are completely disconnected, the nerve fibers cannot regenerate. A surgical procedure is the sole treatment for a severed nerve. Only the peripheral nerves, those existing outside the brain and spinal cord, can be surgically repaired. *See also* COMA.

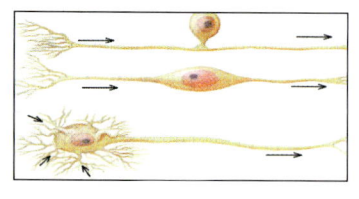

Nerves. Left, every nerve is composed of a bundle of nerve cells. Nerve impulses from the central nervous system enter the nerve through structures called dendrites. They then move down the length of the nerve to exit at projectile fibers called axons.

Nervous Breakdown

Nonscientific term used popularly to describe individuals who have suffered a mental collapse.

A nervous breakdown is generally accompanied by incapacitating anxiety, episodes of debilitating tearfulness and withdrawal, or bouts of shouting, hysteria, and paranoia. The term generally describes an individual who is suffering a mental crisis that is in immediate need of aggressive treatment, possibly including hospitalization. The term nervous breakdown carries a stigma insofar as it implies mental instability and pathological tendencies, but, in fact, many people experience an emotional crisis resulting in an inability to function normally for a period of time. *See also* EMERGENCY FIRST STEPS.

Nose, Broken

A fracture of the nasal bone.

From the forehead, the nasal bones connect to the skull (cranium), and extend down to form the bridge of the nose, which is very difficult to fracture. The rest of the bridge is cartilage. When hit with a sharp blow from the side, the bones and cartilage may be displaced, while blows to the front of the nose will knock the bones outward, flattening the nasal structure.

Diagnosis and Treatment. Broken noses are common injuries, and are often not taken seriously. There usually is a great deal of swelling around the nose, and sometimes only x-rays can reveal the fracture. If a nose fracture is suspected, ice applied immediately will help to reduce the swelling and thus make diagnosis and treatment easier. If there appears to be a deformity or excessive bleeding, a doctor should be called, as the nose may need to be reset. The manipulation and realignment may be conducted with only local anesthetic, except for in extreme cases, when general anesthetic may be necessary.

Prognosis. Most nose fractures heal without complication, but those that are not treated properly may need to be surgically rebroken and reset in order to correct the problem. If the nose does not heal in proper alignment, it may eventually cause breathing problems or a susceptibility to sinus infections. *See also* FRACTURE.

Nosebleed

Nosebleed

Also known as epistaxis

Bleeding from inside the nose.

Nosebleeds can occur frequently and without apparent injury. They are usually not an indication of a serious problem, but in rare cases may indicate that there is an urgent disorder.

Causes. Nosebleeds are more likely to occur in the dry winter months when the humidity is low and when mucous membranes are dry and brittle, cracked or split. Persistent nosebleeds may result from poor blood clotting or a blood disease such as hemophilia.

Nosebleeds frequently result from minor trauma, such as a blow or when a child puts a finger or an object in his or her nose and breaks the fragile blood vessels. Such nosebleeds generally occur in the forward part of the nasal passages and can be treated at home. Nosebleeds originating deeper in the nasal passages can bleed "backwards" down the throat. They are, as a consequence, more serious.

When a person is taking a blood thinning medication, such as coumadin or heparin, or regular doses of aspirin, the blood may not clot properly. To stop a nosebleed, a doctor may apply a blood clotting agent to the bleeding area or apply cauterization. Packing the bleeding nostril with gauze or sponge will generally control the bleeding, but should only be done by trained medical personnel.
See also BLEEDING, TREATMENT OF.

Nosebleed. To treat a nosebleed, sit down and lean forward slightly (top). Pinch the nostrils closed and breathe through the mouth (bottom) until the bleeding has stopped.

TREATING NOSEBLEEDS AT HOME
A person with a nosebleed should remain calm and sit with his or her head tilted forward slightly (to prevent the blood from draining back into the throat), breathing from the mouth. If there is nothing caught in the nostrils, they should be held shut, and a cold compress should be applied for five or ten minutes. If there is something caught in the nostril, the clear nostril should be pinched shut, and the person should breathe in through his or her mouth and blow out gently through the nose. Once the obstructing object has been removed, pressure and a cold compress should be applied to the area. If the bleeding continues for more than half an hour, medical attention should be sought.

Operating Room

Numbness

Lack of sensation in part of the body due to interference with the transmission of nerve impulses along the sensory serves.

Numbness is manifested as either a loss of sensation or feeling, or a burning or tingling sensation in the body. Tingling is an indication of impairment or blockage of the nerves in the area. Unlike numbness, tingling suggests the nerve is not completely dead or severed, but rather just injured or temporarily blocked due to pressure. Numbness can also occur harmlessly, such as when a person's foot "falls asleep" because it was in a position that temporarily restricted blood flow.

Causes. The main causes for numbness are local injury to the nerves under the skin because of:
- lack of blood supply to the area;
- pressure on the nerves, caused by a herniated disk, tumor, or abscess;
- diabetes or other chemical abnormalities;
- vitamin B_{12} deficiency;
- hypothyroidism;
- carpal tunnel syndrome;
- stroke;
- multiple sclerosis because of damage to the nerve pathways in the central nervous system; or
- long term radiation or chemotherapy drugs.

Treatment. A physician can determine the area of sensory impairment and the extent of nerve damage. The treatment corresponds to the extent and site of damage. *See also* COMA *and* STROKE.

Operating Room

A specially designed and equipped hospital room in which physicians perform surgical procedures on patients.

An operating room is designed to provide optimal conditions for surgeons to operate efficiently without bacterial contamination of themselves or the patients.

Basic elements of the operating room include power supply, lighting, ventilation, and water supply. The power supply is conventional electricity with emergency generator back-up, including some use of

Pain Relief

hydraulics and air compressors. The overall bright and diffuse lighting is supplemented by specific operating lamps to spotlight the operation site. A strong ventilation system provides a consistent supply of clean, filtered air to the operating room. There is a nearby stainless steel sink and water supply at which surgeons, assistants, and nurses can "scrub down" with bactericidal soaps and sterile brushes.

The focal point of the room is the operating table on which the patient is positioned. The instrument table (which holds sterile scalpels, dissectors, clamps, forceps, detractors, and other surgical tools) is located next to the scrub nurse, who dispenses the instruments to the chief surgeon. A circulating nurse provides additional assistance. A monitor screen shows the patient's vital signs (heartbeat, blood pressure, and brain waves), and a viewing screen or light box permits quick glances at x-rays and CAT or MRI scans. Two clocks show the actual time and the elapsed time of the operation, respectively.

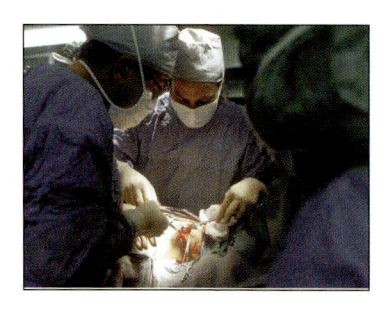

Breast Biopsy. An operating room is specially designed and equipped to facilitate surgical procedures. Here, a surgeon is performing a breast biopsy on a woman.

The anesthesiologist, at the head of the table, carefully monitors the patient's vital signs and controls the amount of anesthetic and oxygen as needed. An intravenous drip to transfuse blood or other fluid by catheter is often necessary.

Transplants, heart bypasses, and brain surgery require additional, highly specialized equipment. Computers, robotics, and television screens are increasingly being used in operating rooms. *See also* SURGERY.

Pain Relief

Treatment of pain, especially with medication.

Pain relievers can be divided into various categories. Analgesics and anti-inflammatory drugs are sold over-the-counter; these include medications such as aspirin, ibuprofen, and acetaminophen. They are all safe for the short-term relief of minor aches and pains; most pain relievers should not be taken for more than ten days.

Plants, Poisonous

Narcotic Analgesics are opium-based. These are reserved for the treatment of intense pain. A narcotic drug is not used to treat chronic pain caused by cancer, head injury, or liver damage. Opiate-related compounds such as codeine, propoxyphene (Darvon), morphine, and meperidine (Demerol) are much stronger than aspirin. These, like all drugs, have a potential for abuse, and may have unpleasant or harmful side effects. They should never be combined with other medicines or alcohol.

Certain antidepressants as well as antiepileptic drugs are used to treat several particularly severe pain conditions, notably the pain arising from shingles and facial neuralgias like tic douloureux. Researchers think that the antidepressant works because it increases the supply of the neurotransmitter, serotonin. A decrease in the amount of serotonin in the body is connected with depression.

Antiepileptic drugs have successfully been used to treat tic douloureux, a condition marked by attacks of facial pain that affects older adults, by restoring the proper balance of incoming and outgoing nerve signals. Tic and other facial pains or neuralgias are often the result of injury to facial nerves when normal transmission of messages to and from the brain is hindered; this causes the nervous system to become hypersensitive. Antiepileptic drugs are effective in calming the excessive brain discharges associated with epileptic seizures.

Some non-drug treatments include: massage, ice packs, or heating pads as these may relieve localized pain that is associated with injury, muscle spasm, or inflammation. *See also* ABDOMINAL PAIN; BANDAGE; BITES; BLEEDING, TREATMENT OF; *and* COMPRESS.

Plants, Poisonous

Plants that become harmful through ingestion or mere contact.

Many plants that are kept in the home or in the garden are toxic. These should be avoided by households with small children or pets. All plants in the home and garden should be identified.

Various popular house plants are poisonous, affecting the stomach, intestines, lungs or heart, However, the toxic parts of plants and their toxicity vary widely among different species. Jewelry and other ornaments made from seeds of poisonous plants like castor beans and rosary peas can be extremely toxic if chewed.

If someone has eaten part of a plant that is or may be poisonous,

Poison

ALERT   ALERT   ALERT

POISONOUS HOUSEHOLD PLANTS

Some plants that people bring into their homes for decoration and color have poisonous properties. If there are small children in the house, these plants should either be removed or kept in a high place—out of reach of small hands. Common poisonous plants include, but are not limited to:

oleander	philodendron	daffodils
hyacinths	narcissus	lily-of-the-valley
lantana	poinsettia	English ivy
jimsonweed	azaleas	rhododendrons
Devil's ivy	caladium	holly
dieffenbachia or dumbcane	may apple	mistletoe
morning glory	schefflera or umbrella tree	iris
yew	peace lily	mountain laurel

call a poison control center immediately. If symptoms are present, such as difficulty breathing, mouth or throat pain, signs of gastrointestinal distress, hallucinations, convulsions, or unconsciousness, first call EMS. If possible, have a sample of the plant that was ingested on hand. *See also* POISONING.

Poison

Any substance that impairs the body's ability to function normally.

All non-food matter is potentially poisonous in large enough doses. Potentially poisonous items include those things that are known for toxicity, such as household cleansers and pesticides, and less obvious threats such as certain plants, medications, vitamins, and alcohol.

All potentially toxic substances, including house plants, should be stored where children do not have access to them. They should be kept in their original packaging so that, should poisoning occur, the toxin can be readily identified. In the case of poisoning, a local poison control center can give first-aid advice. Treatment varies depending on the nature of the poison; an action, such as inducing vomiting, that may be helpful in some cases may be vitally harmful in others. *See also* POISONING.

Poison Ivy, Oak, & Sumac

Poison Ivy, Oak, & Sumac

Three plants that cause contact dermatitis, or an itchy rash, due to an allergic reaction to their oils.

In and of themselves, these three plants are relatively harmless, however, more than 50 percent of all people are allergic to the oils that they produce. These oils produce a rash that usually takes the form of patches or streaks spread out across the skin that has been exposed. A rash may take a matter of some time to appear, or be recognized, so affected areas are often unknowingly scratched, spreading the oils and the rash all over the body. The longest time a dermatitis may take to become evident is a day or two. About a week later, the rash is at its worst, and may require hospitalization for a short period of time.

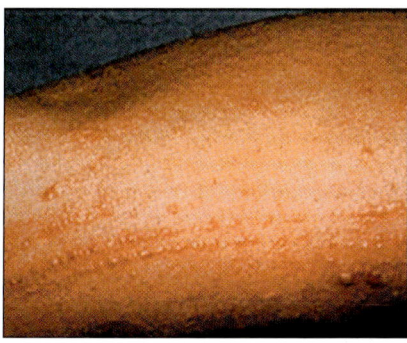

Poisonous Plants. Left, poison sumac a relatively harmless plant that produces an oil that most people are allergic to. The allergy is manifested in a red rash, right, on the area of the body that has been affected.

Poison ivy is found all over the continental United States; poison oak is generally indigenous to the west coast, and poison sumac tends to grow around the Mississippi river bed. Symptoms for all three are nearly indistinguishable.

Treatment. First scrub the exposed skin with soap and water to remove any remaining oils; wash hands and nails frequently because itching spreads the rash. Do not scratch the rash. Calamine lotion and commercial hydrocortisone creams may relieve itching. If the rash is severe, covering most of the body or areas around the eyes or genitals, consult a doctor. *See also* POISONOUS PLANTS.

Poisoning

Poisoning

The introduction of a poisonous substance into the body.

Poisoning results from any of a variety of substances entering the body. These substances may enter the body through various means, such as inhalation, skin absorption (merely by touching the substance), ingestion, or injection.

Almost 95 percent of poisoning deaths occur in adults, a large number of whom poison themselves or overdose intentionally. However, over half of all poisoning cases, involve small children, usually under the age of six. If poisoning is suspected, immediately call for emergency medical help. A regional poison control center can provide vital information.

Indications that poisoning has occurred, in both children and adults, may include burns around the mouth and on clothing, chemical stains in the area near the victim, chemical odor on the victim's breath or open medicine bottles. Symptoms may include vomiting, convulsions, breathing difficulties, and unconsciousness.

If poisoning is suspected, the following procedures are recommended:

- Call for emergency medical help, and consult and a poison control center. The number of your poison control center should be kept by the telephone at all times. The poison control center will provide you with detailed first aid instructions.

- If the poisonous substance is known, check for any first aid instructions written on the label. Follow these instructions if the poison control center cannot be reached quickly.

- Never induce vomiting unless instructed by a poison control center or a physician. If so instructed, vomiting may be induced with syrup of ipecac.

- Carefully remove any clothing that may have poison on it and flush affected eyes and skin with cool or lukewarm water.

See also BANDAGE; COMA; JELLYFISH STINGS; POISON; POISON IVY, OAK, & SUMAC; SNAKEBITES; SPIDER BITES; SCORPION STINGS; *and* STINGS.

Punchdrunk

A condition in which the patient exhibits uncoordinated movement, speech or disorientation.

Punchdrunk is characterized by slurred speech, an impaired ability to concentrate, and awkward, clumsy movements. While the condition is unrelated to alcohol consumption, it is often compared to a state of drunkenness. It is caused by repeated brain injury or concussions in which there is a loss of consciousness. The name is indicative of the fact that there is a high incidence among boxers. *See also* CONCUSSION.

Rabies

Also known as hydrophobia

A viral infection, transmitted from many animals to humans, which attacks the central nervous system (the brain and spinal cord).

The virus that causes rabies is transmitted to humans from the saliva of infected animals, usually by a bite but also by contamination of an open cut. Worldwide, there are an estimated 15,000 cases of human rabies each year. Less than five cases are reported in the United States annually. Raccoons, bats, foxes, skunks, dogs, and cats are all potential sources of the virus. The virus remains dormant for a period of from ten days to as long as a year. This incubation period gives the victim plenty of time to get a preventive vaccination after a bite. The incubation period will be shortest if the bite is on the head or neck.

Symptoms. The virus that causes rabies travels up the spinal column to the brain and then back down to the salivary glands. Symptoms include pain at the site of infection, followed by numbness or tingling. There is also mental depression and restlessness, changing to irritability and uncontrollable excitement. In advanced stages of the disease, the patient will start to produce copious quantities of saliva. There may be spasms in the throat, which make swallowing extremely painful.

Treatment. Once the symptoms appear, the rabies vaccination will have no effect. Treatment should begin before any symptoms appear. The disease was once considered to be 100 percent fatal, but there have been some survivors when the lung, heart, and brain symptoms were treated promptly. Death is usually caused by asphyxiation due to blocked air passages or from convulsions, exhaustion, or paralysis.

Radiation Sickness

Prevention. People in professions that put them at high risk for contracting rabies (veterinarians and laboratory workers who handle animals) should be vaccinated, as should people who are traveling to poorer countries overseas. Since the efficacy of the rabies vaccine declines over time, revaccination is needed every two years. *See* BITES.

AFTER A BITE
- *Even if the victim has been vaccinated, clean a bite wound as quickly as possible with soap and water. Deep punctures should be flushed with soapy water.*
- *Get the victim to an emergency room where he or she can be inoculated with rabies immunoglobulin and injected with rabies vaccine.*
- *Report the bite to animal control authorities. Usually the animal will be killed to determine if it has rabies; however, a veterinarian may confine the animal for ten days and keep it under observation. If it does not develop symptoms of rabies, the veterinarian may conclude that it did not have the disease at the time of the bite.*

Radiation Sickness

An illness caused by exposure to radiation.

Radiation sickness is caused by radiation poisoning. The condition may be acute or chronic, and may occur as a result of cumulative exposure to small doses of radiation, undue exposure to solar radiation, or exposure to a nuclear explosion or other single large dose of radiation.

Symptoms. The symptoms of radiation sickness vary from mild and temporary to severe, depending on the type of radiation, the dose, and the rate at which exposure was experienced. The symptoms include weakness, loss of appetite, vomiting, diarrhea, a tendency to bleed, increased susceptibility to infection, and increased risk of cancer. Radiation sickness can be fatal.

Treatment. If exposure to radiation occurs, emergency medical assistance is needed immediately. All infected clothes and skin should be washed vigorously with water and a special solution, if available.

It is always advisable to avoid unnecessary exposure to radiation. When exposed to x-rays, individuals should wear shields over the parts of the body not being treated or studied.

Rape

Sexual intercourse that is forced on a nonconsenting individual.

In the United States, a rape is reported every six to seven minutes. In addition, it is estimated that 80 to 90 percent of rapes go unreported. Almost half of all rapists are between the ages of 15 and 25. These individuals often feel hatred or violent emotions towards their victims, and may also feel insecure about their own sexual performance. Rape is most often perpetrated by a male upon a female, but many cases of rape in which the woman is the rapist have also been reported. Rape may also occur between individuals of the same sex.

Incidence. The highest incidence of rape is found among women between the ages of ten and 19. However, the incidence of rape among victims over the age of 65 has increased by 800 percent over the last 15 years.

Effects. Emotional reactions to rape vary among victims. These may include withdrawal, crying, hostility, anxiety, or inappropriate laughter. Physical symptoms other than from the rape itself may also be present, as physical abuse of the victim often occurs along with rape.

Treatment. In general, treatment of rape victims focuses on the emotional effects of the rape on the victim, while attempting to obtain enough physical evidence to verify the rape and prosecute the offender. The potential of pregnancy or sexually transmitted diseases must also be addressed. The victim may be referred to a rape crisis center to receive support from other victims and psychotherapy. *See also* NERVOUS BREAKDOWN *and* MORNING AFTER PILL.

Recovery Position

First aid position designed to allow free breathing.

If a person has been in an accident or is unconscious but shows no obvious injury, it is safest to put the individual in the recovery position until emergency medical assistance arrives.

The recovery position is designed to allow free breathing and vomiting without clogging air passages. It assists in blood circulation and allows the victim to rest comfortably. A victim suspected to have suffered head, neck, or spinal injury should never be moved. The recovery position should not be utilized, and individuals should wait until medical personnel arrive.

Recovery Position

Placing the Victim in the Recovery Position. Assuming the victim is on his or her back, the caregiver should kneel beside the body, turning the victim's face toward the caregiver. The victim's head should be tilted back to open the airway, and false teeth or any other obstructions should be removed from the mouth. The arm of the victim that is closest to the caregiver should be placed by the victim's

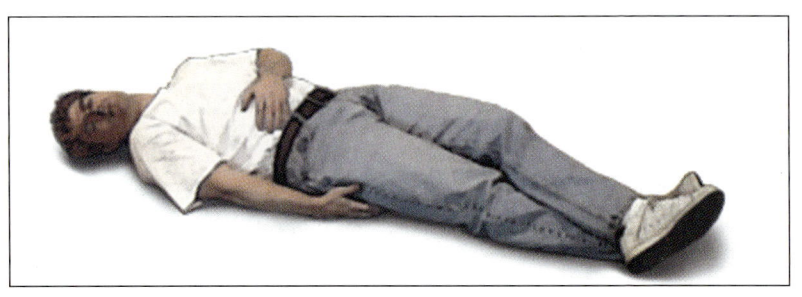

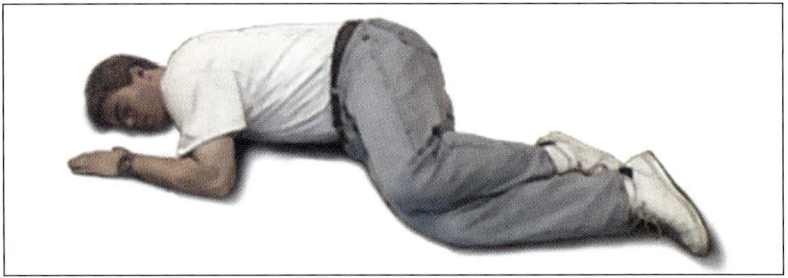

Recovery Position. The photos above show the correct recovery position an injured person should be placed in to allow free breathing, blood circulation, and a comfortable rest until medical assistance arrives.

side and tucked under the buttock. The other arm should lay across the victim's chest. The far leg is then lifted over the near leg so that the legs cross at the ankle. Supporting the head and grasping the clothing at the hip, the victim should be rolled toward the caregiver until the individual is on his or her stomach. However, the head should be controlled so that the face is clear of foreign objects and turned in the same direction as the body. The near arm and leg should be adjusted so that they form a right angle to the body, preventing the victim from rolling onto his or her face. Lastly, the far arm and leg should be adjusted so that they are straight and parallel to the body. *See also* EMERGENCY FIRST STEPS.

Running Injuries

Rib, Fractured

A break in one or more of the ribs.

The most common causes of a fractured rib are a direct blow or fall. Rib fractures are extremely painful, with swelling and tenderness in the area of the break.

Most rib fractures are clean breaks, where the ends of the broken bone remain in alignment and can heal on their own without complications. Patients may simply be given painkillers and instructed to hold the injured side when breathing deeply. If the bone end splinters or is displaced, there is a chance that it can pierce a lung or the spleen. These cases may require an operation in which the ribs are wired into place to avoid damage to the organs. *See also* FRACTURE *and* SHOCK.

Running Injuries

Injuries commonly associated with jogging and running as regular exercise.

Enormous pressure is placed on feet and legs during running. The type and location of the resulting pain can identify the injury. Often, such injuries are preventable.

TYPES

Stress Fractures. The metatarsal bones of the foot are particularly vulnerable to stress fractures, since they take the brunt of the pressure during running. These fractures can be so fine that they are not visible in x-rays, but they can produce pain in the front of the foot.

> ### PREVENTING RUNNING INJURIES
>
> *To prevent running injuries, runners should wear footwear that complements the unique characteristics of their feet (flatfoot or inward-tilting ankles, for example). Footwear should be snug and provide adequate support and stability. Shoes should be replaced before the insole cushioning becomes exceedingly worn down. Long periods of running on an uneven surface increases stress on the ankles and knees. A proper running regimen includes warm-up exercises, preparing the body for strenuous activity. Both beginning and advanced runners should keep their routine and distance within reasonable limits.*

Cornell Illustrated—Emergency Medicine & First Aid Guide • 181

Running Injuries

Shin splints is a term used to refer to damage to the muscles that lie parallel to the shin (tibia). These muscles are located in the front and inner leg.

Tendonitis is a tear or inflammation in one of the tendons that control the movement of joints. The tendons most vulnerable to tendonitis are those that run from the calf to the back of the heel and those that run diagonally across the back of the knees.

Runner's knee is pain caused by the rubbing of the kneecap (patella) against the end of the thigh bone.

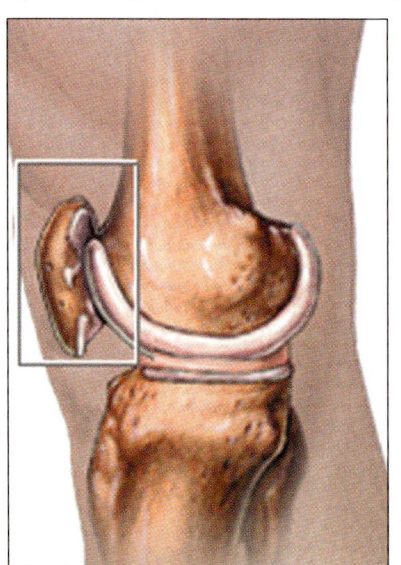

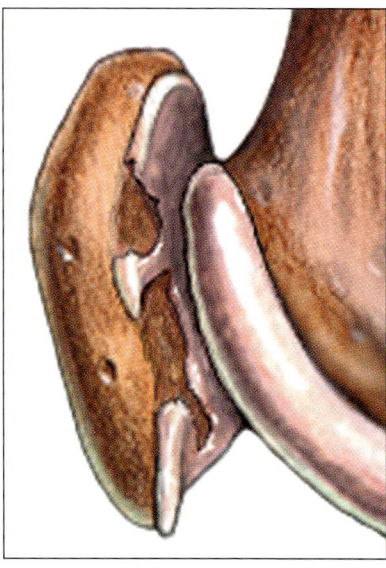

Runner's Knee. The diagrams above show the rubbing of the kneecap (patella) against the end of the thigh bone. The friction caused by these bones can be very painful.

TREATMENT

Most running injuries will heal without treatment if the patient stops running for a given period of time, often weeks. If the patient does not stop running, the pain may subside quickly at first but will become intense and unremitting with time, signalling worsening of the condition. *See also* SPORTS INJURIES.

Seizure

Scorpion Stings

Potentially venomous stings from the tail of a scorpion.

Scorpions are arthropods whose venom is used to capture prey and for self-defense. They are most active at night in warm weather, are not aggressive, and sting only when threatened. Their stings can range from the transiently painful, much like a bee or wasp sting, to the potentially deadly.

Of all of the species of scorpion native to the United States, only one is considered life-threatening. The bark scorpion (*Centruroides exilicauda*), which is between one-half and an inch-and-a-half in size, is found mainly in Arizona and adjacent areas. The venom of this species can cause severe swelling and pain at the sting site, numbness, breathing difficulties, muscle twitching, and convulsions. Death rarely occurs, however, and an antivenin does exist.

In most cases, scorpion stings cause localized pain, hypersensitivity, numbness, and tingling; bites to healthy adults can be treated at home by applying ice packs and elevating the sting area to heart level. However, a poison control center should be contacted in any case where a scorpion sting is suspected. Children, the elderly, and those with respiratory problems are most at risk. *See also* POISONING.

Seizure

Repeated and abnormal electrical discharges from the brain that results in a lack of body control.

A seizure or convulsion can be caused by any event that disturbs the brain's electrical activity. Patients who experience seizures are characterized as suffering from a form of epilepsy.

Cause. Seizures can be the result of a severe head injury, brain damage at birth, a stroke, an infection, a tumor in the brain, or alcohol withdrawal. Seizures may consist of abnormal electrical activity in a small confined area of the brain, or it can spread to other parts of the brain. A very small percentage of patients with seizures experience sensations (auras) prior to the onset of a seizure.

Symptoms. Neuromuscular signs and symptoms of a seizure include tingling of the skin, uncontrollable twitching of the face or limbs, spasms, and tremors. Other potential signs and symptoms include hal-

Seizure, Febrile

lucinations, phobias, or a sense of deja vú, which is a feeling of familiarity. Abnormal electrical activity spread throughout the brain, produces a generalized seizure, referred to as grand mal. A grand mal seizure which continues for more than a few minutes is referred to as "status epilepticus." In these cases, consciousness is typically lost.

Treatment. It is very important that anyone suffering a seizure receive medical help immediately. The most important thing to do for any seizure victim is to move any dangerous objects that could potentially strike him or her away from the patient to prevent them from injuring themselves. Under no circumstances should any object be placed in the victim's mouth. It may obstruct the airway, or cause injury. *See also* CHOKING.

Seizure, Febrile

Jerking of the limbs accompanied by loss of consciousness, occurring mainly in children.

A febrile seizure usually occurs in young children between the ages of three months and five years. This type of seizure tends to run in families. It is estimated that as many as five percent of all children will experience a febrile seizure. The seizures are short in duration and usually occur only once.

Cause and Symptoms. Febrile seizures may be the result of abnormal electrical activity in the brain, brought on by a high fever. This type of seizure generally occurs early on in the course of the fever. Febrile seizures are usually not the result of a brain abnormality. They frequently stem from the high fevers that accompany acute infectious diseases such as tonsillitis (infection of the tonsils) or otitis media (middle ear infection). The seizures include a short period (lasting from a few seconds to up to a few minutes) of wrenching and jerking movements. The child may be exhausted upon regaining consciousness. Even though a particular child has experienced one febrile seizure, the child will not necessarily experience a febrile seizure every time he or she has a fever. However, children who have febrile seizures regularly have a greater chance of developing epilepsy in the future.

Treatment. It is very important to move any dangerous objects out of reach of a child who is having a febrile seizure. If the seizure continues for longer than five minutes, emergency medical attention

Septic Shock

should be sought. In all cases, a doctor should be consulted. Single seizures are generally not treated with anticonvulsant drugs.

Prevention. The most effective method of preventing febrile seizures is to treat the high fever with acetaminophen or ibuprofen, given every four hours. It is especially important not to give aspirin to a child who may have a viral infection, due to the risk of developing Reye's syndrome, which can be fatal. *See also* SHOCK.

Septic Shock

> Condition in which the blood pressure drops precipitously as a result of septicemia (the infection of the blood with bacteria) or toxemia (the presence of the toxins produced by bacteria in the blood).

Septicemia is an infection of the blood by bacteria that are introduced into the bloodstream during surgery of the intestines, by insertion of a contaminated needle, after a serious burn, from bedsores, from a wound, or through other means. The bacteria produce toxins in the blood, causing toxemia, and a sudden drop in blood pressure, called septic shock, is the body's response to these toxins.

INCIDENCE

Septic shock is most common in infants, the elderly, and people with compromised immune systems.

SYMPTOMS

In a patient with septic shock, the blood vessels dilate and the blood pressure falls suddenly. The heart rate goes up in an effort to compensate for the drop in blood pressure, but flow to the organs is reduced, which is particularly dangerous for the brain and the kidneys.

Early symptoms of septic shock include shaking, shivering, chills, fever, and flushed skin tones. Breathing also tends to become rapid and shallow. Even with medical intervention, septic shock is an extremely serious condition. Almost 50 percent of people who experience septic shock do not survive.

TREATMENT

Treatment for septic shock must be provided promptly. The patient is moved to an intensive care unit where fluids are injected, or administered through and I.V., in order to increase blood pressure. Drugs to constrict the blood vessels may also be administered. Antibiotics will be prescribed to fight the infection. If the lungs are affected, the patient may be put on a ventilator. *See also* SHOCK.

Shock

Shock

Dangerous drop in blood pressure that results in inadequate flow to the tissues of the body.

Although sometimes applied to states of mental or emotional distress, medical shock is the result of decreased blood flow to the brain and vital organs. Shock is a secondary effect of severe injury or illness.

ALERT ALERT ALERT
THE SHOCK POSITION
Lay the person on his or her back and cover him or her with a blanket to keep warm. Elevate the legs slightly (but not if the person has had a venomous bite). If there is absolutely no possibility of a neck injury, turn the head to the side so that vomiting will not block air passages. Do not offer beverages or any other food. Loosen clothing that may inhibit breathing. Seek professional medical help immediately.

Causes. Shock may be caused by massive blood loss, blood vessel blockage or widening, or the inability of the heart to pump blood. These conditions are produced by heart attack, injury, allergic reaction, bacterial infection, electric shock, poisoning, heat stroke, extensive burns, some metabolic disorders, drug overdose, and spinal cord injury. Shock is life-threatening.

ALERT ALERT ALERT
ANAPHYLACTIC SHOCK
If a person is allergic to food (especially in the case of nuts), he or she may go into anaphylactic shock. Symptoms include swelling of tongue and face, gasping and choking, hives, a weak and rapid pulse, dizziness, nausea, vomiting, and unconsciousness. A serious case of anaphylactic shock can kill within fifteen minutes. People who know that they are sensitive to certain substances will often wear a medical ID bracelet or tag so that the proper treatment can be administered quickly.

Symptoms. In early stages a person may be tired, dizzy upon standing, easily fatigued, nauseated, and thirsty. In later stages the skin pales, and lips and fingernails may show a bluish coloration (cyanosis). The skin is cool and sweaty; the pulse becomes weak and rapid; breathing may be shallow or fast. Blood pressure can be immeasurably low.

Treatment. A person administering first aid should check to see that there has been no damage to the person's neck or spine, and that the individual is breathing. If necessary, cardiopulmonary resuscitation

Shoulder Dislocation

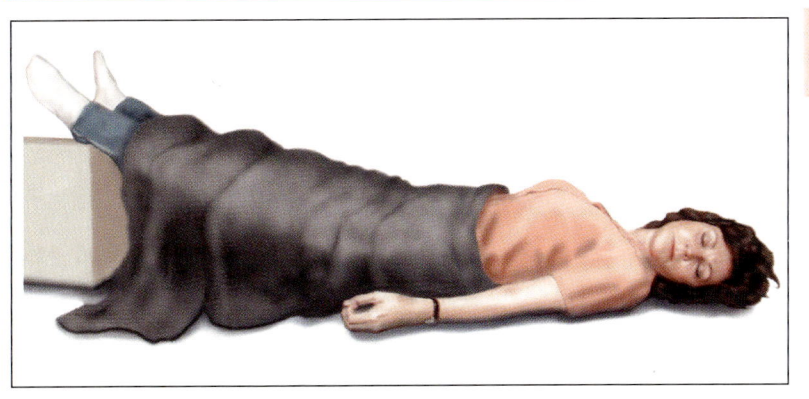

The Shock Position. One of the first steps in many emergency first aid treatments is to put an individual in the shock position, as pictured above. In the shock position, a person's feet should be elevated and the body kept somewhat warm. Only turn the head if there is absolutely no chance that the injury is affecting the head or neck.

(CPR) should be administered; any bleeding that may be evident must be controlled with direct pressure. The patient should be kept in a supine position (the shock position) and kept warm. Medical assistance, from trained professionals, should be alerted as soon as possible. *See also* BANDAGE.

ALERT   ALERT   ALERT

SEPTIC SHOCK

A bacterial invasion of the bloodstream (septicemia and toxemia) can be so severe that a person goes into shock. Only blood tests can reveal the presence of septic shock. In this case, circulation may be preserved until relatively late in the course, and then become severely compromised causing shock. If there is reason to believe a person is suffering from septic shock, he or she should be put in the shock position until emergency medical assistance arrives.

Shoulder Dislocation

Irregular movement of the head of the upper arm bone (humerus) out of the shoulder joint.

The humerus has a round head that rolls into the shoulder joint, giving it a wide range of movement. If the hand takes the weight of the body during a fall, for example, the humerus can be jarred out of place. This

Skin Allergy

is known as an anterior (forward) dislocation, because the head of the humerus slides in front of the joint. Posterior (backward) dislocations, in which the humerus is jarred back behind the joint, are more rare; it would take an extremely sharp direct blow, or violent twisting to send the bone backward. *See also* BANDAGE.

The main symptom of a dislocated shoulder is pain, that is usually made worse by movement. Anterior dislocations are visible to the eye, but posterior ones may not be noticed. X-rays can confirm the diagnosis. Treatment consists of moving the bone back into place, followed by immobilization in a sling during healing. Severe dislocations may also damage surrounding muscles and nerves, which may require further surgery. *See also* FIRST AID.

Skin Allergy

Also known as contact dermatitis

An adverse and marked reaction to irritants or allergens, which cause burning sensations, stinging, itching, or redness of the skin.

Skin allergies are classified as irritant or allergic contact dermatitis. Irritant contact dermatitis is the result of a product irritating the skin. Bath soap, detergents, antiperspirants, cosmetics, moisturizers, and shampoos are the most common causes of allergies. Allergic contact dermatitis is a reaction to a certain ingredient in a product, which may take days to appear. Symptoms include redness, swelling, and clear blisters. Itching is usually a prominent symptom, and it can be difficult to determine if a reaction is allergic or irritant. *See also* ALLERGY.

There are several causes of reactions but fragrances are the most common. Products that are labeled "unscented" may actually contain a fragrance, designed to cover over chemical scents. Products labeled "fragrance-free" or "without perfume" cannot have any fragrances. Preservatives in cosmetics and skin-care products also cause skin allergies. Cosmetics that contain water must also contain a preservative to prevent bacteria and fungi from developing. Many people are also allergic to lanolin, found in cosmetics and skin cleansers. Products that use the term "hypoallergenic" sometimes contain lanolin. *See also* ALLERGEN.

Metals such as nickel, chrome, and cobalt also cause allergies. Costume jewelry made of alloys usually contain these metals. Body-piercing is frequently a cause of allergic reactions. Piercing locations such as the ears, lips, nose, septum, tongue, navel, and genitalia may produce skin reactions. Latex, used in surgical gloves and condoms, is also a common source of allergies for many people. Dermatologists believe that about two of every 1,000 people have severe reactions to chemicals and metals.

To prevent allergic skin reactions, rinse clothes twice after washing. Choose clothes that are pure cotton, and avoid blends. Avoid all perfumes and dyes, and do not use nail polish or hair spray. *See also* BLISTER.

Skull, Fractured

A fracture in any of the bones that make up the skull (cranium).

Eight bones make up the cranium, surrounding and protecting the brain and facial bones. As with other bones, a direct or heavy blow can cause a fracture. The bones of the skull are relatively strong and most fractures are closed; that is, they are clean fractures in which the bones remain beneath the skin, and there is little serious tissue damage. There may be few symptoms, so a person who has suffered any kind of direct blow to the head should have it x-rayed as soon as possible to check for fractures, and, if necessary, she or he will be monitored for complications. Even if the fracture is minor, or if there is no break, there still may be damage to the brain, such as internal bleeding (hemorrhage). A CAT scan can detect these injuries. Otherwise, a closed skull fracture may require little beside rest.

Open fractures, when the skin is broken and bones or blood vessels are damaged, can be much more dangerous and may be life-threatening. These injuries often require surgery, especially if bone fragments have to be removed and tissue repaired. Hemorrhages may need to be drained, or the membrane that covers the skull (meninges) may require repair. As with all open fractures, antibiotics are necessary to prevent infection. *See also* BANDAGE *and* COMA.

Sleep Apnea

Brief interruptions of breathing during sleep.

A person with sleep apnea experiences frequent episodes of breathing pauses, lasting about 10 seconds, that can occur 30 or more times an hour, usually accompanied by snoring. Sleep apnea occurs at all ages and to both sexes, but it appears to be more common in men. Con-

Sleep Apnea

Stributing factors include weight, blood pressure, and obstructions in the nose and throat. Heavy drinking or use of sleeping pills can also play a serious role.

Types. There are two forms of sleep apnea. The less common form, central sleep apnea, occurs when the brain does not send the periodic signals that control breathing. The more common form, obstructive sleep apnea, usually occurs when the tongue and the muscles of the throat relax during sleep, partially blocking the airway. Obstructive sleep apnea also results from enlargement of the tonsils or adenoids.

ALERT   ALERT   ALERT

Sleep Apnea and Children

Sleep apnea also regularly occurs in children aged three to 12, and it is usually caused by enlarged tonsils or adenoids. Some research has found that ethnicity plays a role in the incidence of sleep apnea, as children of African descent are affected two to three times more often than Caucasian children. If a child snores, is restless during sleep, gasps for breath and sleeps with his or her mouth open, apnea may be the cause. Morning headaches, crankiness, and daytime sleepiness are also common in affected children.

In many cases, the interruptions caused by sleep apnea go unnoticed during the night, but the loss of steady sleep shows up during the daytime, in the form of excessive sleepiness, and regular morning headaches. A higher risk of heart disease has been noted in persons with sleep apnea, but it is not clear whether heart disease is associated with the weight issues that increase with the incidence of sleep apnea, or with the condition itself.

Treatment. Treatment for sleep apnea starts with lifestyle changes such as weight loss, reduced alcohol intake, and ending sleeping-pill use. If the condition occurs only when a person sleeps on her or his back, a position-changing device may help.

When lifestyle changes are not effective, continuous positive airway pressure, usually referred to as CPAP, can be used. A person wears a mask over her or his nose, and a blower forces air through the mask into the airway. Some people may undergo surgery to remove tonsils, adenoids, or other tissue that blocks the airway. If sleep apnea is severe enough to pose a major danger to life, it can be relieved by tracheostomy—a surgery in which a small hole is cut in the windpipe. The hole is opened only at night, so that air can enter the respiratory tract without obstruction.

Sling

A type of bandage used to immobilize, support, or elevate an arm.

Slings are often an important part of first aid for fractures, sprains or other injuries in which the arm or hand needs some form of stabilization until help is reached. Slings also are used to elevate arms or hands in emergency situations, as they can help to stop or slow blood flow and reduce attendant swelling. A person may need to keep an arm or hand in a sling throughout the healing process in order to support and immobilize the injured area. Slings are usually made of a triangular bandage, but in emergencies, just about anything will do. *See also* FIRST AID; FRACTURE; *and* SPLINT.

Snakebites

The bite of a snake, which may or may not be venomous.

Only two families of the hundreds of kinds of snakes native to the United States are venomous. The pit vipers—which include copperheads, rattlesnakes, and water moccasins—are characterized by triangular, wedge-shaped heads, small pits under the eyes, and large fangs; consequently, they leave visible bite marks. They are responsible for close to 99 percent of snake-bites in this country. Coral snakes, which are fairly small and thin, have a highly neurotoxic venom that will cause respiratory paralysis. The coral snake's fangs are much smaller than those of pit vipers, and their bites are therefore less obvious. Bites of both types of native venomous snakes can be treated effectively with antivenin. Since antivenin is made with horse serum, people who are sensitive to horse products may experience a severe allergic reaction.

Symptoms of venomous snakebites include weakness, dizziness, nausea, head-ache, difficulty breathing, tissue damage, shock, and tingling lips and tongue.

Treatment. A bite from any snake must be treated as an emergency; since many snakebite victims cannot positively identify the species that bit them, physicians insist that all snakebites receive prompt attention. Bites incurred from nonpoisonous species may cause an allergic reactions in some people. Most frequently, doctors treat venomous snakebites by administering antivenin, an antidote to snake venom.

Spider Bites

S Before medical care arrives, some simple first aid can be applied to the individual who has been bitten. First, wash the area with soap and water. Keep the bite still, and below the heart. Then go to the hospital or call an ambulance. Never treat snakebites with any of the following: ice, ice packs, or any other cooling substance, tourniquets, incisions, or electric shock. Never try to orally suck the venom from the bite. If the victim is unable to reach the hospital within 30 minutes, a bandage (loose enough to slip a finger underneath) may be wrapped two to four inches above the bite. A suction device available in commercial snakebite kits may be used to draw venom from the wound. *See also* VENOMOUS BITES AND STINGS.

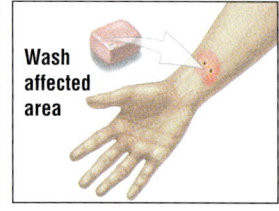

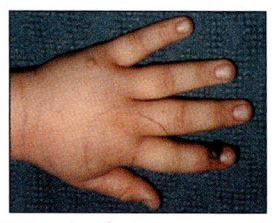

Snakebites. Above left, an illustration of a snake; in the U.S. only pit vipers and coral snakes are venomous, but many different varieties of snakes may bite. The first and most important thing to do when any snake bites is to wash out the wound with warm soapy water, as pictured in the middle. At the right, a finger has been bitten by a snake. Such bites can cause tissue death; this bite has caused swelling and some characteristic tissue death on the first finger.

Prevention. The majority of snakebites that occur could be prevented, since most snakes bite humans only to protect themselves. Give any snake that you pass plenty of space—snakes can often strike the distance of half their length. Do not walk in tall grasses unless you are wearing leather hiking boots and long pants. If you see a snake do not try to catch or kill it—this is how many preventable bites occur. *See also* BITES.

Spider Bites

Potentially venomous bites from spiders.

The bites of most spiders are not particularly dangerous. However, the bites of certain species can be poisonous and deadly.

Bites of some species of tarantulas, black widows (*Lactrodectus mactans*—a black spider identified by a red hourglass-shaped mark on its underside), and brown recluses (*Loxosceles reclusa*—brown spiders with

Splint

Spider Bites. Left, the characteristic black widow spider with the small hourglass marking; they are usually about one and a half inches long. These spiders infest the warmer regions of the United States and much of Mexico. When they are hatched, they are usually white or light yellow—they take on their distinctive color later in life.

a violin-shaped marking on top), in particular, are known for their toxicity. These species thrive in dark places in warm, dry climates. The venom of these spiders causes a localized skin reaction at the site of the bite and a systemic reaction that will include intense pain, nausea, and fever. *See also* TOXIN.

The bite itself may feel like a slight pinprick and thus go unnoticed. However, in a matter of hours, the bite will swell and become tender. Breathing difficulties will also ensue. If these symptoms are exhibited, a health care professional must be sought as soon as possible. An accurate description of the spider will help emergency medical technicians properly treat the bite. If the bite is on a limb, keep it still and apply a snug bandage between the bite and the heart to retard the spread of the venom. Do not elevate the limb—allow it to hang down. Also, apply an ice-filled towel to the bite and wait for help to arrive. *See also* VENOMOUS BITES AND STINGS.

Splint

Appliance used for immobilization of an injured body part.

Splints are often applied as part of first aid for a fracture. A splint is important if a victim needs to be moved from an accident scene, as jarring may cause more damage. A splint may also be applied to keep a body part stable during the healing process. Bones begin to repair themselves rapidly, so the sooner bone ends are reunited the better the chance there is of the fracture healing without any further complications. *See also* SPRAIN.

A splint is usually made from lightweight material (acrylic, polyethylene foam, plaster of Paris, or aluminum). Ambulances or emergency workers carry portable, inflatable splints. In emergencies, a splint may be made from any non-bending material (such as wood, metal, or stiff corrugated cardboard). A person's injured leg can be splinted to the

Sports Injuries

S uninjured one. To apply an emergency splint, gently support the injured limb while sliding the splint material underneath the fractured area. Secure it firmly with tape or string, but make sure it is not so tight as to cut off circulation. Try to move the limb as little as possible while waiting for or traveling to a physician. *See also* FIRST AID *and* FRACTURE.

Sports Injuries

Injuries directly related to participation in a sport or other athletic activity.

Sports injuries fall into two categories. Traumatic, or acute, injuries result from a single instance of extreme trauma (though risk factors make some individuals particularly vulnerable to acute injury). The cause of the injury might be direct force to the body, such as when a football player suffers a concussion from a blow to the head, or it might be more subtle, such as when a runner pulls a hamstring during a race. The second type of sports injury, called an overuse injury, is due to overuse or repetitive strain. Over time, for example, a runner might develop swelling in the knees from the repeated stress of running.

TYPES

Approximately 95 percent of sports injuries involve minor trauma to soft tissue, affecting muscles, ligaments, or tendons. These injuries fall into three categories: contusions, sprains, and strains. A contusion (bruise) is an injury to soft tissue, often produced by a blunt force, such as kick, fall, or blow. It results in pain, swelling, and discoloration in the injured area. Sprains, which account for one-third of all sports injuries, result from a partial or complete tear of a ligament, a strong band of tissue that connects bones to one another and stabilizes joints. A sprain is most often caused by a forced or awkward twisting of the ligament, and usually affects the ankles, knees, or wrists. A strain is an injury to a muscle or tendon. In most cases, strains are caused by overuse of the affected muscle or tendon. Repeated stress on a tendon can cause inflammation of the tendon (tendinitis) or inflammation of the fluid-filled sacs that allow tendons to move easily over bones (bursitis). Tendinitis and bursitis often occur at the same time.

Fractures (bone breaks) account for nearly all of the remaining five percent of sports injuries. They are usually caused by a blow to the bone or a fall. The bones of the arms and legs are the most vulnerable to fracture, while the bones of the spine and skull are the least likely to

Sports Injuries

be affected by sports-related fractures. The bones of the legs and feet are the most susceptible to stress fractures, which occur when muscle strains or contractions make bones bend. Stress fractures are especially common in ballet dancers, in long-distance runners, and in people whose bones are thin.

The most common type of fatal sports injury is a brain injury, or brain concussion. A concussion is a brain injury that can result from even a minor blow to the head.

Concussions can be minor injuries, or they can even be fatal. More than 8 million sports injuries occur each year in the U.S. Young children are most likely to suffer from sports-related injuries. Each year, about 3.2 million children between the ages of 5 and 14 are injured while participating in athletic activities. Annually, more than 775,000 boys and girls under the age of 14 are treated in hospital emergency rooms for sports-related injuries.

SYMPTOMS

Symptoms of sports injuries depend on the type of injury. Soft-tissue injuries commonly cause swelling, pain or tenderness in the area of the injury, discoloration, or weakness in an affected joint. Fractures may cause symptoms including: mild to severe pain, bruising, swelling, paleness, weakness or immobility of the affected bone, or numbness. Concussions can result in disturbed balance, impaired speech, hearing or vision loss, or even loss of consciousness.

TREATMENT

Immediate treatment for almost all acute athletic injuries is rest, ice, compression (pressure on the injured area), and elevation. These four treatments are commonly referred to by the acronym RICE. Rest helps the injured person avoid hemorrhaging or swelling. Ice limits inflammation and reduces the pain. Compression and elevation help reduce edema; that is, the accumulation of fluids in tissue spaces or body cavities. To reduce pain, especially in fracture cases, the injured area is regularly immobilized in a medically appropriate manner using supportive bandaging and splinting techniques.

The best treatment for injuries due to overuse is to abstain from the activity that is causing the problem. Medication or ice might also be used to limit swelling. The injured can often prevent recurrence by identifying the motion or set of motions that is putting physical stress on the affected site. Tennis players, golfers, and others often consult a trained professional to identify the source of an injury.

Sprain

S | Sprain

Tearing or overstretching of ligaments caused by a sudden pull.

The bone ends that meet in a joint are held together by strands of ligaments, tough fibrous tissue that allow the bones to move but prevent the joint from moving too much or in an incorrect way. When that does occur, the ligaments may be torn or overstretched. All of the ligaments in an area may tear, or, in less severe cases, only a few may be damaged. Some of the most common sprains happen to the knee and the ankle, which may twist abnormally while changing direction rapidly (as in a sporting activity) or falling awkwardly. A severe sprain may lead to joint dislocation.

Symptoms of a sprain include pain and swelling. X-rays can ensure there is no fracture. Initial treatment usually consists of ice and elevation of the injured area to reduce pain and swelling. Analgesics or mild painkillers may be prescribed. A cast is usually not necessary, although sometimes a light brace or support may be recommended. Rest is helpful at first, but normal, weight-bearing activity seems to be more successful than keeping weight off the injury during the entire healing process. For the most severe cases, physical therapy may be needed to strengthen or retrain an area where there has been nerve damage. *See also* FRACTURES *and* SLING.

Stings

Lesions caused by stinging insects.

Stings from bees, yellow jackets, wasps, hornets, tarantulas, and fire ants may be painful; but for those who are allergic they can prove extremely dangerous. Since bees' stingers contain venom, remove them by sweeping a stiff, flat object (such as a credit card) against the sting; fingernails also work. If a severe reaction occurs, which may include hives, swelling of the mouth, face and hands, difficulty breathing, confusion, anxiety, nausea, vomiting, or loss of consciousness; immediately call EMS. Do so as well if the victim has been stung many times, as can occur with fire ants and bees. Monitor the victim's airway, breathing, and circulation, and give an antihistamine while waiting for medical personnel.

If stings in the mouth cause swelling and obstruct the airway, call

Stroke

EMS immediately, then administer artificial respiration. Also, those who know that they are allergic to stings should carry around a sting kit for emergencies. These kits include epinephrine or adrenaline to inject immediately after what would otherwise be a possibly fatal sting. If there is no allergic reaction, wash the sting with soap and water, then treat with hydrocortisone cream, calamine lotion, or a paste of baking soda and water. Ice will reduce the swelling. *See also* POISONING.

> **ALERT ALERT ALERT**
> **STINGS FROM MARINE WILDLIFE**
> *Insects such as bees, yellow jackets, hornets (with the most potent sting), and fire ants are not the only creatures that people are regularly stung by. Jellyfish, men-of-war, stone fish, stingrays and a number of other sorts of marine wildlife will also sting unsuspecting bathers. Stings from these animals generally have symptoms similar to those of insects; however, treatment options are more delicate: Never remove stingers from marine wildlife with your bare hands. This could be potentially harmful. Also, do not raise the stung body part; the poison should not be allowed to move throughout the body.*

Strangulation

Twisting or compression of a tube or vessel in the body.

Strangulation disrupts the flow of blood or air, or the ability of an organ to function. Commonly, the term refers to the cessation of air flow through the windpipe by pressure on the neck. Compression of the jugular veins stops the flow of blood to and from the head, leading to a loss of consciousness, brain damage, and finally death. Medically, the term often refers to a pinched or twisted part of the intestine. Accidental strangulation is a risk especially for children. In order to prevent this, avoid toys, furniture, and clothes with dangling strings, cords, or ropes be avoided. *See also* BLEEDING, TREATMENT OF.

Stroke

A disruption in brain function caused by a sudden obstruction or the rupture of an artery leading to the brain.

A brief interruption of the flow of blood to any part of the brain has an immediate effect on the functions controlled by that region; an inter-

Stroke

ruption that lasts as few as four minutes can cause brain cell death. Until recently, researchers believed that new brain cells are not produced after maturity, so the damage caused by a stroke was believed to be permanent. However, about a third of all strokes are fatal.

Strokes are identified by the nature of the cause of the blood vessel blockage. A hemorrhagic stroke results from rupture of a blood vessel in or near the brain. Ischemic strokes can be classified as those caused by a thrombus, a clot that has formed on the wall of an artery, and those caused by an embolism, a clot that has traveled to the brain from elsewhere in the body. Cerebral thrombosis causes about half of all strokes, and cerebral embolism causes about a quarter of them.

Symptoms. The symptoms of a stroke depend on its cause and the part of the brain that is damaged; however, there are features common to all strokes. The major symptoms of a stroke include: a sudden feeling of weakness or numbness in the face or an arm or leg on one side of the body; a sudden loss of speech abilities, feeling, or vision in one or both eyes; fainting, near-fainting or light headedness; confusion; a severe headache; sudden loss of either short-term or long-term memory; and unexplained dizziness. *See also* COMA.

In the case of a stroke caused by cerebral thrombosis, the symptoms occur gradually, sometimes fading and progressing over several days. The symptoms of a stroke caused by an embolism usually come on quickly. A stroke caused by a subarachnoid hemorrhage is signaled by the sudden onset of a headache, with nausea, vomiting, and confusion; it may also be accompanied by seizures. These symptoms require an immediate call for medical help, since permanent brain damage can be prevented or reduced if treatment begins quickly.

Treatment. If a stroke patient is unconscious, steps must be taken to maintain breathing. For an ischemic stroke, anticoagulant medications can be given, not so much to dissolve the clot causing the stroke but to prevent the formation of new clots. The clot-dissolving medication—tissue plasminogen activator (tPA)—has been shown to limit brain damage if it is infused within the first hours after a it occurs. The treatments aimed at ischemic stroke cannot be used for hemorrhagic strokes, since the need in those cases is to limit the amount of bleeding. Surgery may be done in some cases of hemorrhagic stroke to repair the damaged blood vessel that is causing the bleeding.

Over the long term, treatment is aimed at physical rehabilitation and the prevention of future strokes. After the acute phase of treatment, rehabilitation can include several types of therapy, designed around individual cases and carried out for prolonged periods of time.

Strychnine Poisoning

Poisoning from the toxic alkaloid strychnine.

Strychnine has been used as a rodenticide for hundreds of years. It causes violent convulsions shortly following ingestion, due to the extreme stimulation of the central nervous system, particularly the spinal cord. Death can result not from these convulsions, but from the paralysis of the brain's central respiratory center.

Strychnine can be fatal if ingested, inhaled, or absorbed through the skin. Exposure to lesser amounts can cause anxiety or restlessness, cramps, stiffness, or twitching. It may also cause kidney damage.

If you suspect that someone you know has been exposed to strychnine, immediately call EMS. If possible, keep her or him in a dark and quiet place until help arrives—stimuli such as loud noises, abrupt movements, and bright lights can bring on seizures. Inducing vomiting is dangerous because convulsions may cause the victim to aspirate and choke. *See also* CHOKING.

While no longer frequently used to control vermin, strychnine may still be found in quite a few households. All pesticides should be used with extreme caution, and if possible, particularly when there are children or pets in the home, use alternative methods of vermin control. *See also* POISONING; POISON; *and* SEIZURE.

Sucking Wound

Wound that penetrates the lung, causing breathlessness and partial collapse of the organ.

A sucking wound leads to the collapse of a lung on the injured side. Occasionally, the injury will cause the lung contents to shift, leading to a partial collapse of the other lung as well. Respiration is not possible if the lung has collapsed and blood cannot be oxygenated. For emergency first aid, a sealing bandage made of any air-proof material (preferably plastic) should be applied to the wound so that air does not enter during the victim's respiration. The dressing must be tightly sealed until professional help arrives. *See also* SHOCK.

Suffocation

S Suffocation

Obstruction of the flow of air into the lungs.

Suffocation can be caused by an obstruction anywhere in the major airways leading to the lungs—the nose and mouth, the pharynx or larynx, or the main airway (trachea) to the lungs; or by noxious gases, such as carbon monoxide, that inhibit the function of the lungs. Unattended to, suffocation can be fatal within minutes. Treatment starts with removal of whatever is blocking respiration—taking a foreign object out of the body or moving the person into open air. Artificial respiration may be necessary to restore normal breathing. Infants are especially at risk of suffocation during sleeping as the result of bedding, pillows, or bed-sharing with parents. Children are at possible risk of strangulation from clothing, scarves, and mittens. Parents should inspect all beds, clothing, and toys to ensure against such accidents.

Suicide

Act of intentionally taking one's own life.

Suicide is the eighth leading cause of death in the United States, resulting in over 30,500 fatalities a year. More Americans have died over the last five years as a result of suicide than from AIDS, and over five million Americans have attempted to kill themselves at least once. Notably, suicide is the third leading cause of death among adolescents and young adults, and the elderly have the highest suicide rates. Suicide can be prevented, if warning signs are identified and treated.

Many people experience periods when life's problems seem overwhelming. During those phases, a person might feel depressed, use drugs or alcohol, and have fleeting thoughts of taking his or her own life. People are at a higher risk of suicide throughout periods of significant change, adolescence, after a break-up, when failing to achieve a cherished goal, or when seriously ill. Those suffering from depression or psychosis are at the highest risk. Although suicide can be based on a sudden impulse, it usually involves energy and planning. As a result, ironically, the riskiest time for a potential suicide is when one's depression is beginning to subside.

How to Help. Threats of suicide and warning signs should be taken seriously. Whether or not a person is at a high risk for suicide at the

Suicide

time he or she exhibits the warning signs, the risk can easily increase if there is no treatment. Do not be afraid to address the issue directly by asking, "Are you feeling so badly that you are thinking of suicide?" Contrary to popular belief, mentioning suicide does not give a person the idea to do it; it helps to get the issue out in the open and allows it to be dealt with. The risk for suicide is increased if the person has thought about how he or she would carry out the plan and if a time has been set to commit suicide. People who exhibit this type of planning should be taken for mental health assessment.

Depression can be treated and the risk for suicide lessened. A friend or family member can be helpful to someone suffering from depression simply by listening attentively and openly to that person. When someone you care about is depressed, the natural inclination may be to cheer the person up, to deny that the situation is really so bad, or to give advice. In all of these cases, what the sufferer will hear is a negation of feelings and a lack of faith in the individual's ability to make a decision. Allowing the person to express the feelings associated with depression is important and does not mean that you will encourage harm or that you agree with the individual; rather it allows the sufferer to feel soothed and understood. However, such a person should have treatment, which can include psychotherapy and/or medication. Such treatments are very effective and will decrease suffering and suicide risk.

Professional Care. Anyone exhibiting the warning signs below should be seen by a physician, who will most likely offer a referral for treatment by a psychiatrist.

ALERT ALERT ALERT

WARNING SIGNS

The following are a list of warning signs a person may exhibit if he or she is contemplating suicide:
- *Behavior that is sad, withdrawn, anxious, exhausted, apathetic, and indecisive;*
- *Difficulty concentrating on school or work;*
- *Changes in sleep patterns, sleeping excessively or suffering from insomnia or nightmares;*
- *Changes in eating habits;*
- *Loss of interest in friends, sex, or any activity that was previously enjoyed;*
- *Feeling out of control, like one is "going crazy";*
- *Statements of helplessness, hopelessness or worthlessness;*
- *Substance abuse problems;*
- *Recent losses including death, divorce, broken relationships, etc.;*
- *Giving away important possessions;*
- *Expression of a wish for it to be "all over" or verbally expressing a desire for death.*

Swallowing Difficulties

Inability to swallow normally.

Swallowing is the action that brings food or liquid from the mouth into the esophagus, then to the stomach. Food is broken down by chewing and by enzymes in saliva. The tongue pushes the food towards the back of the mouth, where muscles in the palate bring it into the pharynx. Then a series of reflexes sends the food from the pharynx into the esophagus. Therefore, conditions that affect any of these parts can result in swallowing difficulties.

There are numerous causes that may result in swallowing difficulties.

Obstruction. A foreign object that is lodged in the esophagus will prevent the passage of food.

Esophageal Stricture. Narrowing of the esophagus prevents food from passing easily into the stomach. This can be caused by a variety of conditions. Acid reflux is one such cause. Stomach acid that washes back into the esophagus is another cause of this condition; it results in the esophagus becoming inflamed and swollen, culminating in a build-up of scar tissue. Swallowing corrosive substances, or persistent viral or bacterial infections that cause inflammation can also lead to a swollen esophagus, leaving a narrow passageway.

Esophageal Spasm. Spasms in the esophagus disrupt the series of reflexes that allow food to pass into the stomach. The spasms may be caused by acid reflux, or a malfunction in the lower esophagus. This malfunction is often caused by a hiatal hernia (a condition in which the upper portion of the stomach moves around between the chest and abdomen).

Esophageal Cancer. Swallowing difficulties may be the result of a tumor in the esophagus. Because of this possibility, problems with swallowing should be taken seriously and investigated to rule out the possibility of cancer.

Pharyngoesophageal Diverticulum. This is a pouch that forms at the entrance of the pharynx. If the sphincter muscle (located at the top of the esophagus) is not functioning properly, it can cause food particles to become trapped in the pouch. It will enlarge and cause swallowing problems. The pouch usually needs to be removed in a surgical procedure.

Other causes of swallowing difficulties are goiters (swollen thyroid glands) or nerve disorders such as a stroke, which can affect the muscles that permit swallowing. A swollen or enlarged tongue will also prevent normal swallowing.

Treatment of swallowing difficulties should be based on the underlying cause. See also EMERGENCY FIRST STEPS and FIRST AID.

Swelling

Build-up of fluid or tissue growth.

Swelling (edema) is the result of an imbalance between the amount of water that is forced out of the capillaries and pumped throughout the body by blood and the rate at which it is taken back into the capillaries. When these processes are not synchronized, fluid builds up, and the area becomes swollen. Swelling may occur in an isolated area or throughout the body.

Causes. Swelling of a specific area often occurs after an injury from a direct blow, such as a fracture or sprain. Other types of swelling that afflict individual areas are joint swelling due to arthritis, insect bites, swollen gums (gingivitis), muscle tears, and many other traumas or infections. Swelling of the legs, feet, and hands is not uncommon during hot weather, and it also often occurs during pregnancy.

Swelling throughout the body may be caused by a variety of serious conditions. Massive edema may be caused by a lack of albumin, a protein that regulates the movement of fluid in the body. Heart failure can cause a build up of blood in the veins. Pressure caused by a tumor may cause the same effect. Nephritis can interrupt the flow of fluid into the tissues, while renal failure and cirrhosis of the liver can cause retention of salt and therefore of water. A high salt intake, therefore, can also cause a general bloating or swelling. Corticosteroids, androgen drugs, and some contraceptives can affect the kidneys, leading to salt retention.

Diagnosis. Generalized swelling may be difficult to detect, as it can be interpreted as weight gain. If the swelling is sudden, or there seems to be identifiable causes such as injury, a physician should be consulted. A doctor may ask some of the following questions:

How long has the swelling been noticeable? Is it always present or does it come and go?

Is it in one particular area or throughout the body?

How much is it swollen? Does a dent remain in the area if you press on it?

Does it hurt? Does anything make it better, or worse?

Treatment. Once the cause of the swelling has been diagnosed, the underlying condition must be remedied. This should bring down the swelling; but if it does not, diuretic drugs meant to increase the flow of urine and restricted salt intake may be prescribed. If related to injuries, ice packs, and keeping the affected area raised may bring down the swelling. *See also* FIRST AID; PUNCHDRUNK; RECOVERY POSITION; SHOCK; SKIN ALLERGY; *and* TRAUMA.

Tendonitis

T | Tendonitis

> Condition in which a tendon becomes inflamed, usually because of injury.

Tendons are strands of fibrous tissue made of collagen and a few blood vessels. These strands connect muscles to bones. They are strong and flexible, but not elastic. Therefore, overstretching or small, repeated stresses on a tendon may cause it to become inflamed. Swimmers, golfers, baseball players, and tennis players may be prone to tendonitis in the arms or shoulders, while runners and soccer, football, and basketball players are more likely to have it in their legs or feet.

Symptoms of tendonitis usually include pain, tenderness, and in more extreme cases, restricted function of the muscle to which the affected tendon is attached. When an area is affected by tendonitis, the tendon also becomes more likely to rupture, so tendinitis should not be taken lightly. Treatment includes resting the affected area, application of ice, and anti-inflammatory drugs. Working to correct improper movement or motion mechanics may prevent recurrence.

Trauma

> Any injury to the body and its effects on the mind.

Physical trauma has a number of causes, from a fall to an automobile accident to a gun shot. A sprain, a broken bone, and a bleeding wound, are examples of trauma. Emotional trauma is a term applied to a person's reaction to a serious physical trauma, however, it is of little medical relevance. Physical trauma is treated with first aid and emergency medical personnel. The psychological condition that often follows any type of trauma is referred to as posttraumatic stress disorder. *See also* FIRST AID.

Tropical Diseases

> Diseases found primarily in tropical and subtropical regions.

Few tropical diseases are confined solely to tropical areas, though most cases of these illnesses are found in these regions due to the climate, poor sanitation, and a lack of resources to combat them. Thousands of tropical diseases exist, though few are widespread; and they are

Urinary Tract Infection

often transmitted through animal hosts.

Mosquitoes transmit a number of tropical diseases. Malaria, for example, is transmitted by mosquitoes. The disease affects the red blood cells, causing them to first swell and burst. Certain strains can produce cerebral malaria, a potentially fatal disease. Other mosquito-borne diseases include dengue fever and encephalitis, both carried by the asian tiger mosquito, as well as yellow fever and infestation by filarial worms (filariasis).

Flies also carry and transmit tropical diseases such as river blindness (onchocerciasis). It is caused by a parasitic worm and transmitted by a black fly common to fast rivers in Africa and South America. The tsetse fly causes African sleeping sickness (trypanosomiasis), a disease affecting the brain and surrounding tissues. Sand-flies can carry leishmania protozoa, which cause leishmaniasis, an infectious disease affecting the skin, nasal passages, and pharynx.

A parasitic worm (schistosome) causes a variety of tropical diseases, known collectively as schistosomiasis. Schistosomes complete a part of their lifecycle in the bodies of freshwater snails. Schistosome infection can damage the liver, intestines, lungs, or urinary bladder.

Urinary Tract Infection

Infection in the bladder, urethra, or another part of the urinary tract

Urinary tract infections are caused by a number of bacteria, including gonorrhea and chlamydia. They can result in cystitis, which is the inflammation of the bladder; urethritis, inflammation of the urethra; polynephritis, inflammation of kidneys; and other problems. In women, the incidence of infections of the urethra (the passageway which carries urine from the bladder) is more common than in men, because the female urethra, while short, is more exposed to outside effects due to the fact that it runs to the vagina. In addition, pregnancy also increases the risk of developing a urinary tract infection. Many factors can increase the risk in both men and women, including birth defects, such as spina bifida, which affects the emptying of urine from the bladder, and injuries to the spinal cord. A stone in the urinary tract or a bladder tumor that affects the flow of urine can also lead to urinary tract infections. But in many cases, these infections occur without any clear underlying cause.

The symptoms of urinary tract infections depend on the region

Urinary Tract Infection

of the tract that is affected. For urethritis, a burning sensation is felt during urination. For cystitis, there is pain in the abdomen, an urge to urinate frequently, with urine that can be discolored by the presence of blood, and an overall feeling of weakness. A kidney infection results in pain in the loins, accompanied by a fever.

Any urinary tract infection must be treated to prevent permanent damage; untreated infections will cause severe damage to the urinary tract that may require surgery. Kidney infections can cause permanent loss of kidney function; if the infection spreads to the rest of the body through the blood, the patient can go into shock rather quickly.

Treatment of an infection starts with a urine specimen that is examined to determine the specific agent causing the infection. In some severe cases, a pyelogram, an x-ray examination, or an ultrasound scan can be done to determine whether a stone, a tumor or a congenital abnormality is responsible. If such a cause is identified, surgery may be needed to correct the defect or remove a tumor. In most cases, however, antibiotic treatment is enough to cure an infection; the antibiotic given to the patient depends on the agent responsible for the infection.

Vaginal Bleeding

Normal and abnormal bleeding from the vagina.

Normal vaginal bleeding occurs approximately once a month for women in their reproductive years; regular menstrual cycles end at menopause. Abnormal vaginal bleeding can occur for a variety of reasons. The bleeding categories are quite broad and include spotting or full bleeding midcycle, unusually heavy periods, staining in postmenopausal women or irregular menstrual periods in teenagers.

Sometimes different medications, such as anticoagulants, can cause bleeding. It is not uncommon to have midcycle staining for the first few months of taking birth control pills. This is known as "breakthrough bleeding." The pill is also responsible for withdrawal bleeding, which is bleeding that occurs when the body's levels of progesterone or estrogen drops suddenly. Postmenopausal women undergoing hormone replacement therapy may also experience irregular bleeding for three to six months, particularly if the dosage is too low.

Vaginal bleeding can be a warning sign of cancer to the reproductive tract, including the vagina, cervix, and ovaries. The presence of an IUD can cause heavier than normal periods. Bleeding is also caused by:

Venomous Bites and Stings

- laceration or other physical injury to the reproductive tract;
- cervical or endometrial polyps;
- ovarian cysts;
- pelvic inflammatory disease; and
- fibroids.

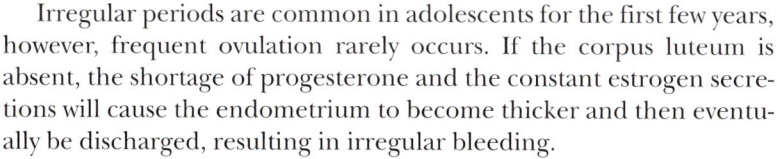

Irregular periods are common in adolescents for the first few years, however, frequent ovulation rarely occurs. If the corpus luteum is absent, the shortage of progesterone and the constant estrogen secretions will cause the endometrium to become thicker and then eventually be discharged, resulting in irregular bleeding.

As a woman approaches menopause, her hormone levels fluctuate, which results in irregular bleeding. Postmenopausal women may experience vaginal atrophy, which can result in bleeding after sexual intercourse. Medical conditions such as hypothyroidism and hyperprolactinemia can increase the frequency of menstruation. *See also* BLEEDING, TREATMENT OF.

Venomous Bites and Stings

Any attack by animal or insect that results in poisons or irritants getting into the tissue or blood.

While insect bites are often nothing more than an annoyance, the bites and stings of some types of bees, ants, wasps, scorpions, and spiders are venomous—some highly toxic, even deadly. Among these are tarantulas, black widow spiders, and brown recluse spiders. Certain marine animals, particularly jellyfish, can produce painful and potentially dangerous stings as well. Even the stings of less venomous insects like honey bees can provoke a life-threatening allergic reaction in some people. *See also* ANAPHYLACTIC SHOCK; JELLYFISH STINGS; *and* STINGS.

ALERT ALERT ALERT

IN CASE OF AN EMERGENCY

If the victim experiences a sudden and severe reaction, or has been bitten or stung multiple times, immediately contact EMS. If the offending creature can safely be killed or captured, do so for accurate identification. Carefully monitor the victim's airway, breathing, and circulation until help arrives. If the bite is on an extremity, apply a snug-fitting bandage (not a tourniquet) between the bite and the heart to slow diffusion of the venom. Do not elevate the bite area above the heart level. After approximately five minutes, or if the bandage causes a loss of sensation, remove it and put an ice pack on the bite.

Vomiting Blood

V Vomiting Blood

The regurgitation of blood from the stomach or esophagus.

Prolonged or vigorous vomiting may cause a tear in the small blood vessels of the throat or esophagus, producing blood in the vomit. This is related to Mallory-Weiss syndrome, which is a laceration or tear of the lower esophagus and the upper part of the stomach. The amount of blood present in the vomit depends on the extent of the damage.

Bleeding ulcers located in the stomach or duodenum are also a source of vomited blood, as are certain types of esophageal irritation or the erosion of the lining of the esophagus or stomach.

Other sources of blood in the vomit include bleeding esophageal varices; ingested blood; severe gastritis or gastroenteritis; severe injury or electrical shock; tumors of the stomach or esophagus; and vascular malformations in the gastrointestinal tract.

Treatments for vomiting blood vary, because they depend upon the specific cause. In general, it is a good idea to drink small amounts of water regularly to prevent dehydration. It is very important to seek medical help. *See also* BLEEDING, TREATMENT OF *and* FIRST AID.

West Nile Virus

Mosquito-borne virus causing inflammation of the brain (West Nile encephalitis).

The virus produces West Nile encephalitis, a brain infection that causes inflammation, impairing nervous system functioning. In North America, the disease spreads primarily in the late summer and early fall. Birds are the carriers for West Nile virus; mosquitoes acquire the virus and pass it to humans after consuming blood from infected birds. West Nile virus multiplies in the bloodstream following infection, crossing the blood-brain barrier to reach the brain, usually within 15 days of infection.

Symptoms include fever, headache, and body aches. More severe infections produce a high fever, stupor, coma, tremors, convulsions, and paralysis. No specific treatment exists for this condition.

Prevention efforts are aimed at mosquito control and eradication. Reducing the amount of standing water and using insecticides can help reduce the risk of infection. *See also* TROPICAL DISEASES.

Appendix A
Further Resources for More Information

This appendix is provided as a resource for those who wish to find more information about specific First Aid and Emergency Medicine issues. The following lists include organizations (both public and private), reading materials, and digital services that many people may find helpful in their search for a broader understanding of what to do in an emergency situation.

Related Organizations

Alcoholics Anonymous
Street Address
475 Riverside Dr.
11th floor
New York, NY 10115
or
Mailing Address
Grand Central Station
P.O. Box 459
New York, NY 10163
www.alcoholics-anonymous.org

Asthma and Allergy Foundation of America
1233 20th Street, NW
Suite 402
Washington, DC 20036
tel: (202) 466-7643
fax: (202) 466-8440
Info: 1-800-7-Asthma (727-8462)
www.aafa.org

American Association of Homes and Services for the Aging
2519 Connecticut Avenue, NW
Washington, DC 20008-1520
tel: 202-783-2224
fax: 202-738-2255
www.aahsa.org

American Association of Poison Control Centers
3201 New Mexico Ave.
Suite 310
Washington, DC 20016
(202) 362-7217
For Poison Emergencies call:
1-800-222-1222
aapcc@poison.org
www.aapcc.org (The AAPCC is an organization of poison centers and interested individuals. It does not manage exposure cases)

American Heart Association
American Heart Association
National Center
7272 Greenville Ave
Dallas, TX 75213
Heart and Stroke Info:
1-800-AHA-USA1 (242-8721)
Stroke Info:
1-888-4-Stroke (478-7653)
www.americanheart.org

Cornell Illustrated Emergency Medicine & First Aid Guide • 209

Appendix A: Resources

American Medical Association
515 N. State Street
Chicago, IL 60610
(312) 464-5000
www.ama-assn.org

American Trauma Society
8903 Presidential Parkway
Suite 512
Upper Marlboro, MD 20772
1-800-556-7890
info@amtrauma.org
www.amtrauma.org

Centers for Disease Control and Prevention
1600 Clifton Road
Atlanta, GA 30333
Hotlines:
National AIDS Hotline:
1-800-342-2437
HIV/AIDS Hotline (Spanish):
1-800-344-7434
Immunization Hotline:
1-800-232-2522
Immunization Hotline (Spanish):
1-800-232-0233
STD Hotline:
1-800-227-8922
Traveler's Health:
1-800-394-8747
Public Inquiries:
(404) 639-3534
1-800-311-3435
www.cdc.gov

Childhelp USA and The National Child Abuse Hotline
15757 N. 78th St.
Scottsdale, AZ 85206
tel: (480) 922-8212
fax: (480) 922-7061
1-800-4-A-Child (422-4453)
TDD: 1-800-2-A-Child (222-4453)
www.chiuldhelpusa.org

Christopher Reeve Paralysis Foundation
500 Morris Ave
Springfield, NJ 07081
tel: (973) 379-2690
fax: (973) 912-9433
1-800-225-0292
info@crpf.org
www.apacure.com

Depressive and Related Affective Disorders Association
Meyer 3-181, 600 North Wolfe St.
Baltimore, MD 21287-7381
(410) 955-4647
drada@jhmi.edu
www.hopkinsmedicine.org/drada

Lyme Disease Foundation
One Financial Plaza, 18th Floor
Hartford, CT -6103
tel: (860) 525-2000
fax: 860-525-Tick (525-8425)
1-800-886-Lyme (886-5963)
lymefnd@aol.com
www.lyme.org

Medic Alert Foundation International
2323 Colorado Ave.
Turlock, CA 95382
1-888-633-4298
www.lyme.org

Medicare
Department of Health and Human Services
1-800-Medicare (633-4227)
www.medicare.gov

Appendix A: Resources

The National Amputation
Foundation
38-40 Church Street
Malverne, NY 11565
tel: (516) 887-3600
fax: 516-887-3667
e-mail: amps76@aol.com
www.nationalamputation.org

National Association of Anorexia
Nervosa and Associated
Disorders
P.O. Box 7
Highland Park, IL 60035
fax: (847) 433-4632
(847) 831-3438
info@anad.com
www.anda.org

National Brain Injury Association
105 North Alfred Street
Alexandria, VA 22314
tel: (703) 236-6000
fax: (703) 236-6001
1-800-444-6443
www.biausa.org

National Center for Missing and
Exploited Children
Charles B. Wang International
Children's Building
599 Prince Street
Alexandria, VA 22314-3175
tel: (703) 274-390
fax: (703)274-2200
1-800-The-Lost (243-5678)
www.missingkids.com

National Depressive and Manic-
Depressive Association
730 N. Franklin Street
Suite 501
Chicago, IL 60610-7240
tel: (312) 642-0049
fax: (312) 642-7243
www.ndma.org

National Health Information
Center
Department of Health and
Human Services
P.O. Box 1133
Washington DC, 20013
www.health.gov/nhic

National Mental Health
Association
1021 Prince Street
Alexandria, VA 22314-2971
tel: (703) 684-7722
fax: (703)684-5968
1-800-969-NMHA (969-6642)
TTY: 1-800-433-5959
www.nmha.org

National Organization for Rare
Disorders
P.O. Box 8923
New Fairfield, CT 06812-8923
tel: (203) 746-6518
fax: (203) 746-6481
1-800-999-6673
www.rarediseases.org

National Stroke Association
9707 E. Easter Lane
Englewood, CO 80112
tel: (303) 649-9299
fax: (303)649-1328
1-800-Strokes (787-6537)
www.stroke.org

National Substance Abuse
Helplines
1-800-DrugHelp (378-4435)
1-800-Cocaine (202-2463)
1-800-Relapse (735-4773)
1-800-Heroine (437-6463)
1-888-Marijuana (627-45862)
www.drughelp.org

Appendix A: Resources

American Red Cross Courses and Programs

The American Red Cross (www.redcross.com) has an impeccable record of public service and training. For further information regarding specific courses or training sessions, contact the local chapter of the American Red Cross. Otherwise, available courses include:

- American Red Cross Community CPR
- American Red Cross Adult CPR
- American Red Cross CPR: Infant and Child
- American Red Cross Basic Aid Training (BAT) (For Children)
- American Red Cross Standard First Aid
- American Red Cross First Aid: Responding to Emergencies
- American Red Cross Basic Water Safety
- American Red Cross Emergency Water Safety
- American Red Cross Safety Training for Swim Coaches
- American Red Cross Basic Lifeguarding
- American Red Cross Child Care Course
- American Red Cross Reaching Adolescents and Parents (RAP)
- American Red Cross Hispanic HIV/AIDS Program
- American Red Cross African American HIV/AIDS Program
- American Red Cross Workplace HIV/AIDS Program

Appendix B
Further Reading

Advanced First Aid Afloat, Peter F. Eastman, M.D., Cornell Maritime Press, 2000.

Altitude Illness: Prevention and Treatment: How to Stay Healthy at Altitude From Resort Skiing to Himalayan Climbing, Stephen Berzruchka, M.D., Mountaineers Books, 1994.

American College of Emergency Physicians First Aid Manual, DK Pub. Merchandise, 2001.

The American Red Cross First Aid and Safety Handbook, Kathleen Handal, M.D., et al., Little Brown & Co., 1992.

Baby & Child Emergency First-Aid Handbook: Simple Step-By-Step Instructions for the most Common Childhood Emergencies, Mitchell J. Einzing, M.D., Meadowbrook Press, 1995.

Backcountry First Aid and Extended Care, 3rd Edition, Buck Tilton, Globe Pequot Press, 1998.

Childhood Emergencies: What to Do, A Quick Reference Guide, Marin Child Care Council, Bull Publishing Co., 2001.

Emergency Medical Treatment: Infants, Children and Adults—A Handbook on What to Do In an Emergency to Keep Someone Alive Until Help Arrives, Stephen N. Vogel, et al., Beechwood Health Books, 1993.

Emergency Survival: A Pocket Guide, Christopher Van Tilburg, Mountaineers Books, 2001.

Field Guide to Wilderness Medicine, Paul S. Auerbach, Howard J. Donner, and Eric A. Weiss, Mosby, 1999.

First Aid and CPR Essentials, Alton L. Thygerson, National Safety Council, Jones & Bartlett, 2000.

Handbook of First Aid and Emergency Care, Jerold B. Leikin, M.D., et al., Random House. 2000.

On-Field Evaluation and Treatment of Common Athletic Injuries, James R. Andrews, M.D., et al., Mosby-Year Book, 1997.

Medicine for the Outdoors: The Essential Guide to Emergency Medical Procedures and First Aid, Paul S. Auerbach, The Lyons Press, 1999.

Mosby's Outdoor Emergency Medical Guide: What to Do in an Outdoor Emergency When Help May Take Some Time To Arrive, David H. Manhoff, et al., Mosby Year-Book, 1996.

Natural First Aid: Herbal Treatments for Ailments & Injuries, Emergency Preparedness, and Wilderness Safety, Brigitte Mars, Storey Books, 1999.

Nols Wilderness First Aid, Todd Schimelpfening, et al., Stackpole Books, 2000.

The Onboard Medical Guide: First Aid and Emergency Medicine Afloat, Paul G. Gill, McGraw-Hill Professional Pub., 1996.

A Parent's Guide to Medical Emergencies: First Aid For Your Child, Janet Zant, et al., Avery–Penguin Putnam, 1997.

The Pocket Guide to CPR for Infants and Children, Gloria Blatti, ed., Pocket Books, 1998.

The Ragged Mountain Press Pocket Guide to Wilderness Medicine and First Aid, Paul G. Gill, Jr., McGraw-Hill Professional Publishing, 1997.

Vehicle Rescue, Harve D. Grant, et al., Prentice Hall, 1996.

Wilderness 911: A Step-By-Step Guide for Medical Emergencies and Improvised Care in the Back Country, Eric A. Weiss, Mountaineers Books, 1999.

Your Offshore Doctor: A Manual of Medical Self-Sufficiency at Sea, Michael H. Beilan, Sheridan House, 1996.

Appendix C
Poison Control Centers

Alabama
Alabama Poison Center
809 University Blvd. East
Tuscaloosa, AL 35401
(205) 345-0600
(800) 462-0800 (Alabama Only)

The Children's Hospital of
Alabama Poison Control Center
1600 Seventh Ave. S.
Birmingham, AL 35233
(800) 292-6675 (statewide)
(205) 933-4050 (local)
(205) 939-9201 (local)
(205) 939-9202 (local)

Alaska
Anchorage Poison Center
Providence Hospital
PO Box 196604
3200 Providence Dr.
Anchorage, AK 99519
(800) 478-3193
(907) 261-3193

Fairbanks Poison Control Center
Fairbanks Memorial Hospital
1650 Cowles St.
Fairbanks, AK 99701
(907) 456-7182

Arizona
Arizona Regional Poison Control System
Arizona Health Sciences Center
Room 3204K
University of Arizona
Tucson AZ 85724
(800) 362-0101

Central Arizona Regional Poison
Management Center
St. Luke's Hospital Medical Center
1800 E. Van Buren St,
Phoenix, AZ 85006

Arkansas
Statewide Poison Control Information
Center
University of Arkansas Center for
Medical Sciences
College of Pharmacy
4301 W. Markham St.
Little Rock, AR 72205
(800) 482-8948 (statewide)
(501) 666-5532 (Pulaski County)

California
Los Angeles County Medical Ass.
Regional Poison Control Center
1925 Wilshire Blvd.
Los Angeles, CA 90057
(213) 484-5151 (for public)
(213) 664-2121 (for physicians)
(800) 825-2722 (for physicians)

Fresno Regional Poison Control Center
of Fresno Community Hospital and
Medical Center
Fresno and R Sts.
Fresno, CA 93715
(800) 346-5922
(209) 445-1222

San Diego Regional Poison Control
Center
University of California, San Diego
Medical Center
225 Dickerson St.
San Diego, CA 92103
(800) 876-4766 (CA only)
(619) 294-6000

UC Davis Medical Center Regional
Poison Center
2315 Stockton Blvd.
Sacramento, CA 95817
(800) 342-9293 (CA only)
(916) 453-3692 (emergency poison information)

Appendix C: Poison Control Centers

Children's Hospital Medical Center of
Northern California
747 52nd Street
Oakland, CA 94609
(415) 428-3248

University of California Poison Control
Center
Irvine Medical Center
101 City Drive S., Rte. 78
Orange, CA 92668
(714) 634-5988

Central-Coast Counties Regional Poison
Control Center
751 Bascom Ave.
San Jose, CA 95128
(800) 662-9886
(408) 299-5112

Colorado

Rocky Mountain Poison Control Center
(also covers Montana and Wyoming)
645 Bannock St.
Denver, CO 80204
(303) 629-1123
(800) 332-3073 (CO only)
(800) 525-5042 (MT only)
(800) 442-2702 (WY only)

Connecticut

Connecticut Poison Control Center
University of Connecticut Health Center
Farmington, CT 06032
(203) 674-3456
(203) 674-3457

Delaware

Poison Information Center
Wilmington Division
501 W. 14th Street
Wilmington, DE 19899
(302) 655-3389

Florida

Tampa Bay Regional Poison Center
Tampa General Hospital
Davis Island, FL 33606
(813) 253-4444
(800) 282-3171 (FL only)

St. Vincent's Medical Center
1800 Barrs St.
Jacksonville, FL 32202
(904) 378-7500
(904) 378-7499 (TDD)

Georgia

Georgia Poison Control Center
Grady Memorial Hospital
80 Butler St. SE
Atlanta, GA 30335
(404) 589-4400
(800) 282-5846 (GA only)
(404) 525-3323 (TDD)

Regional Poison Control Center Medical
Center of Central Georgia
777 Hemlock St.
Macon, GA 31202
(912) 744-1427
(912) 744-1146
(912) 744-1000

Hawaii

Hawaii Poison Center
Kapiolani-Children's Medical Center
1319 Punahou St.
Honolulu, HI 96826
(800) 362-3585
(808) 941-4411

Idaho

Idaho Emergency Medical Poison Center
St. Alphonsus Regional Medical Center
1055 N. Curtis Rd.
Boise, ID 83704
(800) 632-8000
(208) 334-2241

Illinois

Chicago and Northeastern Illinois
Regional Poison Control Center
Ruch-Presbyterian-St. Luke's Medical
Center
1753 W. Congress Pkwy.
Chicago, IL 60612
(800) 942-5969
(217) 753-3330

Appendix C: Poison Control Centers

Indiana
Indiana Poison Center
Wishard Memorial Hospital
1001 W. Tenth Street
Indianapolis, IN 46202
(317) 630-7351
(800) 382-9097 (IN only)
(317) 630-6666 (TDD)

Parkview Memorial Hospital
2200 Randalia Dr.
Ft. Wayne, IN 46805
(219) 484-6636

Iowa
University of Iowa Hospitals and Clinic
Poison Control Center
Iowa City, IA 52242
(800) 272-6477
(319) 356-2922

Variety Club Poison and Drug
Information Center
Iowa Methodist Medical Center
1200 Pleasant St.
De Moines, IA 50309
(800) 362-2327
(515) 283-6254

Kansas
Mid-America Poison Center
University of Kansas Medical Center
39th and Rainbow Blvd.
Kansas City, KN 66103
(800) 332-6633
(913) 588-6633

Wesley Medical Center
550 N. Hillside Ave.
Witchita, KN 67214
(316) 688-2277

Kentucky
Kentucky Regional Poison Control
Center of Kosair Children's Hospital
PO Box 35070
Louisville, KY 40232
(800) 722-5725 (KY only)
(502) 589-8222 (Louisville only)

Louisiana
Louisiana Regional Poison Control
Center
Louisiana State University School of
Medicine
1501 Kings Hwy.
Shreveport, LA 71130
(318) 425-1524
(800) 535-0525 (LA only)

Maine
Maine Poison Control Center at Maine
Medical Center
22 Bramhall St.
Portland, ME 04102
(800) 442-6305 (ME only)
(207) 871-2381 (ER)

Maryland
Maryland Poison Center
University of Maryland School of
Pharmacy
20 N. Pine St.
Baltimore, MD 21201
(410) 528-7701
(800) 492-2414 (MD only)

Massachusetts
Massachusetts Poison Control System
300 Longwood Ave.
Boston, MA 02115
(617) 232-2120
(800) 682-9211
(617) 277-3323 (TDD)

Michigan
Blodgett Regional Poison Center
Blodgett Memorial Medical Center
1840 Wealthy St. SE
Grand Rapids, MI 49506
(800) 442-4112 (for area code 616 only)
(800) 632-2727 (MI only)

Poison Control Center
Children's Hospital of Michigan
3901 Beaubien Blvd.
Detroit, MI 48201
(313) 745-5711
(800) 462-6642 (area code 313 only)
(800) 572-1655 (rest of MI)

Appendix C: Poison Control Centers

Minnesota
Hennepin Regional Poison Center
Henepin County Medical Center
701 Park Ave.
Minneapolis, MN 55415
(612) 347-3141
(612) 347-6219 (TDD)

Minnesota Poison Control System
St. Paul Ramsey Medical Center
St. Paul, MN 55101
(612) 221-2113
(800) 222-1222 (MN only)

Mississippi
Regional Poison Control Center
2500 N. State St.
Jackson, MS 39216
(601) 354-7660

Missouri
The Children's Mercy Hospital
24th and Gillham Rd.
Kansas City, MO 64108
(816) 234-3000
Cardinal Glennon Children's Hospital
Regional Poison Center
1465 S. Grand Blvd.
St. Louis, MO 63104
(314) 772-5200
(800) 392-9111 (MO only)

Montana
Rocky Mountain Poison Control Center
(also covers Colorado and Wyoming)
645 Bannock St.
Denver, CO 80204
(303) 629-1123
(800) 332-3073 (CO only)
(800) 525-5042 (MT only)
(800) 442-2702 (WY only)

Nebraska
Mid-Plains Poison Control Center
8301 Dodge St.
Omaha, NE 68114
(402) 390-5400 (Omaha)
(800) 642-9999 (NE only)
(800) 228-9515 (CO, IA, KN, MO, SD, and WY)

New Hampshire
New Hampshire Poison Information Center
2 Maynard St.
Hanover, NH 03756
(800) 562-8236 (NH only)
(603) 646-5000 (outside NH)

New Jersey
New Jersey Poison Information and Education System
201 Lyons Ave.
Newark, NJ 07112
(201) 923-0764
(800) 962-1253 (NJ only)
(201) 926-8008 (TDD)

New Mexico
New Mexico Poison and Drug Information Center
University of New Mexico
Albuquerque, NM 87131
(505) 843-2551
(800) 432-6866 (NM only)

New York
Long Island Regional Poison Control Center
Nassau County Medical Center
2201 Hempstead Tpk.
East Meadow, NY 11554
(516) 542-2323 (TDD)
(516) 542-2324
(516) 542-2325

New York City Poison Control Center
455 1st Ave., Rm 123
New York, NY 10016
(212) 340-4494
(212) 764-7667
(800) 225-0658 (outside NY)

Southern Tier Poison Center
Binghamton General Hospital
Mitchell Ave.
Binghamton, NY 13903
(607) 723-8929

Appendix C: Poison Control Centers

Western New York Poison Control Center at Children's Hospital of Buffalo
219 Bryant St.
Buffalo, NY 14222
(716) 878-7654
(716) 878-7655

Finger Lakes Poison Center
LIFE LINE
University of Rochester Medical Center
Box 777
Rochester, NY 14620
(716) 275-5152
(716) 275-2700 (TDD)

Central New York Poison Control Center
Upstate Medical Center
750 E. Adams St.
Syracuse, NY 13210
(315) 476-4766
(800) 252-5655 (outside Onandaga County)

North Carolina
Duke University Poison Control Center
Duke University Medical Center
Box 3007
Durham, NC 27710
(919) 684-8111;
(800) 672-1697 (NC only)

North Dakota
North Dakota Poison Information Center
St. Luke's Hospital
Fifth St. N. and Mills Ave.
Fargo, ND 58122
(800) 732-2200 (ND only);
(800) 280-5575

Ohio
Central Ohio Poison Center
Columbus Children's Hospital
700 Children's Dr.
Columbus, OH 43205
(614) 228-1323;
(800) 682-7625 (OH only)

Cincinnati Regional Poison Control System and Drug and Poison Information Center
University of Cincinnati Medical Center
231 Bethesda Ave., M.L. #144
Cincinnati, OH 45267
(513) 872-5111;
(800) 872-5111

Oklahoma
Oklahoma Poison Control Center
Oklahoma Children's Memorial Hospital
P.O. Box 26307
940 N.E. 10th
Oklahoma City, OK 73126
(800) 522-4611 (OK only)
(405) 271-5454

Oregon
Oregon Poison Control and Drug Information Center
Oregon Health Sciences University
3181 SW Sam Jackson Park Rd.
Portland, OR 97201
(800) 452-7165;
(503) 225-8968

Pennsylvania
Delaware Valley Regional Poison Control Center
One Children's Center
34th and Civic Center Blvd.
Philadelphia, PA 19104
(215) 386-2100

Pittsburgh Poison Center
One Children's Place
3705 5th Ave. at DeSota St.
Pittsburgh, PA 15213
(412) 647-5600 (administration);
(412) 681-6669 (emergency)

Rhode Island
Rhode Island Poison Center
Rhode Island Hospital
593 Eddy St.
Providence, RI 02902
(401) 277-5727;
(401) 277-8062 (TDD)

Appendix C: Poison Control Centers

South Carolina
Palmetto Poison Center
University of South Carolina College of Pharmacy
Columbia, SC 29208
(800) 922-1117;
(800) 765-7359

South Dakota
Mid-Plains Poison Control Center
(See Nebraska)

Tennessee
T.C. Thompson Children's Hospital
910 Blackford St.
Chattanooga, TN 37403
(615) 778-6100

Texas
North Central Texas Poison Center
P.O. Box 35926
Dallas, TX 75235
(214) 920-2400;
(800) 441-0040 (TX only)

Texas State Poison Center
University of Texas Medical Branch
Galveston, TX 77550
(409) 765-1420;
(713) 654-1701 (Houston);
(516) 478-4490 (Austin);
(800) 392-8548 (TX only)

Utah
Intermountain Regional Poison Control Center
50 N. Medical Dr., Bldg. 428
Salt Lake City, UT 84132
(801) 581-2151
(800) 662-0062 (UT only)

Vermont
Vermont Poison Center
Medical Center Hospital of Vermont
Colchester Ave.
Burlington, VT 05401
(802) 658-3456 (poison info)
(802) 656-2721 (education programs)

Virginia
Blue Ridge Poison Center
University of Virginia Hospital
Charlottesville, VA 22908
(800) 552-3723
(800) 222-5927 (TDD, VA only)
(804) 924-5543

Central Virginia Poison Center
Medical College of Virginia
Richmond, VA 23298
(804) 786-9123 (24-hour emergency number)

Washington
Seattle Poison Center
Children's Hospital and Medical Center
4800 Sand Point Way NE
PO Box C5371
Seattle, WA 98105
(206) 526-2121

Washington, DC
National Capital Poison Center
Georgetown University Hospital
3800 Reservoir Rd. NW
Washington, CD 20007
(202) 625-3333

West Virginia
West Virginia Poison Center
West Virginia University School of Pharmacy
3110 McCorckle Ave. SE
Charleston, WV 25304
(304) 348-4211
(800) 642-3625 (WV only)

Wisconsin
Green Bay Poison Control Center
St. Vincent Hospital
PO Box 13508
Green Bay, WI 54307
(414) 433-8100

Wyoming
Wyoming Poison Center
Hathaway Bldg., Rm 527
Cheyenne, WY 82001
(800) 442-2702

Index

Article titles are set in **boldface**.

A

Abdominal pain, 11–13
  alert, 12
Accidents, 13–15
Acting out, 16
AIDS (acquired immune deficiency syndrome), 16–18
Airway obstruction, 19, 131–132
Alcohol dependence, 19–20
Allergic reaction, 20–21
  alert, 55
  foods, 129–130
Ambulances, 22, *22*
Amenorrhea, 162
Amputation, 23
Anaphylactic shock, 20, 24
  alert, 24, 187
Aneurysm, 24–25, *25*, 30, 68
Angina pectoris, 26, 26–27, 71, 71
Anoxia, 27
Antepartum hemorrhage, 28
Anthrax, 28–29, *29*
Antifreeze poisoning, 29
Antiseptics, 29
Aortic aneurysm, 30
Apnea, 30, 56
Appendicitis, 13, 31
Arrhythmia, cardiac, 31–32, 71
Arsenic, 33
Asphyxia, 33
Asthma attack, 20–21, 34–35
  alert, 34

Atelectasis, 36
Atrial fibrillation, 37
Avulsion, 38

B

Back spasms, 39
Bandages, 40, *40*, 105–106, *106*
Barbiturate drugs, 41
  alert, 41
Bends, 42, 89
Beta-blocker drugs, 42–43
  alert, 43
Betamethasone, 43
Biliary colic, 44
Birth control, 79–80, 166
Birth defects, 44–45
Bites, 45–46. see also Stings
  insects, 156–158
  snakes, 191–192
  spiders, 192–193
Black eye, 46, 123
Bleeding, 46–47, *47*
  alert, 47
  coughing up blood, 82
  during pregnancy, 28
  emergency treatment, 118–119
  gastrointestinal, 138–139
  in the brain, 54
  internal, 158
  nasal, 170
  shock alert, 49
  treatment of, 47–49, *48*
  vaginal, 206–207
Blisters, 50
Blood poisoning, 50–51
  alert, 51
Blood pressure, 51–52, *52*

Boils, 53
Botulism, 53
Brain hemorrhage, 54
Breathing
  airway obstruction, 19
  apnea, 30
  asthma attack, 20, 34–35
  choking, 74–75
  difficulty, 55–57
  emergency treatment, 118
Bronchodilator drugs, 57–58
  alert, 58
Bruises, 58
Burns, 14, 59–60
  first aid alert, 60
  in the eye, 122–123

C

Cadmium poisoning, 61
Caffeine, 61–62
  alert, 58, 61
Carbon monoxide, 62
  alert, 62
Cardiac arrest, 63
  alert, 63
Cardiopulmonary resuscitation (CPR), 64–66, *65*, *66*
Cardiovascular disorders, 67–68. see also Heartbeat
  angina pectoris, 26, 26–27
  caffeine alert, 61
  carditis, 69
  coronary heart disease, 81
  pericarditis, 71
Carditis, 69

Cornell Illustrated Emergency Medicine & First Aid Guide • 221

Index

Catastrophic health insurance, 69
Cauliflower ear, 70
Causalgia, 70
Centers for Disease Control, 70–71
Chest pain, 71–72
  alert, 72
  angina pectoris, 26–27
Childbirth, 73
Children
  abdominal pain, 13
  acting out, 16
  cardiopulmonary resuscitation (CPR), 65, 65–66
  choking alert, 75
  concussion alert, 79
  dehydration alert, 92
  drug poisoning alert, 110
  electrical shock alert, 115
  protective devices, 14
  safety precautions, 15
  sleep apnea alert, 190
Chlorate poisoning, 74
  alert, 74
Choking, 74–76, 146
Cold injury, 76
Coma, 77
Complications, 78
Compresses, 78
Concussion, 79, 195
  alert, 79
Contact dermatitis, 188–189
Contraception, 79–80, 166
Coronary heart disease, 81–82
  alert, 81
Coughing up blood, 82–83
Cramps, 83–84
Crohn's disease, 84–86
  alert, 85
Crush syndrome, 86

D

Dacryocystitis, 87
Deafness, 87–88
Decompression sickness, 42, 89
Defibrillation, 89–90, *90*
Dehydration, 90–91
  alert, 85
Dehydration in infants, 92–93
Delirium, 93–94
Dementia, 94
Dengue, 94–95
Dental emergencies, 95–96
Depression, 96–98
Detergent poisoning, 99
Diarrhea, 93, 99–101
  alert, 100
Discharge, 102, 112
Dislocation, joint, 102–103, *103*
  alert, 103
Dizziness, 103–104
Doom, sense of, 12
Double vision, 104–105
Dressing, 40, *40*, 105–106, *106*
Drowning, 15, 107–108
Drug overdose, 108–109
Drug poisoning, 110
  alert, 110
Dysentery, 111
Dysmenorrhea, 111–112, 162–163

E

Earache, 113–114
Eardrum, perforated, 114
Ears
  discharge from, 112
  foreign body in, 112–113, 132
Electrical injury, 15, 114–116
  child protection alert, 115

Embolism, 116–117
  alert, 117
Emergency hospitalization, 119
Emergency, first steps, *118*, 118–119
Epileptic seizures, 120–121
  alert, 121
Extradural hemorrhage alert, 122
Eyes
  foreign body in, 123–124, *124*
  injuries to, 122–123

F

Facial pain, 125
Fainting, 125
Falls in elderly, 126
Feces, abnormal, 126–127
Fever, 127–129
  alert, 128
First aid, priorities, 14, 118–119
Food allergy, 129–130
Food poisoning, 53, 130–131
Foreign body, 131–132
Fractures, 132–134, *133*, 147
  nose, 169
  rib, 181
  skull, 189
Frostbite, 76, 135, *135*

G

Gallstones, 136, *136*
Gangrene, 137, *137*
Gastritis, 137–138, *138*
Gastrointestinal bleeding, 138–139
Glands, swollen, 139–140

H

Index

Head injury, 140–141
Head, neck, and back injuries, 141–142
Headaches
  concussion, 79
  hemorrhage alert, 122
  migraine, 164–165
Health insurance, 69
Hearing loss, 87–88
Heart attack, *142*, 142–144
  alert, 81, 143
  cardiac arrest, 63
Heartbeat
  arrhythmia, cardiac, 31–32
  atrial fibrillation, 37
  defibrillation, 89–90
Heart disease. *see* Cardiovascular disorders
Heartburn, 12
Heat exhaustion, 144
Heat stroke, 145
Heimlich maneuver, 75, 146, *146*
Hiccup, 147
Hip fracture, 147
HIV (human immunodeficiency virus) infection, 16–18
Hives, 147–148
Hospitals
  emergency use, 119
  types of, 148–149
Hot flashes, 149
Hyperemesis, 150
Hyperglycemia, 150–151
  alert, 150
Hypertension, 51–52, *52*, 68
  alert, 52
Hyperventilation, 151
Hypotension, 151–152
  alert, 152
Hypothermia, 153
Hypovolemia, 154

I

Ice packs, 154
Indigestion, 155
Infants
  cardiopulmonary resuscitation (CPR), 66, *66*
  dehydration alert, 92–93
Injury, 155, 204
Insect stings and bites, 156–158, *157*
  alert, 157–158
Internal bleeding, 158
  alert, 47
Ipecac, 158

J

Jellyfish stings, 159

K

Kidney failure, 159–160
Kidney pain, 12
Kidney stones, 160–161

L

Labor (childbirth), 73
Life support, 161
Loss of consciousness, 161

M

Menorrhagia, 163
Menstrual pain, 12
Menstruation, disorders of, 111–112, 162–163
Mercury poisoning, 163–164
Migraine, 164–165
Mitral valve prolapse, 71
Morning after pill, 80, 166
Mushroom poisoning, *166*, 166–167
  alert, 167
Myocardial infarction, 142–143

N

Nausea, 167
Neck rigidity, 168
Nerve injury, 168
Nerve pain, 70
Nerves, 168
Nervous breakdown, 169
Nose, broken, 169
Nosebleed, 170, *170*
Numbness, 171

O

Obesity, 56
Oligomenorrhea, 163
Operating room, 171–172

P

Pain relief, 172–173
Pelvic organ inflammation, 12
Peptic ulcer, 12
Pericarditis, 71
Plants, poisonous, 173–174
  alert, 174
Poison ivy, oak, sumac, 175
Poisoning, 15, 176
  antifreeze, 29
  arsenic, 33
  barbiturate drugs, 41
  cadmium, 61
  carbon monoxide, 62
  chlorate, 74
  detergents, 99
  from drugs, 110
  food poisoning, 130–131
  mercury, 163–164
  mushrooms, 166–167
  plants, 173–174
  strychnine, 199

Poisons, 174
Pregnancy
  antepartum hemor-
    rhage, 28
  birth defects, 44–45
  caffeine, 61
  vomiting during, 150
Pressure points, 48, *48*
Protective devices, for
  children, 14
Punchdrunk, 177
Pus, 102

R
Rabies, 177–178
Radiation sickness, 178
Rape, 179
Recovery position, 118,
  179–180, *180*
Rib, fractured, 181
Rotavirus, 93, 99
Running injuries,
  181–182

S
Scorpion stings, 183
Seizures, 183–184
  epileptic, 120–121
  febrile, 129, 184–185
Septic shock, 185
  alert, 51, 185
Septicemia, 50–51
Shock, 186–187
  allergy alert, 55
  anaphylactic, 20
  bleeding alert, 49
  septic, 187
  septic shock alert, 51
  Shock (electrical),
    114–116
Shock position, 187
Shoulder dislocation,
  187–188
Skin allergy, 188–189
Skull, fractured, 189
Sleep apnea, 189–190
  alert, 190
Sling, 191
Snakebites, 191–192, *192*
Spasms, in the back, 39
Spider bites, 192–193
Splint, 193–194
Sports injuries, 181–182,
  194–195
Sprains, 196
Status epilepticus, 120
Stings, 196–197. *see also*
  Bites
  insects, 156–158
  jellyfish, 159
  marine wildlife alert,
    197
  scorpions, 183
Strangulation, 197
Stroke, 197–198
  embolism, 116–117
Strychnine poisoning,
  199
Substance abuse, 19–20,
  41
Sucking wound, 199
Suffocation, 200
Suicide, 200–201
  alert, 201

Swallowing difficulties,
  202
Swelling, 203
Swimmer's ear, 113

T
Tendonitis, 204
Thrombosis, 68
Tourniquets, 49
Transient ischemic attack
  (TIA), 117
Trauma, 155, 204
Triage, 119
Tropical diseases,
  204–205

U
Urination, difficulty in,
  205–206

V
Vaginal bleeding,
  206–207
**Venomous bites and
  stings**, 207
  alert, 207
Vomiting
  during pregnancy, 150
  of blood, 207

W
West Nile virus, 207
Withdrawal, from
  alcohol, 19–20

Image Credits
T: Top M: Middle R: Right

2: Cornel; 5: Cornell; 8: Corbis; 14-L,M,R: Corbis; 15: Troy Schremmer; 22: L,M,R: Corbis; 26: Rachel Soltis; 29: CDC; 40-L: Corbis; 40-R: Troy Schremmer; 47: Corbis; 48: Rachel Soltis; 52: Corbis; 65: ADAM; 71: Rachel Soltis; 75: ADAM; 88: Corbis; 101: ADAM; 108: ADAM; 116-T, B: ADAM; M: Rachel Soltis; 124: ADAM-L,R: Corbis; M: Reference Works; 133: ADAM; 135: ADAM; 136: ADAM; 137: ADAM; 142: ADAM; 146: ADAM; 157-Top L, R: ADAM Lower L: CDC; 166: Corbis; 168: Reference Works; 170: ADAM; NCI; 174-R: CDC; L: ADAM; 180: ADAM; 182: ADAM; 187: ADAM; 192: ADAM; 193: ADAM.